The Lingo Guide
for Builders

*Covers all construction trades from demolition
to roofing and everything in between*

I0150679

Dedicated to David, Caleb and Silas with love.

Published by:
The Lingo Guide
Nashville, TN

Contact:
info@thelingoguide.com
www.thelingoguide.com

Copyright (c) 2006 The Lingo Guide®, LLC
ISBN 978-1-62880-052-4
Digitally printed on acid free paper.
Ideas into Books®
WESTVIEW
P.O. Box 605
Kingston Springs, Tennessee 37082

The Lingo Guide for Builders is meant solely as a tool to assist in advancing communications between English and Spanish speakers. It is not meant to be used for any legally binding communications nor is the editor, publisher, or author responsible for any errors, omissions, or damages resulting from the use of information contained in *The Lingo Guide for Builders*.

CONTENTS

Basics

BASIC TERMS
Términos Básicos

A

access – acceso (ahk-SEH-soh)
addition – adición (ah-dee-see-ON)
anchor – ancla (AHN-klah)
apprentice – aprendiz (ah-PREN-dis)
attic – ático / desván (AH-tee-koh / dehs-VAN)

B

backfill – relleno (reh-YEH-noh)
baseboard – zócalo (SOH-kah-loh)
basement – sótano (SOH-tah-noh)
bathroom – baño (BAHN-yo)
bathtub – bañera (bahn-YEH-rah)
block, blocking – traba / trabar / bloque / bloquear (TRAH-bah / trah-BAHR / BLOH-keh / bloh-keh-AHR)
blueprints – planos (PLAH –nos)
bracing – refuerzo (reh-fooh-EHR-soh)
building – edificio / edificación (eh-dee-FEE-see-oh / eh-dee-fee-kah-see-ON)

C

carpenter – carpintero (car-peen-TEH-roh)
caulking – enmasillado (ehn-mah-see-YAH-doh)
ceiling – techo interno / cielorraso (TEH-choh eehn-TEHR-noh / see-eh-loh-RAH-soh)
ceramic tile – baldosa cerámica (bahl-DOH-sah seh-RAH-me-kah)
chalk line – línea de marcar, tendel / línea de gis / línea de demarcación / línea de tiza (LEE-neh-ah deh mahr-KAHR, tehn-DEHL / LEE-neh-ah deh his / LEE-neh-ah deh deh-mahr-kah-see-ON / LEE-neh-ah deh TEEH-sah)
chase – canaleta / museca (kah-nah-LEH-tah / moo-SEH-kah)
chimney – chimenea (chee-meh-NEH-ah)
circuit breaker – interruptor de circuito (een-teh-roop-TOHR deh seer-koo-EEH-toh)
coarse – grueso / áspero (groo-EH-soh / AHS-peh-roh)
code – código (KOH-dee-goh)
column – columna (koh-LOOM-nah)
concrete – concreto (kohn-KREH-toh)

conduit – conducto (kohn-DOOK-toh)
connection – conexión / unión (koh-nek-see-ON / oo-nee-ON)
connector – conector (koh-nehk-TOHR)
contractor – contratista (kohn-trah-TEEHS-tah)
cracked walls – paredes agrietadas (pah-REH-dehs ah-gree-eh-TAH-dahs)
cracks – rajas / grietas (RAH-hahs/gree-EH-tahs)
crown – corona (koh-ROH-nah)
curb – bordillo / guarnición / borde de acera (bore-DEE-yoh / gwahr-nee-see-ON / BORH-deh deh ah-SEH-rah)

D

damper – regulador (reh-goo-lah-DOOR)
deck, decking – cubierta / balcón (koo-bee-EHR-tah / bahl-KOHN)
design drawings – planos de diseño (PLAH-nohs deh dis-EN-yo)
diesel – diesel (deeh-sel)
dig – excavar (ex-kah-VAHR)
door – puerta (pooh-EHR-tah)
doorway – entrada (ehn-TRAH-dah)
dormer – ventanilla sobresaliente / dórmer (vehn-tah-NEEH-yah soh-breh-sah-leeh-EHN-teh / dormer)
double plate – solera doble (soh-LEH-rah DOH-bleh)
drain / drainage – desagüe / drenaje (deh-SAH-gweh/dreh-NAH-heh)
drywall – drywall / muro en seco / (drái uól / MOO-roh ehn SEH-koh)
duct – conducto (kohn-DOOK-toh)
dwelling – vivienda / residencia (vee-vee-EHN-dah / reh-see-DEHN-see-ah)

E

electrical outlet – enchufe / toma corriente (ehn-CHOO-feh / TOH-mah koh-ree-EHN-teh)
electrician – electricista (eh-lehk-tree-SEES-tah)
electricity – electricidad (eh-lehk-tree-see-DAHD)
elevator – elevador / ascensor (eh-leh-vah-DOOR / ah-sehn-SOHR)
enclosed – encerrado (ehn-seh-RAH-doh)
enclosure – cerramiento (seh-rah-me-EHN-toh)
engineer – ingeniero (een-heh-nee-EH-roh)
exhaust – escape (ehs-KAH-peh)
exit – salida (sah-LEE-dah)
extension cord – cable de extensión (KAH-bleh deh ex-ten-see-ON)
exterior wall – muro / pared exterior (MOO-roh / pah-REHD ex-teh-ree-OHR)

F

façade – fachada (fah-CHAH-dah)
facing brick – ladrillo frontal (lah-DREE-yoh frohn-TAHL)

fan – abanico / ventilador (ah-BAH-nee-koh / vehn-tee-lah-DOOR)

faucet – llave / grifo (YAH-veh / GREE-foh)

felt – fieltro (fee-EHL-troh)

fence – cerca / medianera (SEHR-kah / meh-dee-ah-NEH-rah)

filled – relleno / rellenado (reh-YEH-noh / reh-yeh-NAH-doh)

finish – acabado (ah-kah-BAH-doh)

finishing nail – clavo sin cabeza (KLAH-voh seen kah-BEH-sah)

fitting – accesorio / conexión (ahk-seh-SOH-ree-oh / koh-nehx-see-ON)

fixture – accesorio (ahk-seh-SOH-ree-oh)

flashing – cubrejuntas / tapajuntas (koo-breh-HOON-tahs / -pah-HOON-tahs)

flashlight – linterna / lámpara / faro (leen-TEHR-nah / LAHM-pah-rah / FAH-roh)

flex conduit – conducto / portacables flexible (kohn-DOOK-toh / pore-tah-KAH-blehs flek-SEE-bleh)

floodlight – iluminación industrial / luz de faro (ee-loo-me-nah-see-ON een-doos-tree-AHL / loose deh FAH-roh)

floor – piso (PEE-soh)

flooring – revestimiento para pisos / material para pisos (reh-vehs-tee-me-EHN-toh PAH-rah PEE-sohs / mah-teh-ree-AHL PAH-rah PEE-sohs)

floor deck – plataforma (plah-tah-FOR-mah)

flue – conducto de humo (kohn-DOOK-toh deh OO-moh)

fluorescent – fluorescente (floh-reh-SEHN-teh)

forms [concrete] – encofrados (ehn-koh-FRAH-dohs)

formwork – encofrado (ehn-koh-FRAH-doh)

foundation – fundación (foon-dah-see-ON)

foundation wall – muro de fundación (MOO-roh deh foon-dah-see-ON)

frame – marco / estructura / armazón (MAHR-koh / ehs-trook-TOO-rah / ahr-mah-ZOHN)

framed – armado (ahr-MAH-doh)

framework – armazón (ahr-mah-SOHN)

fuel – combustible (come-boos-TEE-blay)

fumes – gases / emanaciones (gases / eh-mah-nah-see-OH-nehs)

furred out, furring – enrasado (ehn-rah-SAH-doh)

fuse – fusible (foo-SEE-bleh)

fuse box – caja de fusibles (KAH-hah deh foo-SEE-blehs)

G

gable – hastial (ahs-tee-AHL)

gable roof – techo a dos aguas (TEH-choh ah dohs AH-gwahs)

gauge [instrument] – calibrador / indicador / medidor (kah-lee-brah-DOOR / een-dee-kah-DOOR / meh-deeh-DOOR)

gauge [thickness] – caliber / grosor (kah-LEE-breh / groh-SOHR)
garage – garaje / cochera (gah-RAH-heh / koh-CHEH-rah)
gasket – arandela / empaque / junta (ah-rahn-DEH-lah / ehm-PAH-keh / HOON-tah)
gas – gas (gas)
gas main – cañería principal de gas (kahn-yeh-REE-ah preen-see-PAHL deh gas)
generator – generador (hey-nehr-rah-DOOR)
girder – viga maestra / jácena (VEE-gah mah-EHS-trah / HAH-seh-nah)
glazed, glazing – vidriado / encristalado (vee-dree-AH-doh / ehn-krees-tah-LAH-doh)
glue – resistol / pegamento / goma / cola (reh-sees-TOHL / peh-gah-MEHN-toh / GOH-mah / KOH-lah)
grade – nivel de terreno (nee-VEHL deh teh-REH-noh)
gravel – grava / gravilla / granzón (GRAH-vah / grah-VEE-yah / grahn-SON)
grommet – arandela / ojal / hembra (ah-rahn-DEH-lah / oh-HAL / EHM-brah)
ground fault circuit – interruptor / fusible de seguridad a tierra (een-teh-roop-TOHR / foo-SEE-bleh deh seh-goo-ree-DAHD ah tee-EH-rah)
ground level – planta baja (PLAHN-tah BAH-hah)
ground wire – cable a tierra (KAH-bleh ah tee-EH-rah)
grout – lechada / mortero de cemento (leh-CHAH-dah / mor-TEH-roh deh seh-MEHN-toh)
gutter – canal / canaleta (kah-NAHL / kah-nah-LEH-tah)
gypsum board – gypsum board / panel de yeso (gypsum board / PAH-nehl deh YEH-soh)

H

hallway – pasillo (pah-SEE-yoh)
handle – manija / mango / agarradera (mah-NEE-hah / MAHN-goh / ah-gah-rah-DEH-rah)
handrail – pasamanos (pah-sah-MAH-nohs)
hangers – ganchos / colgadores (GAHN-chohs / kohl-gah-DOH-rehs)
hardboard – tablero duro (tah-BLEH-roh DOO-roh)
hatch – compuerta (kohm-pooh-EHR-tah)
header – cabecera / cabezal (kah-beh-SEH-rah / kah-beh-SAHL)
heater – calefactor / calentador (kah-leh-fahk-TOHR / kah-lehn-tah-DOOR)
heating – calefacción (kah-leh-fahk-see-ON)
hinge – bisagra (bee-SAH-grah)
hip roof – techo a cuatro aguas (TEH-choh ah koo-AH-troh AH-gwahs)
hole – hoyo / agujero / boquete / hueco (OH-yoh /

ah-goo-HEH-roh / boh-KEH-the / ooh-EH-koh)
hose – manguera (mahn-GEH-rah)
house plans – planos de casa (PLAH-nohs deh CAH-sah)

I

incline – declive / inclinación / pendiente / inclinar / ladear
(deh-KLEE-veh / een-klee-nah-see-ON / pehn-deeEHN-the / een-klee-NAHR / lah-deh-AHR)
insulating – aislante (eyes-LAHN-teh)
insulation – aislamiento (eyes-lah-meEHN-toh)
insurance – seguro (say-GOOH-ro)
interior room – cuarto interior (koo-AHR-toh een-teh-ree-OHR)
interlocking – enclavamiento / entrelazado
(ehn-klah-vah-meEHN-toh / ehn-treh-lah-SAH-doh)

J

job site – lugar de la obra (loo-GAHR deh lah OH-brah)
joint – unión (oo-nee-ON)
joint compound – pasta de muro (PAHS-tah deh MOO-roh)
joist – vigueta (vee-GEH-tah)
joist [floor] – vigueta del piso (vee-GEH-tah dehl PEE-soh)
joist hanger – estribo para vigueta (ehs-TREE-boh PAH-rah
vee-GEH-tah)
joist [load-bearing] – viga de carga (VEE-gah deh KAHR-gah)
junction – empalme / unión (ehm-PAHL-meh / oo-nee-ON)

K

kitchen sink – fregadero / lavaplatos (freh-gah-DEH-roh /
lah-vah-PLAH-tohs)

L

ladder – escalera (ehs-kah-LEH-rah)
latching device – dispositivo de traba (dees-poh-see-TEE-voh deh
TRAH-bah)
lawn – césped / pasto / grama / chipica / zacate (SEHS-pehd /
PAHS-toh / GRAH-mah / chee-PEE-kah / sah-KAH-teh)
layout – croquis / diseño / diagramación (kroh-KEYS / dee-SEHN-yo
/ dee-ah-grah-mah-seeOHN)
lift – levantamiento / alzada (leh-vahn-tah-meEHN-toh / ahl-SAH-dah)
light – luz (luz)
lightbulb – bombilla (bohm-BEE-yah)
light fixture – accesorio de iluminación (ahk-sehs-OR-ee-oh deh
ee-loo-me-nah-see-ON)
limestone – piedra caliza (pee-EH-drah kah-LEE-sah)
link, linkage – enlace / tirante / conexión (ehn-LAH-she / tee-RAHN-
the / koh-nek-see-ON)

lintel – dintel (deen-TEHL)

lock – candado / cerradura / cerrojo (kahn-DAH-doh / seh-rah-DOO-rah / seh-ROH-hoh)

lock bolt – perno de seguridad (PEHR-noh deh seh-goo-ree-DAHD)

lot – terreno / lote (teh-REH-noh / LOH-teh)

lumber – madera de construcción (mah-DEH-rah deh kohns-trook-see-ON)

M

mailbox – buzón de correos (boo-SOHN deh koh-REH-ohs)

main – principal / matriz (preen-see-PAHL / mah-TREES)

main breaker – interruptor principal (een-teh-roop-TOHR preen-see-PAHL)

main vent – ventilación principal (vehn-tee-lah-see-ON preen-see-PAHL)

manhole – boca de acceso / pozo de entrada / tapa de alcantarilla (BOH-kah deh ahk-SEH-soh / POH-soh deh ehn-TRAH-dah / tah-pah deh al-can-tah-REE-yah)

mason – albañil (ahl-bah-NYEE-eel)

masonry – mampostería (mahm-pohs-teh-REE-ah)

mastic – mastique (mahs-TEEK)

metal deck – plataforma metálica (plah-tah-FOR-mah meh-TAH-lee-kah)

meter – medidor (meh-dee-DOOR)

molding – moldura (mohl-DOO-rah)

mortar – mortero / argamasa (mohr-TEH-roh / AR-gah-MAH-sah)

N

nailing strip – listón para clavar (lees-TOHN PAH-rah klah-VAHR)

nails – clavos (KLAH-vohs)

nosings – vuelos (vooh-EH-lohs)

O

occupancy – capacidad / ocupación / cupo (kah-pah-see-DAHD / oh-koo-pah-see-ON / KOO-poh)

offset – desplazamiento / pieza en "S"/ pieza de inflexión / desvío / desnivel (dehs-plah-sah-meEHN-toh / peeEH-sah ehn EH-she / peeEH-sah deh een-flehk-see-ON / dehs-VEE-oh / dehs-knee-VEHL)

open air – aire libre (EYE-reh LEE-breh)

opening – abertura (ah-behr-TOO-rah)

overhang – voladizo / vuelo / saledizo (voh-lah-DEE-soh / voo-EH-loh / sah-leh-DEE-soh)

overlap – traslape / sobresolape / superposición (trahs-LAH-peh / soh-breh-soh-LAH-peh / soo-pehr-poh-see-see-ON)

oxidizers – oxidantes (ohk-see-DAHN-tehs)

P

pallet – estante / tarima / plataforma (ehs-TAHN-teh / tah-REE-mah / plah-tah-FOR-mah)

painter – pintor (peen-TOHR)

paneling – empanelado (ehm-pah-neh-LAH-doh)

particle board – madera aglomerada / madera contra enchapada (mah-DEH-rah ah-gloh-meh-RAH-dah / mah-DEH-rah KOHN-trah-ehn-chah-PAH-dah)

partition – tabique / separación / division (tah-BEE-keh / seh-pah-rah-see-ON / dee-vee-see-ON)

passageway – pasillo (pah-SEE-yoh)

pavement – pavimento (pah-vee-MEHN-toh)

performance – desempeño / comportamiento / rendimiento (deh-sehm-PEHN-yo / kohm-pohr-tah-me-EHN-toh / rehn-dee-me-EHN-toh)

permit – permiso [de construcción] (pehr-MEE-soh [deh kohns-trook-see-ON])

pipe, piping – cañería / caño / tubería / tubo (kah-nee-eh-REE-ah / KAHN-yo / too-beh-REE-ah / TOO-boh)

plank – tablón (tah-BLOHN)

plaster – azotado / enjarre / enlucido / yeso (ah-soh-TAH-doh / ehn-HAH-reh / ehn-loo-SEE-doh / YEH-soh)

plastering – revoque / enlucido / repello / forjado (reh-VOH-keh / ehn-loo-SEE-doh / reh-PEH-yoh / fohr-HAH-doh)

plumber – fontanero / plomero (fohn-tah-NEH-roh / ploh-MEH-roh)

plumbing – plomería / cañería / tubería (ploh-meh-REE-ah / kah-nee-eh-REE-ah / too-beh-REE-ah)

plywood – tableros de madera contrachapada / plywood (tah-BLEH-rohs deh mah-DEH-rah kohn-trah-chah-PAH-dah / plái uúd)

poles / posts – postes (POHS-tehs)

portable – portátil (pore-TAH-teel)

power outlet – tomacorriente / enchufe (toh-mah-koh-ree-EHN-the / ehn-CHOO-feh)

power strip – zapatilla eléctrica (sah-pah-TEE-yah eh-LEHK-tree-kah)

premises – local / sitio (loh-KAHL / SEE-tee-oh)

pressure – presión (preh-see-ON)

primed – imprimado (eem-pree-MAH-doh)

primer – imprimador (eem-pree-mah-DOOR)

property line – línea / límite de propiedad / deslinde (LEE-neh-ah / LEE-me-teh deh proh-pee-eh-DAHD / dehs-LEEN-deh)

pump – bomba (BOHM-bah)

R

rack – cremallera / tarima (kreh-mah-YEH-rah / tah-REE-mah)

rafter – cabria / viga (KAH-bree-ah / VEE-gah)

rail – carril / baranda (kah-REEL / bah-RAHN-dah)
railing – baranda / pasamanos (bah-rahn-DAH / PAH-sah MAH-nohs)
rate – proporción (proh-pore-see-ON)
rebar – barra de refuerzo (BAH-rah deh reh-fooh-EHR-soh)
register – rejilla / registro (reh-HE-yah / reh-HIS-troh)
regulator – regulador (reh-goo-lah-DOOR)
reinforced masonry – mampostería reforzada
(mahm-pohs-teh-REE-ah reh-fohr-SAH-dah)
reinforcement – refuerzo / armadura (reh-fooh-EHR-soh /
ahr-mah-DOO-rah)
release – descarga / liberación / desenganche (dehs-CAR-gah /
lee-beh-rah-see-ON / des-ehn-GAHN-cheh)
relief valve – válvula / llave de alivio (VAHL-voo-lah / YAH-veh
deh ah-LEE-vee-oh)
removal – eliminación / remoción (eh-lee-me-nah-see-ON /
reh-moh-see-ON)
repair – reparación (reh-pah-rah-see-ON)
residence – residencia (reh-see-DEHN-see-ah)
restroom – baño / sanitario (BAHN-yo / sah-nee-TAH-ree-oh)
rib – costilla (kohs-TEE-yah)
ridge – cresta / cumbrera (KREHS-tah / koom-BREH-rah)
ridgeboard – tabla de cumbrera (tah-blah de koom-BREH-rah)
rim – borde / orilla (BOHR-deh / oh-REEH-yah)
ring shank nail – clavos con fuste corrugado (KLAH-vohs kohn FOOS-
steh koh-roo-GAH-doh)
riser [stair] – contrahuella [escalera] (kohn-trah-ooh-EH-yah
[ehs-kah-LEH-rah])
rivet – remache (reh-MAH-cheh)
rock – roca / piedra (ROH-kah / pee-EH-drah)
roof covering – revestimiento de tejado (reh-vehs-tee-meEHN-toh deh
teh-HAH-doh)
roof drain – desagüe de tejado (deh-SAH-gweh deh teh-HAH-doh)
roof [flat] – tejado plano (teh-HAH-doh PLAH-noh)
roof sheeting – entarimado de tejado (ehn-tah-ree-MAH-doh deh
teh-HAH-doh)
roofing – techado (teh-CHAH-doh)
roofing square – cuadro de tejado / cubierta de tejado
(koo-AH-droh deh teh-HAH-doh / koo-be-EHR-tah deh teh-HAH-doh)
room – cuarto / sala / habitación (koo-AHR-toh / SAH-lah /
ah-bee-tah-see-ON)
rubble – escombro (ehs-KOHM-broh)
runner – larguero (lahr-GEH-roh)

S

sandstone – arenisca (ah-reh-NEES-kah)
scaffold – andamio (ahn-DAH-me-oh)
scope – alcance (ahl-KAHN-seh)
screw – tornillo (tohr-NEE-yoh)
sealant – sellador (seh-yah-DOOR)
self-closing – auto cierre (AH-oo-toh see-EH-reh)
setback – retraso (reh-TRAH-soh)
sewage – aguas negras / cloacas (AH-gwahs NEH-grahs / kloh-AH-kahs)
sewer – cloaca / alcantarilla (kloh-AH-kah / ahl-kahn-tah-REE-yah)
shaft – recinto (reh-SEEN-toh)
sheathing – entablado (ehn-tah-BLAH-doh)
sheet – pliego / chapa / plancha / lámina (pleeEH-goh / CHAH-pah / PLAHN-chah / LAH-me-nah)
sheet metal – lamina / chapa / metálica / laminado (LAH-me-nah / CHAH-pah / meh-TAH-lee-kah / lah-me-NAH-doh)
sheetrock – sheetrock (sheetrock)
shelf – repisa (reh-PEE-sah)
shingle – teja / tejamanil (TEH-hah / teh-hah-mah-NEEL)
shingle [asphalt] – teja de asfalto (TEH-hah deh ahs-FAHL-toh)
shingle [wood] – teja de madera / ripio (TEH-hah deh mah-DEH-rah / REE-pee-oh)
shiplap – traslape / rebajo a media madera (trahs-LAH-peh / reh-BAH-hoh ah MEH-dee-ah mah-DEH-rah)
shower door – puerta de ducha (pooh-EHR-tah deh DOO-chah)
shower stall – ducha (DOO-chah)
shower head – regadera (reh-gah-DEH-rah)
shrinkage – contracción / encogimiento / reducción (kohn-trahk-see-ON / ehn-koh-he-me-EHN-toh / reh-dook-see-ON)
shut-off valves – válvulas de cierre (VAHL-voo-lahs deh see-EH-reh)
sidewalk – acera (ah-SEH-rah)
sill plate – solera inferior (soh-LEH-rah EEN-feh-ree-ohr)
sink – lavabo (lah-VAH-boh)
site – sitio (SEE-tee-oh)
slab – losa (LOH-sah)
sleeve – manga (MAHN-gah)
slope – pendiente / talud / declive (pehn-dee-EHN-teh / tah-LOOD / deh-KLEE-veh)
smoke – humo (OO-moh)
smoke detector – sensor de humo / detector de humo (sen-SOHR deh OO-moh / deh-tehk-TOHR deh OO-moh)
soffit – sofito (soh-FEE-toh)

span – vano / claro / espacio (VAH-noh / KLAH-roh / ehs-PAH-see-oh)

spigot – llave / grifo / canilla / espiga (YAH-veh / GREE-foh / kah-NEE-yah / ehs-PEE-gah)

spike – clavo para madera (KLAH-voh PAH-rah mah-DEH-rah)

splice – empalme / traslape / junta / union (ehm-PAHL-meh / trahs-LAH-peh / HOON-tah / oo-nee-ON)

sprinkler – rociador (roh-see-AH-door)

stairs – escaleras (ehs-kah-LEH-rahs)

steel – acero (ah-SEH-roh)

steeple – campanario (kahm-pah-NAH-ree-oh)

steps – escalones (ehs-kah-LOH-nehs)

stone – piedra / roca (pee-EH-drah / ROH-kah)

stress – esfuerzo (ehs-fooh-EHR-soh)

strip – listón (lees-TOHN)

stripping – tiras metálicas (TEE-rahs meh-TAH-lee-kahs)

structure – estructura (ehs-trook-TOO-rah)

stucco – revoque / enlucido / estuco (reh-VOH-keh / ehn-loo-SEE-doh / ehs-TOO-koh)

stud – montante / parante / barrote (mohn-TAHN-the / pah-RAHN-the / bah-ROH-teh)

stud bearing wall – muro con montante / parante (MOO-roh kohn mohn-TAHN-the / pah-RAHN-teh)

stud finder – stud finder / busca montantes (studfinder / BOOS-kah mohn-TAHN-tehs)

subfloor – contrapiso / bajopiso / piso subterráneo (kohn-trah-PEE-soh / bah-hoh-PEE-soh / PEE-soh soohb-teh-RAH-neh-oh)

subroof – base de tejado (BAH-seh deh teh-HAH-doh)

supervisor – supervisor / inspector (soo-pehr-vee-SOHR / eens-pehk-TOHR)

support – apoyo / soporte (ah-POH-yoh / soh-PORE-teh)

swinging door – puerta pivotante / puerta giratoria (pooh-EHR-tah pee-voh-TAHN-the / pooh-EHR-tah heeh-rah-TOH-reeh-ah)

switch plate – placa de interruptor / apagador (PLAH-kah deh een-teh-roop-TOHR / ah-pah-gah-DOOR)

T

tar paper – papel de brea (PAH-pehl deh BREH-ah)

temporary – provisional (proh-vee-see-oh-NAHL)

termite – termita (tehr-ME-tah)

threshold – umbral / entrada (OOM-brahl / ehn-TRAH-dah)

tile [floor] – azulejo / baldosa (ah-soo-LEH-hoh / bahl-DOH-sah)

tile [masonry] – ladrillo cerámico (lah-DREE-yoh seh-RAH-me-koh)

timber – madera (mah-DEH-rah)

toilet – sanitario / excusado / retrete / baño
(sah-nee-TAH-ree-oh / ex-koo-SAH-doh / reh-TREH-the / BAHN-yo)
tongue and groove – machihembrado (mah-chee-ehm-BRAH-doh)
tool – herramienta (eh-rah-me-EHN-tah)
treated wood – madera tratada (mah-DEH-rah trah-TAH-dah)
truss – cercha / reticulado / armadura / cabreada / caballete
(SEHR-chah / reh-tee-koo-LAH-doh / ahr-mah-DOO-rah / kah-breh-ah-
DAH / kah-bah-YEH-teh)

U

underlayment – capa base / bajo piso (KAH-pah BAH-she /
BAH-hoh PEE-soh)
urinal – urinal / urinario / mingitorio (oo-ree-NAHL / oo-ree-
NAH-ree-oh / mean-he-TOH-ree-oh)
use – uso / usar / utilizar (OO-soh / oo-SAHR oo-tee-lee-SAHR)

V

vacuum – vacío / aspiradora (vah-SEE-oh / ahs-pee-rah-DOH-rah)
vent – respiradero / ventilación (rehs-pee-rah-DEH-roh /
vehn-tee-lah-see-ON)
vestibule – vestíbulo (vehs-TEE-boo-loh)
vinyl siding – revestimiento de vinilo (reh-vehs-tee-me-EHN-toh
deh vee-NEE-loh)
vise – morsa / prensa (MORE-sah / PREHN-sah)
voltage – voltaje (vohl-TAH-heh)
volts – voltios (VOHL-tee-ohs)

W

wainscot, wainscoting – friso / alfarje / revestimiento (FREE-soh /
ahl-FAHR-heh / reh-vehs-tee-me-EHN-toh)
walkway – camino / pasillo (kah-ME-noh / pah-SEE-yoh)
wall – muro / pared (MOO-roh / PAH-rehd)
wallboard – plancha de yeso / cartón de yeso (PLAHN-chah de
YEH-soh / car-TOHN deh YEH-soh)
washer and dryer – lavadora y secadora (lah-vah-DOH-rah ee seh-kah-
DOH-rah)
washer – arandela / planchuela de perno (ah-rahn-DEH-lah /
plan-choo-EH-lah deh PEHR-noh)
water heater – calentador de agua (kah-lehn-TAH-door deh AH-gwa)
water main – tubería principal / matriz (too-beh-REE-ah preen-see-
PAHL / mah-TREES)
wax seal – empaque / empacadura de cera (ehm-PAH-keh / ehm-
pah-kah-DOOH-rah deh SEH-rah)
weeds – yerbas / yerbajos / malezas / paja / yuyos (YEHR-bahs /
yehr-BAH-hohs / mah-LEH-sahs / PAH-hah / yoo-yohs)
welding – soldadura (sohl-dah-DOO-rah)

window – ventana (vehn-TAH-nah)
window sill – soporte de ventana / repisa (soh-PORE-teh deh vehn-TAH-nah / reh-PEE-sah)
wire – alambre / cable (ah-LAHM-breh / KAH-bleh)
wire tie – alambre de paca / alambre para empacar / alambre para amarrar (ah-LAHM-breh deh PAH-kah / ah-LAHM-breh PAH-rah ehm-pah-KAHR / ah-LAHM-breh PAH-rah ah-mah-RAHR)
wood framing – bastidores de madera (bahs-tee-DOH-rehs deh mah-DEH-rah)
work – trabajo (trah-BAH-hoh)

BASIC TOOLS
Herramientas Básicas

axe – hacha (AH-chah)
bar – barreta (bah-REH-tah)
blower – sopladora (soh-plah-DOH-rah)
broom – escoba (ehs-KOH-bah)
brush – pincel / brocheta / brocha (PEEN-sehl / broh-CHEH-tah / BROH-chah)
carpenter's apron – mandil de carpintero (mahn-DEEL deh car-peen-TEH-roh)
carpenter's square – escuadra de carpintero (ehs-koo-AH-drah deh car-peen-TEH-roh)
C-clamp – prensa de "C" (PREHN-sah deh SEH)
clamp – prensa (PREHN-sah)
chain pipe wrench – llave de cadena (YAH-veh de kah-DEH-nah)
chain saw – sierra de cadena (see-EH-rah deh kah-DEH-nah)
circular saw – sierra circular [de mano] (see-EH-rah seer-koo-LAHR [deh MAH-nohl)
compound mitre saw – sierra de corte angular (see-EH-rah deh KOHR-teh ahn-goo-LAHR)
drill – taladro (tah-LAH-droh)
drill bit – barrena (bah-REH-nah)
electric drill – taladradora [eléctrica] (tah-lah-drah-DOH-rah [eh-LEHK-tree-kah])
electric saw – sierra eléctrica (see-EH-rah eh-LEHK-tree-kah)
file – lima (LEE-mah)
flashlight – linterna / faro (leen-TEHR-nah / FAH-roh)
flathead screwdriver – desarmador / destornillador de paleta (deh-sahr-mah-DOOR / dehs-tohr-nee-yah-DOOR deh pah-LEH-tah)
framing square – escuadra (ehs-koo-AH-drah)
funnel – embudo (ehm-BOO-doh)

hammer – martillo (mahr-TEE-yoh)
hand saw – serrucho (seh-ROO-choh)
hoe – azadón (ah-sah-DOHN)
hose – manguera (mahn-GEH-rah)
jigsaw – sierra de vaivén (see-EH-rah deh vah-ee-VEHN)
jointer – cepillo automático (seh-PEE-yoh ah-oo-toh-MAH-tee-koh)
ladder – escalera [de mano] (ehs-kah-LEH-rah [deh MAH-noh])
level – nivel (nee-VEHL)
mallet – mazo (MAH-soh)
mitre box – caja de corte angular (KAH-hah deh KOHR-teh ahn-goo-LAHR)
mitre saw – sierra de retroceso (see-EH-rah deh reh-troh-SEH-soh)
mixer – mezcladora / revolvedora (mehs-klah-DOH-rah / reh-vohl-veh-DOH-rah)
nail gun – clavadora automática (klah-vah-DOH-rah ah-oo-toh-MAH-tee-kah)
phillips screwdriver – desarmador / destornillador de punta en cruz (dehs-ahr-mah-DOOR / dehs-tohr-nee-yah-DOOR deh POOHN-tah ehn- kroohs)
pick – pico (PEE-koh)
pick-axe – zapapico (sah-PAH-pee-koh)
plane – cepillo de carpintero (seh-PEE-yoh deh car-peen-TEH-roh)
pliers – alicates / pinzas (ah-lee-KAH-tehs / PEEN-sahs)
plumb line – hilo de plomada (EE-loh deh ploh-MAH-dah)
power washer – lavado a presiòn (lah-VAH-doh ah preh-see-ON)
pump – bomba (BOHM-bah)
radial saw – sierra fija (see-EH-rah FEE-hah)
rake – rastrillo (rahs-TREE-yoh)
rebar bender – doblador de varilla (doh-blah-DOOR deh vah-REE-yah)
reciprocating saw – sierra alternante (see-EH-rah ahl-tehr-nanh-the)
roller – aplanadora / rodillo (ah-plah-nah-DOH-rah / roh-DEE-yoh)
router – fresadora (freh-sah-DOH-rah)
safety glasses – gafas / lentes de seguridad (GAH-fahs/LEHN-tehs deh seh-goo-ree-DAHD)
sander – lijadora (lee-hah-DOH-rah)
saw – sierra (see-EH-rah)
sawhorse – burro (BOO-roh)
screwdriver – destornillador / desarmador (dehs-tohr-nee-yah-DOOR / dehs-ahr-mah-DOOR)
sheet metal shears – tijeras para metal (tee-HEH-rahs PAH-rah meh-TAHL)
shovel – pala (PAH-lah)
sledgehammer – marro / mazo (MAH-roh / MAH-soh)
square – escuadra (ehs-koo-AH-drah)

soldering torch – soplete (soh-PLEH-the)
stapler – engrapadora (ehn-grah-pah-DOH-rah)
staple gun – engrapadora automática (ehn-grah-pah-DOH-rah ah-oo-toh-MAH-tee-kah)
table saw – sierra fija / sierra de mesa (see-EH-rah FEE-hah / see-EH-rah deh MEH-sah)
tool box – caja de herramientas (KAH-hah deh eh-rah-me-EHN-tahs)
torch – antorcha (ahn-TOHR-cah)
T-square – regla "T" (REH-glah teh)
utility knife – navaja (nah-VAH-hah)
wheelbarrow – carretilla (kah-reh-TEE-yah)
wrench – llave (YAH-veh)
wrench [adjustable] – llave francesa (YAH-veh frahn-SEH-sah)
wrench [plumbers] – llave inglesa perico (YAH-veh een-GLEH-sah per-REE-koh)
work light – lámpara de trabajo (LAHM-pah-rah deh trah-BAH-hoh)

BASIC SUPPLIES
Provisiones Básicas

buckets – baldes / cubetas / cubos (BAHL-dehs / kooh-BEH-tahs / KOOH-bohs)
caulk – masilla (mah-SEE-yah)
caution tape – cinta de precaución (SEEN-tah deh preh-kah-ooh-see-OHN)
chalk – tiza / gis (TEEH-sah / heehs)
flags – banderines (bahn-deh-REEH-nehs)
flashlight – linterna / faro (leehn-TEHR-nah / FAH-roh)
gloves – guantes (gooh-AHN-tehs)
glue – goma / pega / cola (GOH-mah / PEH-gah / KOH-lah)
grass seed – zacate / semilla de pasto / grama / chipica (sah-KAH-teh / seh-MEEH-yah deh PAHS-toh / GRAH-mah / cheeh-PEEH-kah)
gravel – grava / granzón (GRAH-vah / grahn-SOHN)
hard hat – casco de seguridad (KAHS-koh deh seh-gooh-reeh-DAHD)
knee pads – protectores de rodillas (proh-tehk-TOH-rehs deh roh-DEEH-yahs)
magic marker – marcador negro (mar-cah-DOR NAY-groh)
marking paint – pintura para demarcar (peehn-TOOH-rah PAH-rah deh-mahr-KAHR)
marking tape – cinta para demarcar (SEEN-tah PAH-rah deh-mahr-KAHR)

nails – clavos (CLAH-vohs)
paper – papel (pah-PEHL)
pen / pencil – lapicera / bolígrafo / lápiz (lah-peeh-SEH-rah / boh-LEEH-grah-foh / LAH-peehs)
rags – trapos (TRAH-pohs)
safety glasses – lentes de seguridad (LEHN-tehs deh seh-gooh-reeh-DAHD)
sand – arena (ah-REH-nah)
screws – tornillos (tohr-NEEH-yohs)
seed & straw – semillas y paja (seh-MEEH-yahs eeh PAH-hah)
sod – césped / pasto (SEHS-pehd / PAHS-toh)
spray paint – pintura en atomizador / pintura sprey (peehn-TOOH-rah enh ah-toh-meeh-sah-DOHR / peehn-TOOH-rah spray)
straw – paja (PAH-hah)
tape measure – cinta para medir (SEEN-tah PAH-rah meh-DEEHR)
utility knife – corta pluma (KOHR-tah PLOOH-mah)

ARCHITECTURAL STYLES
Estilos Arquitectónicos

A-frame – marco en A (MAHR-koh ehn ah)
American classic – clásico americano (KLAH-see-koh ah-meh-reeh-KAH-noh)
beach house – casa de playa (KAH-sah deh PLAH-yah)
bungalow – bungalow (boohn-gah-LOW)
cabin – cabaña (kah-BAHN-yah)
chalet – chalet (chah-LEHT)
contemporary – contemporáneo (kohn-tehm-poh-RAH-neh-oh)
cottage – cabaña (kah-BAHN-yah)
country estate – campestre (kahm-PEHS-treh)
craftsman – artesano (ahr-teh-SAH-noh)
duplex – dúplex (DOOH-pleks)
estate home – residencia (reh-see-DEHN-see-ah)
farm house – granja (GRAHN-hah)
four-square – cuatro cuadrado (kooh-AH-troh kooh-ah-DRAH-doh)
French country – estilo francés (ehs-TEEH-loh frahn-SEHS)
loft – desván (dehs-VAHN)
mediterranean style – estilo mediterráneo (ehs-TEEH-loh meh-deeh-teh-RAH-neh-oh)
old-world style – estilo antiguo / viejo mundo (ehs-TEEH-loh ahn-TEEH-gooh-oh / vee-EH-hoh MOON-doh)
ranch – rancho (RANH-choh)
victorian – victoriano (veehk-toh-reeh-AH-noh)

waterfront house – casa a orillas de la playa (KAH-sah ah oh-REEH-yahs deh lah PLAH-yah)

zero-lot line – casa sin terreno (KAH-sah seen teh-REH-noh)

APPLIANCES
Electrodomésticos

air purifier – purificador de aire (pooh-reeh-fee-kah-DOHR deh AH-eeh-reh)

blender – licuadora (leeh-kooh-ah-DOH-rah)

coffee pot – cafetera (kah-feh-TEH-rah)

convection oven – horno (OR-noh)

dehumidifier – deshumidificador (dehs-ooh-meeh-deeh-fee-kah-DOHR)

dishwasher – lavadora de platos (lah-vah-DOH-rah deh PLAH-tohs)

dryer – secadora (seh-kah-DOH-rah)

electric stove / oven – estufa eléctrica / horno eléctrico (ehs-TOOH-fah eh-LEHK-tree-kah / OR-noh eh-LEHK-tree-koh)

freezer – congelador (kohn-heh-lah-DOHR / freezer)

garbage disposal – dispensador de basura (deehs-pehn-sah-DOHR deh bah-SOOH-rah)

gas stove / oven – estufa de gas / horno de gas (ehs-TOOH-fah deh gas / OR-noh deh gas)

hot water heater – calentador de agua (kah-lehn-tah-DOHR deh AH-goo-ah)

ice maker – fabricador de hielo (fah-breeh-kah-DOHR deh eeh-EH-loh)

juicer – exprimidor (ehks-pree-mee-DOOR)

microwave – microondas (meeh-kroh-OHN-dahs)

mixer – batidora (bah-teeh-DOH-rah)

refrigerator – refrigerador / nevera / heladera (reh-free-heh-rah-DOHR / neh-VEH-rah / eh-lah-DEH-rah)

toaster – tostador (tohs-tah-DOHR)

vent hood – campana de la estufa (kahm-PAH-nah deh lah ehs-TOOH-fah)

warming tray – bandeja de calentamiento (bahn-DEH-hah deh kah-lehn-tah-meeh-EHN-toh)

washing machine – lavadora (lah-vah-DOOR-ah)

water filter – filtro de agua (FEEL-troh deh AH-goo-ah)

HOUSE TERMS & ACCESSORIES
Términos de Casa y Accesorios

1st floor – primer piso (PREEH-mehr PEEH-soh)

2nd floor – segundo piso (seh-GOOHN-doh PEEH-soh)

3rd floor – tercer piso (tehr-SEHR PEEH-soh)

acreage – acres de terreno (AH-krehs deh teh-REH-noh)

attic – ático / desván / tapanco (AH-teeh-koh / dehs-VAHN / tah-PAHN-koh)

awnings – toldos (TOHL-dohs)

basement – sótano (SOH-tah-noh)

bird feeder – comedero de pájaros (koh-meh-DEH-roh deh PAH-hah-rohs

carport – enramada / cobertizo para carros (ehn-rah-MAH-dah / coh-behr-TEE-soh pah-rah CAH-rohs)

chimney cap – tapa de chimenea (TAH-pah deh cheeh-meh-NEH-ah)

computer – computadora (kohm-pooh-tah-DOH-rah)

copula – cópula (KOH-pooh-lah)

curtains – cortinas (kohr-TEEH-nahs)

fenced – encercado (ehn-serh-KAH-doh)

five-acre track – terreno de cinco acres (teh-REH-noh deh SEEN-koh AH-krehs)

flat panel TV – televisión plana (tay-lay-vee-see-ON PLAH-nah)

fire pit – fogón / fosa de fuego (foh-GOHN / FOH-sah deh foo-EH-goh)

full-light basement – sótano iluminado (SOH-tah-noh eeh-looh-meeh-NAH-doh)

garage – garaje (gah-RAH-heh)

gardening shed – cobertizo para jardinería (koh-behr-TEEH-soh PAH-rah hahr-deeh-neh-REEH-ah)

hammock hut – choza para colgar hamaca (CHOH-sah PAH-rah kohl-GAHR ah-MAH-kah)

intercom systems – sistema recíproco de comunicación (sis-tay-mah ray-SEE-proh-coh deh co-moo-ne-cah-see-ON)

mailbox – buzón de correo (booh-SOHN deh koh-REH-oh)

mirrors – espejos (ehs-PEH-hohs)

one acre – un acre (oohn AH-kreh)

out building – construcción fuera de la casa / construcción aparte (kohn-stroohk-see-OHN fooh-EH-rah deh lah KAH-sah / kohn-stroohk-see-OHN ah-PAHR-the)

patio furniture – muebles de patio (mooh-EH-blehs deh patio)

plasma screen TV – televisión plasma (tay-lay-vee-see-OHN plahs-mah)

play house – casa de juego / casa de muñecas (KAH-sah de hooh-EH-goh / KAH-sah deh mooh-NYEH-kahs)

pool – piscina / pileta / alberca (peehs-SEE-nah / peeh-LEH-tah / ahl-BEHR-kah)

pool house – casa de piscina / pileta / alberca (KAH-sah deh peehs-SEE-nah / peeh-LEH-tah / ahl-BEHR-kah)

porch swing – columpio de porche (koh-LOOHM-peeh-oh deh POHR-cheh)

privacy fence – cerca de privacidad (SEHR-kah deh preeh-vah-see-DAHD)

shades – persianas (pehr-see-AH-nahs)

shutters – contraventanas / postigos (KOHN-trah-vehn-TAH-nahs / pohs-TEEH-gohs)

stained glass windows – vidrios ahumados para ventanas (VEEH-dreeh-ohs ah-ooh-MAH-dohs PAH-rah lahs vehn-TAH-nahs)

stepping stones – sendero / camino de piedras (sehn-DEH-roh / kah-MEEH-noh deh peeh-EH-drahs)

stereo / audio speaker – estéreo (es-TEHR-ee-oh)

telephones – teléfonos (teh-LEH-foh-nohs)

tent – carpa (KAHR-pah)

tool shed – cuarto para herramientas (kooh-ahr-TOH PAH-rah eh-rah-meeh-EHN-tahs)

trailer – remolque / traila (reh-MOHL-keh / TRAH-eeh-lah)

tree house – casita de árbol (kah-SEE-tah deh AHR-bohl)

weather vane – veleta (veh-LEH-tah)

WI-FI wireless fidelity – conecciòn al internet sin cable (koh-nehk-she-ON al in-tehr-net seen cah-blay)

window boxes – jardineras / canteros de ventana (hahr-deeh-NEH-rahs / kahn-TEH-rohs deh vehn-TAH-nah)

wrought iron – hierro colado (eeh-EH-roh koh-LAH-doh)

wrought iron fence – cerca de hierro / reja (SEHR-kah deh eeh-EH-roh / REH-hah)

ROOM TYPES
Habitaciones

bathroom – baño (BAHN-yoh)

bedroom – dormitorio / recámara / cuarto (dohr-meeh-TOH-reeh-oh / reh-KAH-mah-rah / kooh-AHR-toh)

billiards room – salón de billar (sah-LOHN deh bee-YAHR)

breakfast room – cuarto para desayunar (kooh-AHR-toh PAH-rah deh-sah-yooh-NAHR)

deck – balcón (bahl-KOHN)

den – salón de estar (sah-LOHN deh ehs-TAHR)

dining room – comedor (koh-meh-DOHR)

eat-in kitchen – cocina comedor (koh-SEE-nah koh-meh-DOHR)

exercise room – cuarto de ejercicios (kooh-AHR-toh deh eh-hehr-SEE-see-ohs)

family room – salón familiar (sah-LOHN fah-meeh-leeh-AHR)

Florida room – salón estilo florida (sah-LOHN ehs-TEEH-loh floh-REEH-dah)

foyer – vestíbulo (vehs-TEEH-booh-loh)

guest house – casa de invitados (KAH-sah deh eehn-veeh-TAH-dohs)

guest room – cuarto para invitados (kooh-AHR-toh PAH-rah eehn-veeh-TAH-dohs)

half bath – medio baño (MEH-deeh-oh BAHN-yoh)

hobby room – salón para pasatiempo (sah-LOHN PAH-rah pah-sah-TEE-ehm-poh)

kitchen – cocina (koh-SEE-nah)

laundry room – salón de lavandería (sah-LOHN deh lah-vahn-deh-REEH-ah)

library – biblioteca (bee-bleeh-oh-TEH-kah)

living room – sala (SAH-lah)

master bath – baño del cuarto matrimonial (BAHN-yoh dehl kooh-AHR-toh mah-treeh-moh-neeh-AHL)

master bedroom – cuarto / dormitorio / recámara matrimonial (kooh-AHR-toh / dohr-meeh-TOH-reeh-oh / reh-KAH-mah-rah mah-treeh-moh-neeh-AHL)

master suite – suit matrimonial (Suite mah-treeh-moh-neeh-AHL)

media room – sala de computadora (sah-LAH deh kohm- pooh-tah-DOH-rah)

mud room – sala para sacudirse los pies (sah-LAH PAH-rah sah-kooh-DEEHR-seh lohs PEEH-ehs)

office – oficina (oh-fee-SEE-nah)

outside kitchen – cocina exterior (koh-SEE-nah ex-teh-ree-OHR)

pantry – despensa (dehs-PEHN-sah)

patio – patio (patio)

playroom – salón de juegos (sah-LOHN deh hooh-EH-gohs)

powder room – tocador (toh-kah-DOHR)

screened-in porch – porche encubierto (POHR-cheh ehn-kooh-bee-EHR-toh)

solarium – solar (SOH-lahr)

study – estudio (ehs-TOOH-deeh-oh)

sunroom – solar / salón iluminado por el sol (soh-LAHR / sah-LOHN ee-loo-me-NAH-doh pohr ehl sohl)

wine room – salón para vinos (sah-LOHN PAH-rah VEEH-nohs)

INSECTS
Insectos

ants – hormigas (ohr-MEEH-gahs)
aphid – afidio (ah-FEE-dee-oh)
bagworm – lombriz / gusano de bolsa (lohm-BREEHS / gooh-SAH-noh deh BOHL-sah)
bee – abeja (ah-BEH-hah)
beetle – escarabajo (ehs-kah-rah-BAH-hoh)
butterfly – mariposa (mah-reeh-POH-sah)
caterpillar – gusano (gooh-SAH-noh)
cricket – grillo (GREEH-yoh)
dragonfly – chicharra / libélula (cheeh-CHAH-rah / leeh-BEH-looh-lah)
fire ant – hormiga de fuego (ohr-MEEH-gah deh fooh-EH-goh)
grasshopper – saltamontes (sahl-tah-MOHN-tehs)
grub worm – lombriz excavadora (lohm-BREEHS ehks-kah-vah-DOH-rah)
Japanese beetle – escarabajo japonés (ehs-kah-rah-BAH-hoh hah-poh-NEHS)
ladybug – mariquita (mah-reeh-KEEH-tah)
leafhopper – salta hojas (SAHL-tah OH-hahs)
leaf roller – enrollador de hojas (ehn-roh-yah-DOHR deh OH-hahs)
midge – mosca de agua (MOHS-kah deh AH-gooh-ah)
mosquito – mosquito / zancudo (mohs-KEEH-toh / sahn-KOOH-doh)
nematode – nematodo (neh-mah-TOH-doh)
praying mantis – mantis religiosa (MAHN-teehs reh-leeh-heeh-OH-sah)
rose chafer – escarabajo de rosa (ehs-kah-rah-BAH-hoh deh ROH-sah)
rose leaf beetle – escarabajo de hoja de rosa (ehs-kah-rah-BAH-hoh deh OH-hah deh ROH-sah)
slug – babosa (bah-BOH-sah)
snail – caracol (kah-rah-KOHL)
spider mites – huevos de araña (ooh-EH-vohs deh ah-RAHN-yah)
squash bug – chinche de calabaza (CHEEHN-cheh deh kah-lah-BAH-sah)
stem borer – perforador de tallos (pehr-foh-rah-DOHR deh TAH-yohs)
tent caterpillar – oruga de cabaña (oh-ROOH-gah deh kah-BAHN-yah)
wasp – avispa (ah-VEEHS-pah)
whitefly – mosca blanca (MOHS-kah BLAHN-kah)
weevil – gorgojo / coco (gohr-GOH-hoh / KOH-koh)

WILDLIFE
Reino Animal

armadillo – armadillo / cachicamo / quirquincho
(ahr-mah-DEEH-yoh / kah-cheeh-KAH-moh / keehr-KEEHN-choh)
beaver – castor (kahs-TOHR)
cat – gato (GAH-toh)
chipmunk – ardilla listada (arh-DEEH-yah leehs-TAH-dah)
coyote – coyote (koh-YOH-teh)
dog – perro (PEH-roh)
deer – venado / ciervo (veh-NAH-doh / see-EHR-voh)
fox – zorro (SOH-roh)
frog – rana (RAH.nah)
groundhog – marmota (mahr-MOH-tah)
lizard – lagartija (lah-gahr-TEEH-hah)
mole – topo (TOH-poh)
mouse / mice – ratón / ratones (rah-TOHN / rah-TOH-nehs)
opossum – zarigüeya / rabipelado / faro (sah-reeh-gooh-EH-yah /
rah-bee-peh-LAH-doh / FAH-roh)
rabbit – conejo (koh-NEH-hoh)
raccoon – mapache (mah-PAH-cheh)
shrew – musaraña (mooh-sah-RAHN-yah)
skunk – zorrillo / zorrino / mofeta (soh-REEH-yoh / soh-REEH-noh /
moh-FEH-tah)
snake – culebra / víbora / serpiente (kooh-LEH-brah / VEEH-boh-rah
/ sehr-peeh-EHN-teh)
squirrel – ardilla (arh-DEEH-yah)
toad – sapo (SAH-poh)
vole – ratón de rampo (rah-TOHN deh KAHM-poh)

COLORS
Los Colores

black – negro (NEH-groh)
blue – azul (ah-SOOL)
brown – marrón / café (mah-RRROHN / kah-FEH)
green – verde (VEHR-deh)
orange – anaranjado (ah-nah-rahn-HAH-doh)
pink – rosado (rrroh-SAH-doh)
purple – púrpura / morado (POO-r-poo-rah / moh-RAH-doh)
red – rojo (RRROH-hoh)
white – blanco (BLAHN-koh)
yellow – amarillo (ah-mah-REE-yoh)

MONTHS
Los Meses del Año

January – enero (eh-NEH-roh)
February – febrero (feh-BREH-roh)
March – marzo (MAHR-soh)
April – abril (ah-BREEL)
May – mayo (MAH-yoh)
June – junio (HOO-nee-oh)
July – julio (HOO-lee-oh)
August – agosto (ah-GOHS-toh)
September – septiembre (sep-tee-EHM-breh)
October – octubre (ohk-TOO-breh)
November – noviembre (noh-vee-EHM-breh)
December – diciembre (dee-see-EHM-breh)

DAYS
Los Días de la Semana

Monday – lunes (LOO-nehs)
Tuesday – martes (MAHR-tehs)
Wednesday – miércoles (me-EHR-koh-less)
Thursday – jueves (hoo-EH-vehs)
Friday – viernes (vee-EHR-nehs)
Saturday – sábado (SAH-bah-doh)
Sunday – domingo (doh-MEEN-goh)

SEASONS & WEATHER DESCRIPTIONS
Descripciones del Tiempo y las Estaciones

spring – primavera (pree-mah-VEH-rah)
summer – verano (veh-RAH-noh)
fall – otoño (oh-TOH-nyo)
winter – invierno (in-ve-ER-no)
hot – caliente (cah-le-EN-tay)
cold – frío (FREE-oh)
rain / raining – lluvia / lloviendo (YOO-vee-ah / yoh-vee-EN-doh)
sunshine / sunny – luz del sol / soleado (loose del sol / soh-lay-AH-doh)
snow / snowing – nieve / nevando (nee-EH-veh / neh-VAN-doh)
drought / dry – sequía / seco (say-KEY-ah / SAY-coh)
ice – hielo (ee-EH-lo)
freeze / freezing – congelado / congelando (cohn-hey-LAH-doh / cohn-hey-LAHN-doh

NUMBERS
Los Números

0 – cero (SEH-roh)
1 – uno (OO-noh)
2 – dos (dohs)
3 – tres (trehs)
4 – cuatro (koo-AH-troh)
5 – cinco (SEEN-koh)
6 – seis (SEH-ees)
7 – siete (see-EH-the)
8 – ocho (OH-choh)
9 – nueve (noo-EH-veh)
10 – diez (dee-EHS)
11 – once (OHN-she)
12 – doce (DOH-she)
13 – trece (TREH-seh)
14 – catorce (kah-TOHR-seh)
15 – quince (KEEN-seh)
16 – dieciseis (dee-eh-see-SEH-ees)
17 – diecisiete (dee-eh-see-see-EH-teh)
18 – dieciocho (dee-eh-see-OH-choh)
19 – diecinueve (dee-eh-see-noo-EH-veh)
20 – veinte (VEIN-teh)
21 – veintiuno (vein-tee-OO-noh)
22 – veintidos (vein-tee-DOHS)
30 – treinta (TREH-in-tah)
31 – treinta y uno (TREH-in-tah ee OOH-noh)
32 – treinta y dos (TREH-in-tah ee DOHS)
40 – cuarenta (kwah-REHN-tah)
50 – cincuenta (seen-koo-EHN-tah)
60 – sesenta (seh-SEHN-tah)
70 – setenta (seh-TEHN-tah)
80 – ochenta (oh-CHEN-tah)
90 – noventa (noh-VEHN-tah)
100 – cien (see-EHN)
200 – doscientos (doh-see-EHN-tohs)
300 – trescientos (treh-see-EHN-tohs)
500 – quinientos (kee-nee-EHN-tohs)
1000 – mil (meel)

BASIC CONVERSATIONAL PHRASES
Frases Básicas en Conversación

Do you speak English?
¿Habla inglés?
(AH-blah een-GLEHS?)

Do you speak Spanish?
¿Habla español?
(AH-blah ehs-pahn-YOHL?)

Hello – Hola (OH-lah)

Good-bye – Adiós (ah-dee-OHS)

Yes – Sí (see)

No – No (noh)

Please – Por favor (pore fah-VOHR)

Thank you – Gracias (GRAH-see-ahs)

What is your name?
¿Cuál es su nombre / Cómo se llama?
(koo-AHL ehs soo NOHM-breh / KOH-moh seh YAH-mah?)

My name is ____.
Mi nombre es ____. (me NOHM-breh ehs ____)
Me llamo ____. (meh YAH-moh ____)

How are you today?
¿Cómo está usted hoy / Cómo le va?
(KOH-moh ehs-TAH oos-TEHD OH-ee / KOH-moh leh vah?)

How is your family?
¿Cómo está su familia?
(KOH-moh ehs-TAH soo fah-ME-lee-ah?)

Very well, thank you.
Muy bien, gracias.
(MOO-ee bee-EHN, GRAH-see-ahs)

I am not well today.
No estoy bien hoy
(noh ehs-TOY bee-EN OH-ee)

I need help.
Necesito ayuda.
(neh-seh-SEE-toh ah-YOU-dah)

I will see you tomorrow.
Nos vemos mañana.
(nohs VEH-mohs mahn-YAH-nah)

I will not be here tomorrow.
No estaré aquí mañana.
(noh ehs-tah-REH ah-KEY mahn-YAH-nah)

Did you have a good weekend?
¿Pasó un buen fin de semana?
(pah-SOH oon boo-EHN feen deh seh-MAH-nah?)

Yes, I had a very good weekend.
Sí, pasé un muy buen fin de semana.
(see pah-SEH oon MOO-ee boo-EHN feen deh seh-MAH-nah)

I am going to the store. Do you need anything?
¿Voy a la tienda, necesita algo?
(VOH-ee ah lah tee-EHN-dah, neh-seh-SEE-tah AHL-goh?)

What time is it?
¿Qué hora es?
(keh OH-rah ehs?)

Where? – ¿Dónde? (DON-deh)

Where is _____ ?
¿Dónde está _____?
(DON-deh ehs-TAH _____?)

Where are_____ ?
¿Dónde están _____?
(DON-deh ehs-TAHN _____?)

What is that? – ¿Qué es eso? (keh ehs EH-soh?)

Congratulations!
¡Felicitaciones!
(feh-leeh-see-tah-see-OH-nehs)

Happy Birthday!
¡Feliz Cumpleaños!
(feh-LEEHS koohm-pleh-AH-neeh-ohs)

Merry Christmas!
¡Feliz Navidad!
(feh-LEEHS nah-veeh-DAHD)

Happy New Year!
¡Feliz Año Nuevo!
(feh-LEEHS AH-neeh-oh nooh-EH-voh)

Happy Easter!
¡Feliz Semana Santa!
(feh-LEEHS seh-MAH-nah SAHN-tah)

Happy Anniversary!
¡Feliz Aniversario!
(feh-LEEHS ah-neeh-vehr-SAH-reeh-oh)

Don't worry. Be happy!
¡No se preocupe. Sea feliz!
(noh seh preh-oh-KOOH-peh SEH-ah feh-LEEHS)

Life is good!
La vida es buena.
(lah VEEH-dah ehs booh-EH-nah)

BASIC JOB Q & A'S
Preguntas y Respuestas Básicas en el Trabajo

Do you have references?
¿Tiene referencias?
(tee-EH-neh reh-feh-REHN-see-ahs?)

Yes, I have references.
Sí, tengo referencias.
(see TEHN-goh reh-feh-REHN-see-ahs)

No, I do not have references.
No, no tengo referencias.
(noh noh TEHN-goh reh-feh-REHN-see-ahs)

We need a copy of your driver's license.
Necesitamos una copia de su licencia de conducir.
(neh-seh-see-TAH-mohs OOH-nah KOH-peeh-ah deh sooh
leeh-SEHN-see-ah deh kohn-doo-SEER)

We need a copy of your green card
Necesitamos una copia de su tarjeta de residencia.
(neh-seh-see-TAH-mohs OOH-nah KOH-peeh-ah deh sooh
tahr-HEH-tah deh reh-see-DEHN-see-ah)

We need a copy of your work permit.
Necesitamos una copia de su permiso de trabajo.
(neh-seh-see-TAH-mohs OOH-nah KOH-peeh-ah deh sooh
pehr-MEEH-soh deh trah-BAH-hoh)

We need a copy of your social security card.
Necesitamos una copia de su tarjeta de seguro social.
(neh-seh-see-TAH-mohs OOH-nah KOH-peeh-ah deh sooh
tahr-HEH-tah deh seh-GOOH-roh soh-see-AHL)

We need a copy of your insurance.
Necesitamos una copia de su seguro.
(neh-seh-see-TAH-mohs oo-nah CO-pee-ah deh soo seh-
GOO-roh)

We need you to sign the forms.
Necesitamos que firme las formas.
(neh-seh-see-TAH-mohs keh FEEHR-meh lahs fohr-MAHS)

What is your phone number?
¿Cuál es su número de teléfono?
(koo-AHL ehs soo NOO-meh-roh deh teh-LEH-foh-noh?)

My phone number is ____.
Mi número es ____.
(me NOO-meh-roh ehs ____)

Follow me to the job site.
Sígame hasta el sitio de trabajo.
(SEE-gah-meh AHS-tah ehl SEE-teeh-oh deh trah-BAH-hoh)

How many men do you have to help you?
¿Cuántos hombres tiene para ayudarlo / a?
(koo-AHN-tohs OHM-brehs tee-EH-neh PAH-rah ah-YOU-dahr-loh / lah?)

How big is your crew?
¿Cuán grande es su cuadrilla / equipo?
(kwahn GRAHN-deh ehs soo KWAH-dree-yah / eh-KEY-poh?)

My crew has _____ men.
Mi cuadrilla / equipo tiene _____ hombres.
(me koo-ah-DREE-yah/eh-KEY-poh tee-EH-neh _____ OHM-brehs)

You have a good crew of men.
Tiene un buen equipo de hombres.
(tee-EH-neh oon boo-EHN eh-KEY-poh deh OHM-brehs)

Do you have your own tools?
¿Tiene sus propias herramientas?
(tee-EH-neh soos PROH-pee-ahs eh-rah-me-EHN-tahs?)

When can you start the job?
¿Cuándo puede comenzar con el trabajo?
(koo-AHN-doh pooh-EH-deh koh-mehn-SAHR kohn EHL trah-BAH-hoh?)

I can begin the job next week.
Puedo comenzar con el trabajo la semana que viene.
(pooh-EH-doh koh-mehn-SAHR kohn ehl trah-BAH-hoh lah seh-MAH-nah keh vee-EH-neh)

How long will it take you to do the job?
¿Cuánto le tomará completar el trabajo?
(koo-AHN-toh leh toh-mah-RAH kohm-pleh-TAHR ehl trah-BAH-hoh?)

It will take a month / week / day to do the job.
Tomará un mes / una semana / un día para terminar el trabajo.
(toh-mah-RAH oon mehs / OO-nah seh-MAH-nah / oon DEE-ah PAH-rah tehr-me-NAHR ehl trah-BAH-hoh)

We need an estimate for the job.
Necesitamos un estimado por el trabajo.
(neh-seh-see-TAH-mohs oon ehs-tee-MAH-do pohr ehl trah-BAH-ho)

Can you give me a bid to do another job?
¿Puede darme un cotizado para hacer otro trabajo?
(pooh-EH-deh DAHR-meh oon coh-tee-ZAH-doh PAH-rah ah-SEHR
OH-troh trah-BAH-hoh?)

We can give you a bid to do another job.
Podemos darle un cotizado para hacer otro trabajo.
(poh-DEH-mohs DAHR-leh oon coh-tee-ZAH-doh PAH-rah ah-SEHR
OH-troh trah-BAH-hoh)

Can you work tomorrow?
¿Puede trabajar mañana?
(pooh-EH-deh trah-bah-HAHR mahn-YAH-nah?)

No, I cannot work tomorrow.
No, no puedo trabajar mañana.
(noh, noh PWAY-doh trah-bah-HAHR mahn-YAH-nah)

I can work every day.
Puedo trabajar todos los días.
(pooh-EH-doh trah-bah-HAHR TOH-dohs lohs DEE-ahs)

How much does this job pay?
¿Cuánto paga este trabajo?
(koo-AHN-toh PAH-gah EHS-teh trah-BAH-hoh?)

Your pay is going to be $ _____ per hour.
Su paga será _____ dólares la hora.
(soo PAH-gah seh-RAH _____ DOH-lah-rehs lah OH-rah)

When is pay day?
¿Cuándo es el día de pago?
(koo-AHN-doh ehs ehl DEE-ah deh PAH-goh?)

I will pay you at the end of the week / day / job.
Le pagaré al final de la semana / del día / del trabajo.
(leh pah-GAH-reh ahl fee-NAHL deh lah seh-MAH-nah / dehl DEE-ah /
dehl trah-BAH-hoh)

BASIC JOB SITE PHRASES
Frases Básicas en el Lugar de Trabajo

Drug use is not tolerated.
No se permite el uso de drogas.
(noh seh pehr-ME-teh ehl OO-soh deh DROH-gahs)

We do not drink on the job site.
No consumimos alcohol en el lugar de trabajo.
(noh kohn-sooh-MEEH-mohs ahl-KOHL ehn ehl looh-GAHR
deh trah-BAH-hoh)

Your work looks good.
Su trabajo se ve bien.
(soo trah-BAH-hoh seh veh bee-EHN)

Hold it there while I nail it.
Sosténgalo allí mientras lo clavo.
(sohs-TEHN-gah-loh ah-YEE me-EHN-trahs loh KLAH-voh)

Pick this up.
Recoja esto.
(reh-KOH-hah EHS-toh)

Raise it a little.
Levántelo un poco.
(leh-VAHN-teh-loh oon POH-koh)

Lower it a little
Bájelo un poco.
(BAH-heh-loh oon POH-koh)

Hammer this.
Martille esto.
(mahr-TEE-yeh EHS-toh)

Get someone to help you.
Consiga a alguien que lo ayude.
(kohn-SEE-gah ah AHL-guee-ehn keh loh ah-YOO-deh)

Let me help you with that.
Déjeme ayudarle con eso.
(DEH-heh-meh ah-you-DAHR-leh kohn EH-soh)

Help me carry this.
Ayúdeme a cargar esto.
(ah-YOU-deh-meh ah kahr-GAHR EHS-toh)

The key will be hidden here.
La llave estará escondida aquí.
(lah YAH-veh ehs-tah-RAH ehs-kohn-DEE-dah ah-KEY)

Please lock the door when you leave.
Por favor cierre la puerta con llave antes de irse.
(pore fah-VOHR see-EH-reh lah pooh-EHR-tah kohn YAH-veh
AHN-tehs deh EER-seh)

The port-a-pot is out back.
El baño portable está allí atrás.
(ehl BAH-nee-oh pore-TAH-bleh ehs-TAH ah-YEE ah-TRAHS)

The dumpster is over there.
El basurero está allá.
(ehl bah-soo-REH-roh ehs-TAH ah-YAH)

Be careful! – ¡Tenga cuidado! (TEHN-gah koo-eeh-DAH-doh!)

Follow me. – Sígame. (SEE-gah-meh)

Push. – Empuje. (ehm-POOH-heh)

Pull. – Jale. (HAH-leh)

Watch out! – ¡Cuidado! (koo-eeh-DAH-doh!)

We need to organize the tools.
Necesitamos organizar las herramientas.
(neh-seh-see-TAH-mohs or-gah-ne-ZAR lahs eh-rah-me-EHN-tahs)

Look in the truck.
Mire en la camioneta.
(MEE-reh ehn lah cahm-ee-YO-neh-tah)

Nice tool belt.
Buèn cinturón de herramientas.
(boo-EHN seen-too-ROHN deh eh-rah-me-EHN-tahs)

We need the house plans.

Necesitamos los planos de la casa.

(neh-seh-see-TAH-mos los PLAH-nos day la CAH-sah)

Do you want to take a lunch break?

¿Quiere tomar un descanso para almorzar?

(kee-EH-reh toh-MAHR oon dehs-KAHN-soh PAH-rah ahl-more-SAHR?)

Where is the hospital / clinic?

¿Dónde está un hospital / una clínica?

(DON-deh ehs-TAH oon ohs-pee-TAHL / OO-nah KLEE-nee-kah?)

Carpentry

CARPENTRY TERMS

CABINET STYLES & TERMS
Estilos de Gabinetes y Términos

arched – con arco / arqueado (kohn ARH-koh / ahr-keh-AH-doh)

back panels – paneles traseros (PAH-neh-lehs trah-SEH-rohs)

ball bearing – rolinera / rodamiento (roh-leeh-NEH-rah / roh-dah-mee-EHN-toh)

beveled glass – vidrio biselado (VEEH-dreeh-oh beeh-seh-LAH-doh)

bottom panels – páneles inferiores (PAH-neh-lehs eehn-feh-reeh-OH-rehs)

cabinet bracing – refuerzo para el gabinete (reh-fooh-ERH-soh PAH-rah ehl gah-bee-NEH-the)

cathedral – catedral (kah-teh-DRAHL)

coping joint – junta de acoplamiento machihembrado (HOOHN-tah deh ah-koh-plah-meeh-EHN-toh mah-cheeh-ehm-BRAH-doh)

custom – hacer a la medida (hah-SEHR ah lah meh-DEEH-dah)

drawer slides – deslizantes de las gavetas / los cajones (dehs-leeh-SAHN-tehs deh lahs gah-VEH-tahs / lohs kah-HOH-nehs)

door / drawer – sobresale de su marco (soh-breh-SAH-leh deh sooh MAHR-koh)

engineered wood – madera manufacturada (mah-DEH-rah mah-nooh-fahk-tooh-RAH-dah)

flat panel door – puerta de panel plano (pooh-ERH-tah deh PAH-nehl PLAH-noh)

framed – enmarcado (enh-mahr-KAH-doh)

framed door – puerta enmarcada (pooh-ERH-tah enh-mahr-KAH-doh)

frameless – sin marco (seen MARH-koh)

full extension – en toda su extensión (enh TOH-dah sooh ehks-tehn-see-OHN)

full overlay door / drawer – puerta / gaveta sin marcos (pooh-EHR-tah / gah-VEH-tah seen MAHR-kohs)

glass insert doors – puertas con vidrios insertados (pooh-EHR-tah kohn VEEH-dreeh-ohs eehn-sehr-TAH-dohs)

hardware – ferretería / herrería (feh-reh-teh-REEH-ah / eh-reh-REEH-ah)

inset door / drawer – puerta / gaveta incrustada (pooh-EHR-tah / gah-VEH-tah eenh-kroohs-TAH-dah)

joinery – ensamblamiento (ehn-sahm-blah-meeh-ENH-toh)

lipped door / drawer – puerta / gaveta con canalete y manija (pooh-EHR-tah / gah-VEH-tah kohn kah-nah-LEH-teh eeh mah-NEEH-hah)

mitered joint – empalme angular (ehm-PAHL-meh ahn-gooh-LAHR)

mullion doors – puertas con travesaños (pooh-EHR-tahs kohn trah-veh-SAHN-yohs)

nail rail – tira de clavos (TEEH-rah kohn CLAH-vohs)

particle board – cartón de aglomerado / contraenchapado (kahr-TOHN deh ah-gloh-meh-RAH-doh / kohn-trah-ehn-chah-PAH-doh)

plywood – plywood / madera prensada (plái uúd / mah-DEH-rah prehn-SAH-dah)

raised panel [solid] – panel levantado / elevado [sólido] (PAH-nehl leh-vahn-TAH-doh / eh-leh-VAH-doh [SOH-leeh-doh])

recessed flat panel – panel plano incrustado (PAH-nehl PLAH-noh eehn-kroohs-TAH-doh)

side panels – paneles / tableros laterales (pah-NEH-lehs / tah-BLEH-rohs lah-teh-RAH-lehss)

solid wood – madera maciza (mah-DEH-rah mah-SEE-sah)

square – escuadra (ehs-kooh-AH-drah)

stock – culata / caja / surtido / reservas (kooh-LAH-tah / KAH-hah / soohr-TEEH-doh / reh-SEHR-vahs)

tempered glass – vidrio templado (VEEH-dreeh-oh tehm-PLAH-doh)

toe-kick board – tablero para rodapies / zócalo (tah-BLEH-roh PAH-rah roh-dah-peeh-EHS / SOH-kah-loh)

top panels – paneles superiores (pah-NEH-lehs sooh-peh-reeh-OH-rehs)

track & roller – herramientas track and roller (eh-rah-meeh-EHN-tahs Track and Roller)

traditional overlay – puerta / gaveta con tope (pooh-EHR-tah / gah-VEH-tah con TOH-pay)

wood veneer – chapa de madera (CHAH-pah deh mah-DEH-rah)

vanities – tocador (toh-kah-DOHR)

CEILING TERMS
Términos de Cielos Rasos / Techos Internos

8 / 9 / 10 / 12 ft. high – ocho / nueve / diez / doce pies de alto (OH-choh / nooh-EH-veh / deeh-EHS / DOH-she peeh-EHS deh AHL-toh)

bead board – tablero para paredes (tah-BLEH-roh PAH-rah pah-REH-dehs)

exposed beams – vigas al descubierto (VEEH-gahs ahl dehs-kooh-bee-EHR-toh)

skylights – tragaluces / claraboyas (trah-gah-LOOH-sehs / clah-rah-BOH-yahs)

smooth finish – acabado liso (ah-kah-BAH-doh LEEH-soh)

speckled – moteado (moh-teh-AH-doh)

tray – bandeja / platón (banh-DEH-hah / plah-TOHN)

vaulted – con bóveda / cúpula (kohn BOH-veh-dah / KOOH-pooh-lah)

COUNTERTOP TERMS
Términos de Mesadas / Mezones

backsplash – salpicado (sahl-peeh-KAH-doh)
butcher block – mezón para cortar / tablón carnicero (meh-SOHN PAH-rah kohr-TAHR / tah-BLOHN car-knee-SEH-roh)
concrete – concreto (kohn-KREH-toh)
cultured stone – piedra cultivada (peeh-EH-drah koohl-teeh-VAH-dah)
glass – vidrio (VEEH-dreeh-oh)
granite – granito (grah-NEEH-toh)
grout color – color de la lechada / cemento (koh-LOHR deh lah leh-CHAH-dah / say-MEN-toh)
honed – afilado (ah-feeh-LAH-doh)
laminate – laminado (lah-meeh-NAH-doh)
marble – mármol (MAHR-mohl)
metals – metales (meh-TAH-lehs)
quartz – cuarzo (kooh-AHR-soh)
sandstone – arenisca (ah-reh-NEEHS-kah)
slate – pizarra (peeh-SAH-rah)
soapstone – esteatita / talco natural (ehs-teh-ah-TEEH-tah / TAHL-koh nah-tooh-RAHL)
solid surface – superficie sólida (sooh-pehr-FEE-see-eh SOH-leeh-dah)
stainless steel – acero inoxidable (ah-SEH-roh eeh-nohk-see-DAH-bleh)
stone – piedra (peeh-EH-drah) [See Stone Names]
stone [natural] – piedra natural (peeh-EH-drah)
stone [synthetic] – piedra sintética (peeh-EH-drah seen-TEH-teeh-kah)
tile – baldoza (bahl-DOH-sah)
travertine – mármol travertino (MAHR-mohl trah-vehr-TEEH-noh)

DOOR & WINDOW TERMS
Términos de Puertas / Ventanas

aluminum – aluminio (ah-looh-MEEH-neeh-oh)
antique door – puerta antigua (pooh-EHR-tah ahn-TEEH-gooh-ah)
awning window – ventanas con toldo (vehn-TAH-nahs kohn TOHL-doh)
bay – bahía (bah-EEH-ah)
casement window – bóveda de ventana (BOH-veh-dah deh vehn-TAH-nah)
decorative – decorativo (deh-koh-rah-TEEH-voh)
double-hung – colgado doble (kohl-GAH-doh DOH-bleh)
French doors – puertas francesas (pooh-EHR-tahs frahn-SEH-sahs)
garage doors – puertas del garaje (pooh-EHR-tahs dehl gah-RAH-heh)
glass – vidrio (VEEH-dreeh-oh)

hollow core doors – puertas de centro hueco (pooh-EHR-tahs deh SEHN-troh WEH-koh)

insulated – con aislamiento (kohn ah-eehs-lah-meeh-EHN-toh)

jamb size – tamaño jamba (tah-MAHN-yoh HAM-bah)

laminated doors – puertas laminadas (pooh-EHR-tahs l ah-meeh-NAH-dahs)

metal doors – puertas de metal (pooh-EHR-tahs deh meh-TAHL)

mullions – travesaños (trah-veh-SAHN-yohs)

paladin – herramientas paladín (eh-rah-meeh-EHN-tahs pah-LAH-deehn)

pane glass – pánel de vidrio (PAH-nehl deh VEEH-dreeh-oh)

picture – cuadro (kooh-AH-droh)

screen door – puerta de rejilla (pooh-EHR-tah deh reh-HEEH-yah)

screen window – ventana de rejilla (vehn-TAH-nah deh reh-HEEH-yah)

skylights – tragaluces / claraboyas (trah-gah-LOOH-sehs / klah-rah-BOH-yahs)

solid core doors – puertas macizas (pooh-EHR-tahs mah-SEE-sahs)

stained glass – vidrio ahumado (VEEH-dreeh-oh ah-ooh-MAH-doh)

storm window – ventana con protección para las tormentas (vehn-TAH-nah kohn proh-tehk-see-OHN PAH-rah lahs tohr-MEHN-tahs)

transoms – travesaño (trah-veh-SAHN-yoh)

wood – madera (mah-DEH-rah)

window glass – vidrio para ventana (VEEH-dreeh-oh PAH-rah vehn-TAH-nah)

window weights – contrapesos de las ventanas (kohn-trah-PEH-sohs deh lahs vehn-TAH-nahs)

EXTERIOR MATERIALS TERMS
Términos de Materiales para Exteriores

aluminum siding – revestimiento de aluminio (reh-vehs-teeh-meeh-EHN-toh deh ah-looh-MEEH-neeh-oh)

block – bloque (BLOH-keh)

brick – ladrillo (lah-DREEH-yoh)

concrete – concreto (kohn-KREH-toh)

copper gutters and downspouts – canaletes y cañerías de cobre (kah-nah-LEH-tehs eeh kahn-yeh-REEH-ahs deh KOH-breh)

gutters and downspouts –canaleta y cañerías de cobre (kah-nah-LEH-tah eeh kahn-yeh-REEH-ahs deh KOH-breh)

house wrap – papel protector para la casa en construcción (pah-PEHL proh-tehk-TOHR PAH-rah lah KAH-sah ehn kohn-stroohk-see-OHN)

shake shingles – tejas de ripia / madera (TEH-hahs deh REEH-peeh-ah / mah-DEH-rah)

siding – revestimiento (reh-vehs-teeh-meeh-EHN-toh)
slate roofing shingles – tejas de pizarra (TEH-hahs deh peeh-SAH-rah)
solar panels – páneles solares (PAH-neh-lehs soh-LAH-rehs)
stone – piedra (peeh-EH-drah) [see stone names]
stucco – estuco (ehs-TOOH-koh)
tile roofing shingles – tejas de baldoza (TEH-hahs deh bahl-DOH-sah)
vinyl siding – revestimiento de vinilo (reh-vehs-teeh-meeh-EHN-toh deh veeh-NEEH-loh)

FLOOR TERMS
Términos de Pisos

brick – ladrillo (lah-DREEH-yoh)
bamboo – bambú (bam-BOO)
carpet – alfombra (ahl-FOHM-brah)
concrete – concreto (kohn-KREH-toh)
hardwood – madera (mah-DEH-rah)
laminate – laminado (lah-meeh-NAH-doh)
stone – piedra (peeh-EH-drah) [see stone names]
tile – baldoza (bahl-DOH-sah)
vinyl – vinilo (veeh-NEEH-loh)

HARDWARE TERMS
Términos de Ferretería / Herrería

back plates – placas traseras (PLAH-kahs trah-SEH-rahs)
brass – latón (lah-TOHN)
bronze – bronce (BROHN-seh)
ceramic – cerámica (seh-RAH-meeh-kah)
chrome – cromo (KROH-moh)
copper – cobre (KOH-breh)
crystal – cristal (kreehs-TAHL)
deadbolt locks – cerraduras sin manijas (seh-rah-DOOH-rahs seen mah-NEEH-hahs)
door knobs – manijas de las puertas (mah-NEEH-hahs deh lahs pooh-EHR-tahs)
door stop – sujetador de puerta (sooh-heh-tah-DOHR deh pooh-EHR-tah)
double cylinder deadbolt – cerradura sin manija con cilindro doble (seh-rah-DOOH-rah seen mah-NEEH-hah kohn see-LEEHN-droh DOH-bleh)
glass – vidrio (VEEH-dreeh-oh)
hinges – bisagras (bee-SAH-grahs)
hooks – ganchos (GAHN-chohs)
knobs – manijas (mah-NEEH-hahs)

locksets – juegos de cerraduras (hooh-EH-gohs deh seh-rah-DOOH-rahs)
nickel – niquel (NEEH-kehl)
paper holder – sostenedor de papel (sohs-teh-neh-DOHR deh pah-PEHL)
pewter – peltre (PEHL-treh)
plastic – plástico (PLAHS-teeh-koh)
porcelain – porcelana (pohr-seh-LAH-nah)
pulls – arrastres / tirantes (ah-RAHS-trehs / teeh-RAHN-tehs)
towel bars – barras para las toallas (BAH-rahs PAH-rah lahs toh-AH-yahs)
silver – plata (PLAH-tah)
window locks – trabas / cerrojos de las ventanas (TRAH-bahs / seh-ROH-hohs deh lahs vehn-TAH-nahs)
wood – madera (mah-DEH-rah)
wrought iron – hierro forjado (eeh-EH-roh fohr-HAH-doh)

TRIM TERMS
Términos de Molduras

baseboard – zócalo / rodapiés (SOH-kah-loh / roh-dah-peeh-EHS)
bay window – ventana estilo balcón (vehn-TAH-nah ehs-TEEH-loh bahl-KOHN)
bead board – tableros para paredes (tah-BLEH-rohs PAH-rah pah-REH-dehs)
built-in bookshelves – estantes para libros incrustados (ehs-TAHN-tehs PAH-rah leeh-BROHS eehn-kroohs-TAH-dohs)
built-in ironing board – mesa de planchar incrustada (MEH-sah deh plahn-CHAHR eehn-kroohs-TAH-dah)
chair rail molding – moldeadura del pasamanos de la silla (mohl-deh-ah-DOOH-rah dehl pah-sah-MAH-nohs deh lah SEE-yah)
closet shelves – estantes / entrepaños del closet (ehs-TAHN-tehs / ehn-treh-PAHN-yohs dehl KLOH-set)
columns – columnas (koh-LOOHM-nahs)
crown molding – moldura en relieve (mohl-DOOH-rah ehn reh-leeh-EH-veh)
custom cabinets – gabinetes fabricados a la medida (gah-bee-NEH-tehs fah-breeh-KAH-dohs ah lah meh-DEEH-dah)
custom millwork – molenillo fabricado a la medida (moh-leh-NEEH-yoh fah-breeh-KAH-doh ah lah meh-DEEH-dah)
deck railing – barandas del balcón (bah-RAHN-dahs dehl bahl-KOHN)
decorative molding – moldura decorativa (mohl-DOOH-rah deh-koh-rah-TEEH-vah)
door casing – cavidad de la puerta (kah-veeh-DAHD deh lah pooh-EHR-tah)

facia – facia (fah-SEE-ah)
fireplace mantel – repisa de la chimenea (reh-PEEH-sah deh lah cheeh-meh-NEH-ah)
hearths – chimeneas (cheeh-meh-NEH-ahs)
kitchen work island – mezón separado en la cocina (meh-SOHN seh-pah-RAH-doh ehn lah koh-SEE-nah)
mantels – repisas (reh-PEEH-sahs)
picture box molding – moldura de caja para cuadros (mohl-DOOH-rah deh KAH-hah PAH-rah kooh-AH-drohs)
rear staircase – escaleras de atrás (ehs-kah-LEH-rahs deh ah-TRAHS)
shelving – estantería (ehs-tahn-teh-REE-ah)
shoe mold – rodapiés (roh-dah-peeh-EHS)
soffit – sofito (soh-FEE-toh)
special woodwork – trabajo especial en madera (trah-BAH-hoh ehs-peh-see-AHL ehn mah-DEH-rah)
staircase – escaleras (ehs-kah-LEH-rahs)
staircase [curved] – escaleras [en curva] (ehs-kah-LEH-rahs ehn COOR-vah)
stair handrails – pasamanos de las escaleras (pah-sah-MAH-nohs deh lahs ehs-kah-LEH-rahs)
stair risers – altura de los peldaños (ahl-TOOH-rah deh lohs pehl-DAHN-yohs)
stair treads – peldaños de las escaleras (pehl-DAHN-yohs deh lahs ehs-kah-LEH-rahs)
wainscoting – revestimiento (reh-vehs-teeh-meeh-EHN-toh)
wood paneling – empanelado de madera (ehm-pah-neh-LAH-doh deh mah-DEH-rah)

WALL TERMS
Términos de las Paredes

bead board – tablero para paredes (tah-BLEH-roh PAH-rah pah-REH-dehs)
concrete block – bloque de concreto (BLOH-keh deh kohn-KREH-toh)
drywall – drywall (drái uól)
foundation walls – paredes con bases (pah-REH-dehs kohn BAH-sehs)
framed – enmarcado (ehn-mahr-KAH-doh)
glass wall panels – paneles de vidrio para paredes (pah-NEH-lehs deh VEEH-dreeh-oh PAH-rah pah-REH-dehs)
house wrap – empapelado para las casas (ehm-pah-peh-LAH-doh PAH-rah lahs KAH-sahs)
paneling – empanelado (ehm-pah-neh-LAH-doh)
plaster – yeso / plaster (YEH-so / plaster)
poured concrete – concreto vaciado (kohn-KREH-toh vah-see-AH-doh)

stucco – estuco (ehs-TOOH-koh)
wainscot – friso (FREE-soh)
wall paper – papel para pared (pah-PEHL PAH-rah pah-REHD)

WOOD TYPES
Tipos de Madera

alder – abedul (ah-beh-DOOHL)
ash – ceniza (seh-NEEH-sah)
aspen – álamo (AH-lah-moh)
beech – haya (AH-yah)
birch – abedul (ah-beh-DOOHL)
Brazilian cherry – cerezo brasileño (seh-REH-soh brah-see-LEHN-yoh)
cherry – cerezo (seh-REH-soh)
hickory – nogal (noh-GAHL)
mahogany – caoba (kah-OH-bah)
maple – arce (AHR-seh)
oak – roble (ROH-bleh)
pine – pino (PEEH-noh)
poplar – álamo (AH-lah-moh)
pressure treated – presurizado (preh-sooh-reeh-SAH-doh)
teak – teca (TEH-kah)

CARPENTRY TOOLS
Herramientas de Carpintería

air compressor – compresor de aire (kohm-preh-SOHR deh EYE-ray)
air hose – manguera de aire (mahn-GEHR-rah deh EYE-ray)
chalk line – línea de tiza / gis (LEEH-neh-ah deh TEEH-sah / heehs)
chop saw – sierra rebanadora (see-EH-rah reh-bah-nah-DOH-rah)
chisel – cinsel (seen-SEHL)
circular saw – sierra circular (see-EH-rah seer-coo-LAHR)
drill – taladro (tah-LAH-droh)
file – lima (LEEH-mah)
hammer – martillo (mahr-TEEH-yoh)
level – nivel (neeh-VEHL)
nailgun – pistola de clavos (peehs-TOH-lah deh CLAH-vohs)
nail puller – saca clavo (SAH-cah CLAH-voh)
nails – clavos (CLAH-vohs)
pry bar – palanca (pah-LAHN-ca)
sander – arenador / lijador (ah-reh-nah-DOHR / lee-ha-DOHR)
screwdriver – destornillador / desarmador (dehs-tohr-neeh-yah-DOHR / dehs-ahr-mah-DOHR)

sledgehammer – almádena (ahl-MAH-day-nah)
square – cuadrado (coo-ah-DRAH-do)
table saw – sierra de mesa (see-EH-rah deh MEH-sah)
tape measurer – cinta de medir (SEEN-tah day may-DEER)

CARPENTRY SUPPLIES
Provisiones de Carpintería

chalk – tiza / gis (TEEH-sah / heehs)
dust mask – mascarilla para el polvo (mahs-kah-REEH-yah
PAH-rah ehl POHL-voh)
extension cord – cable de cable de extensión
(CAH-blay day eks-ten-see-ON)
fan– ventilador (ven-tee-lah-DOOR)
heater – calentador (cah-len-tah-DOOR)
horses – burros / caballetes (BOOH-rohs / kah-bah-YEH-tehs)
joist hangers – estribo para viguetas (ehs-TREE-boh PAH-rah veeh-
GEH-tahs)
knee pads – protectores de rodillas / rodilleras
(proh-tehk-TOH-rehs deh roh-DEEH-yahs / roh-dee-YEH-rahs)
ladder – escalera (ehs-kah-LEH-rah)
nails – clavos (CLAH-vohs)
sandpaper – lija (LEEH-hah)
scaffolding – andamiaje (ahn-dah-meeh-AH-heh)
screws – tornillos (tohr-NEEH-yohs)
stud finder – stud finder / busca montantes (stud finder /
BOOS-kah mohn-TAHN-tehs)
tool belt – cinturón herramientas (seen-toor-ON er-ah-mee-EHN-tahs)

FRAMING PHRASES
Frases de Enmarcar

See Page 32 for Basic Job Q & A's
and Job Site Phrases

How long have you been framing?
¿Cuánto hace que trabaja enmarcando?
(koo-AHN-toh AH-seh keh trah-BAH-hah ehn-mahr-CAN-doh?)

I have been framing for _____ years.
Hace _____ años que trabajo en enmarcando.
(AH-seh _____ AHN-yohs keh trah-BAH-hoh ehn ehn.mar.KAHN.doh)

The supplies will be delivered tomorrow.
Mañana entregarán los materiales.
(Mahn-YAH-nah ehn-treh-gah-RAHN lohs mah-teh-ree-AH-lehs)

Where is the hammer?
¿Dónde está el martillo?
(DON-deh ehs-TAH ehl mahr-TEE-yoh?)

Where are the nails?
¿Dónde están los clavos?
(DON-deh ehs-TAHN lohs KLAH-vohs?)

We need more nails.
Necesitamos más clavos.
(neh-seh-see-TAH-mohs mahs KLAH-vohs)

Where is the tape measurer?
¿Dónde está la cinta de medir?
(DON-deh ehs-TAH lah SEEN-tah deh meh-DEEHR?)

Where is the level?
¿Dónde está el nivel?
(DON-deh ehs-TAH ehl nee-VEHL?)

Where is the laser level?
¿Dónde está el nivel láser?
(DON-deh ehs-TAH ehl nee-VEHL LAH-sehr?)

Look in the toolbox.
Mire en la caja de herramientas
(MEE-rah ehn la CAH-ha deh er-rah-mee-EHN-tas)

Where are the shake shingles?
¿Dónde están las tejas de madera?
(DON-deh ehs-TAHN lahs TEH-hahs deh mah-DEH-rah?)

We need to install shake shingles.
Necesitamos instalar tejas de madera.
(neh-seh-see-TAH-mos eens-tah-LAHR TEH-hahs deh mah-DEH-rah)

We need more wood.
Necesitamos más madera.
(neh-seh-see-TAH-mohs mahs mah-DEH-rah)

We need more 2x4 / 2x6 / 2x8 / 2x10.
Necesitamos más de 2 por 4 / 2 por 6 / 2 por 8 / 2 por 10.
(neh-seh-see-TAH-mohs mahs deh dohs pore koo-AH-troh / dohs pore
SEH-ees / dohs pore OH-choh / dohs pore dee-EHS)

We need to stack the lumber there.
Necesitamos apilar la madera allí.
(neh-seh-see-TAH-mos ah-pee-LAHR lah mah-DEH-rah ah-YEE)

We need more scaffolding.
Necesitamos más andamiaje.
(neh-seh-see-TAH-mohs mahs ahn-dah-mee-AH-heh)

We need walk boards.
Necesitamos tablas para caminar.
(neh-seh-see-TAH-mohs TAH-blahs PAH-rah kah-me-NAHR)

We need the framing nail gun.
Necesitamos la clavadora automática.
(neh-seh-see-TAH-mohs lah klah-vah-DOH-rah ah-oo-toh-MAH-tee-kah)

We need the coil nailer.
Necesitamos la pistola para clavos enrollados en tiras / pistola de clavos con tambor.
(neh-seh-see-TAH-mohs lah pees-TOH-lah PAH-rah KLAH-vohs ehn-roh-YAH-dohs ehn TEE-rahs / pees-TOH-lah PAH-rah KLAH-vohs kohn tam-BOHR)

We need to frame this floor according to the blueprints.
Necesitamos construir un armazón / una estructura conforme los planos del arquitecto.
(neh-seh-see-TAH-mos kohns-troo-EER oon ahr-mah-SOHN / OO-nah ehs-trook-TOO-rah kohn-FOR-meh lohs PLAH-nohs dehl ahr-key-TECH-toh)

Can you cut?
¿Puede realizar cortes?
(pooh-EH-deh reh-ah-lee-SAHR KOHR-tehs?)

We need to fix the soffits.
Necesitamos arreglar los sofitos.
(neh-seh-see-TAH-mos ah-reh-GLAHR lohs soh-FEE-tohs)

We need to build a deck.
Necesitamos construir una cubierta / un balcón.
(neh-seh-see-TAH-mos kohns-TROO-eer OO-nah koo-beeEHR-tah / oon bahl-KOHN)

We need to lap side the rear of the building.
Necesitamos revestir con tablas con traslapo / solapo la parte trasera del edificio.
(neh-seh-see-TAH-mos reh-vehs-TEER kohn TAH-blahs kohn trahs-LAH-poh / soh-LAH-poh lah PAHR-teh trah-SEH-rah dehl eh-dee-FEE-see-oh)

We need to trim out the house after the drywall is done.
Necesitamos darle las terminaciones a la casa una vez finalizado el drywall.
(neh-seh-see-TAH-mos DAHR-leh lahs tehr-me-nah-see-OH-nehs ah lah KAH-sah OO-nah vehs fee-nah-lee-SAH-doh ehl drái uól)

We need to frame for a hip roof.
Necesitamos construir un armazón / una estructura para un techo a cuatro aguas.
(neh-seh-see-TAH-mos kohns-troo-EER oon ahr-mah-SOHN / OO-nah ehs-trook-TOO-rah PAH-rah oon TEH-choh ah koo-AH-troh AH-gwahs)

We need to frame for the gutters.
Necesitamos construir un armazón / una estructura para las canaletas.
(neh-seh-see-TAH-mos kohns-troo-EER oon ahr-mah-SOHN / OO-nah ehs-trook-TOO-rah PAH-rah lahs kah-nah-LEH-tahs)

We need to frame for a window here.
Necesitamos construir un bastidor / marco para una ventana aquí.
(neh-seh-see-TAH-mos kohns-troo-EER oon bahs-tee-DOOR / MAHR-koh PAH-rah OO-nah vehn-TAH-nah ah-KEY)

We need to frame for a dormer.
Necesitamos construir una armazón / una estructura para una ventana vertical de buhardilla / un aposento salidizo.
(neh-seh-see-TAH-mos kohns-troo-EER oo-nah ahr-mah-SOHN / OO-nah ehs-trook-TO-rah PAH-rah OO-nah vehn-TAH-nah vehr-tee-KAHL deh boo-ahr-DEE-yah / oon ah-poh-SEHN-toh sah-lee-DEE-soh)

We need a gable.
Necesitamos un hastial / gable.
(neh-seh-see-TAH-mohs oon ahs-tee-AHL /gable)

We need to get the stairs in.
Necesitamos colocar las escaleras.
(neh-seh-see-TAH-mos koh-loh-CAR lahs ehs-kah-LEH-rahs)

The stairs go here.
Las escaleras van aquí.
(las es-cah-LEHR-as vahn ah-KEY)

What is the pitch of the roof?
¿Cuál es la inclinación del techo?
(koo-AHL ehs lah een-klee-nah-see-ON dehl TEH-choh?)

We need to dry this in until the roofer gets here.
Necesitamos secar esto mientras llega el techista.
(neh-seh-see-TAH-mos seh-KAHR EHS-toh meEHN-trahs yeh-GAH ehl teh-CHEESE-tah)

We need to install doors / windows.
Necesitamos instalar las puertas / ventanas.
(neh-seh-see-TAH-mos eens-tah-LAHR lahs pooh-EHR-tahs / vehn-TAH-nahs)

That wall needs to be furred out.
Hay que enrasar esa pared.
(AH-ee keh ehn-rah-SAR EH-sah pah-REHD)

We need to plumb this.
Necesitamos colocarle plomería a esto.
(neh-seh-see-TAH-mos koh-loh-CAR-leh ploh-meh-REE-ah ah EHS-toh)

We need more support here.
Necesitamos más apoyo aquí.
(neh-seh-see-TAH-mohs mahs ah-POH-yoh ah-KEY)

We need a special beam here.
Necesitamos una viga especial aquí.
(neh-seh-see-TAH-mohs OO-nah VEE-gah ehs-peh-seeAHL ah-KEY)

We need to get an inspection.
Necesitamos obtener una inspección.
(neh-seh-see-TAH-mos ohb-teh-NEHR OO-nah eens-pek-see-ON)

We need to clean up the job site daily.
Necesitamos limpiar el área de trabajo a diario.
(neh-seh-see-TAH-mos leem-pee-AHR ehl AH-reh-ah deh trah-BAH-hoh ah dee-AH-ree-oh)

FLOORING PHRASES (Carpet / Tile / Wood)

CARPET PHRASES
Frases de Alfombra

See Page 32 for Basic Job Q & A's and Job Site Phrases

How long have you been installing carpet?
¿Cuánto hace que trabaja colocando alfombra?
(koo-AHN-toh AH-seh keh trah-BAH-hah koh-loh-CAN-doh ahl-FOHM-brah?)

I have been installing carpet for _____ years.
Hace _____ años que trabajo colocando alfombra.
(AH-seh _____ AHN-yohs keh trah-BAH-hoh koh-loh-CAN-doh ahl-FOHM-brah)

We need to measure for carpet.
Necesitamos tomar medidas para la alfombra.
(neh-seh-see-TAH-mos toh-MAHR meh-DEE-dahs PAH-rah lah ahl-FOHM-brah)

The carpet is on order.
La alfombra ya está pedida.
(lah ahl-FOHM-brah yah ehs-TAH peh-DEE-dah)

The carpet will be delivered tomorrow.
Mañana entregarán la alfombra.
(Mahn-YAH-nah ehn-treh-gah-RAHN lah ahl-FOHM-brah)

We need to go pick up the carpet.
Necesitamos ir a recoger la alfombra.
(neh-seh-see-TAH-mohs eer ah ray-coh-HAIR lah ahl-FOHM-brah)

We need to unload the truck.
Necesitamos descargar el camión.
(neh-seh-see-TAH-mohs days-car-GAR ehl cah-mee-ON)

We need to bring the carpet in here.
Necesitamos traer la alfombra para acá.
(neh-she-see-TAH-mohs trah-EHR lah ahl-FOHM-brah PAH-rah ah-CAH)

We need the hot iron and tape.
Necesitamos la plancha caliente y la cinta.
(neh-seh-see-TAH-mohs lah PLAHN-chah kah-lee-EHN-teh
ee lah SEEN-tah)

We need the carpet stretcher.
Necesitamos el aplanador para alfombra.
(neh-seh-see-TAH-mohs ehl ah-plah-nah-DOOR PAH-rah ahl-FOHM-brah)

We need sharp utility blades.
Necesitamos cuchillas de navaja afiladas.
(neh-seh-see-TAH-mohs koo-chee-YAHS deh nah-VAH-hah
ah-fee-LAH-dahs)

We need to install the pad first.
Necesitamos colocar primero el bajoalfombra.
(neh-seh-see-TAH-mos koh-loh-CAR pree-MEH-roh ehl bah-hoh-ahl-
FOHM-brah)

We need to install the tack boards.
Necesitamos instalar una cartelera / tabla de tachuelas.
(neh-seh-see-TAH-mos eens-tah-LAHR OO-nah kahr-teh-LEH-rah / TAH-
blah deh tah-choo-EH-lahs)

We need to put the carpet in the bedroom / closet.
Necesitamos alfombrar la habitación / el closet.
(neh-seh-see-TAH-mos ahl-fohm-BRAHR lah ah-bee-tah-see-ON / ehl
KLOH-set)

We need to clean up the job site daily.
Necesitamos limpiar el área de trabajo a diario.
(neh-seh-see-TAH-mos leem-pee-AHR ehl AH-reh-ah deh trah-BAH-hoh
ah dee-AH-ree-oh)

TILE FLOOR PHRASES
Frases de Baldosa

*See Page 32 for Basic Job Q & A's
and Job Site Phrases*

How long have you been installing tile?
¿Cuánto hace que trabaja colocando baldosa?
(koo-AHN-toh AH-seh keh trah-BAH-hah koh-loh-CAN-doh
bahl-DOH-sah?)

I have been installing tile for _____ years.
Hace _____ años que trabajo colocando baldosa.
(AH-seh _____ AHN-yohs keh trah-BAH-hoh koh-loh-CAN-doh bahl-
DOH-sah)

Where is the tile?
¿Dónde está la baldosa?
(DON-deh ehs-TAH lah bahl-DOH-sah?)

We need more tile.
Necesitamos más baldosa.
(neh-seh-see-TAH-mohs mahs bahl-DOH-sah)

We need to go pick up the tile.
Necesitamos ir a recoger las baldosas.
(neh-seh-see-TAH-mohs eer ah ray-coh-HAIR las bahl-DOH-sahs)

We need to bring the tile in here.
Necesitamos traer las baldosas para acá.
(neh-seh-see-TAH-mohs trah-EHR las bahl-DOH-sahs PAH-ra ah-CAH)

We need to unload the truck.
Necesitamos descargar el camión.
(neh-seh-see-TAH-mohs days-car-GAR el cah-mee-ON)

We need to stack the tile here.
Necesitamos apilar las baldosas aquí.
(neh-she-see-TAH-mohs ah-peel-AHR las bahl-DOH-sahs ah-KEY)

Where is the grout?
¿Dónde está la lechada?
(DON-deh ehs-TAH lah leh-CHAH-dah?)

We need more grout.
Necesitamos más lechada.
(neh-seh-see-TAH-mohs mahs leh-CHAH-dah)

We need to clean off the grout residue.
Necesitamos limpiar la lechada.
(neh-seh-see-TAH-mos leem-pee-AHR lah leh-CHAH-dah)

We need a 5-gallon bucket.
Necesitamos un balde de 5 galones.
(neh-seh-see-TAH-mohs oon BAHL-deh deh SEEN-koh gah-LOH-nehs)

We need clean water.
Necesitamos agua limpia.
(neh-seh-see-TAH-mohs AH-gwah LEEM-pee-ah)

We need a clean sponge.
Necesitamos una esponja limpia.
(neh-seh-see-TAH-mohs OO-nah ehs-POHN-hah LEEM-pee-ah)

We need the tile saw.
Necesitamos el serrucho para baldosa.
(neh-seh-see-TAH-mohs ehl seh-ROO-choh PAH-rah bahl-DOH-sah)

We need the grinder.
Necesitamos el molinillo.
(neh-seh-see-TAH-mohs ehl moh-lee-NEE-yoh)

Can you cut tile?
¿Puede cortar baldosa?
(pooh-EH-deh kohr-TAHR bahl-DOH-sah?)

Where is the saw?
¿Dónde está el serrucho?
(DON-deh ehs-TAH ehl seh-ROO-choh?)

We need to install ceramic tile in the bathroom / kitchen.
Necesitamos instalar baldosa cerámica en el baño / la cocina.
(neh-seh-see-TAH-mos eens-tah-LAHR bahl-DOH-sah seh-RAH-me-kah ehn ehl BAH-neeoh / lah koh-SEE-nah)

We need to clean up the job site daily.
Necesitamos limpiar el área de trabajo a diario.
(neh-seh-see-TAH-mohs leem-pee-AHR ehl AH-reh-ah deh trah-BAH-hoh ah dee-AH-ree-oh)

WOOD FLOOR PHRASES
Frases para Pisos de Madera

See Page 32 for Basic Job Q & A's and Job Site Phrases

How long have you been installing and refinishing wood floors?
¿Cuánto hace que trabaja colocando pisos de madera?
(koo-AHN-toh AH-seh keh trah-BAH-hah koh-loh-CAN-doh PEE-sohs deh mah-DEH-rah?)

I have been installing and refinishing wood floors for _____ years.
Hace _____ años que trabajo colocando pisos de madera.
(AH-seh _____ AHN-yohs keh trah-BAH-hoh koh-loh-CAN-doh PEE-sohs deh mah-DEH-rah)

We need to go pick up the hardwood floors.
Necesitamos ir a recoger los pisos de madera.
(neh-seh-see-TAH-mohs eer ah ray-coh-HAIR los PEE-sohs deh mah-DEH-rah)

We need to unload the truck.
Necesitamos descargar el camión.
(neh-seh-see-TAH-mohs days-car-GAR el ca-mee-ON)

We need to bring the hardwood in here.
Necesitamos traer la madera para pisos para acá.
(neh-seh-see-TAH-mohs tra-EHR la mah-DEH-rah PAH-ra PEE-sohs PAH-rah ah-CAH)

We need to stack the wood here.
Necesitamos apilar las baldosas aquí.
(neh-seh-see-TAH-mohs ah-peel-AHR las bahl-DOH-sahs ah-KEY)

Where are the knee-pads?
¿Dónde están los protectores de rodillas?
(DON-deh ehs-TAHN lohs proh-tech-TOH-rehs deh roh-DEE-yahs?)

Where are the safety masks?
¿Dónde están las máscaras protectoras?
(DON-deh ehs-TAHN lahs MAHS-kah-rahs proh-tech-TOH-rahs?)

Where are the mineral spirits?
¿Dónde está el aguarrás?
(DON-deh ehs-TAH ehl ah-gwah-RAHS?)

We need to lay this floor.
Necesitamos colocar este piso.
(neh-seh-see-TAH-mos koh-loh-CAR EHS-teh PEE-soh)

We need to refinish the hardwood floors.
Necesitamos realizar el acabado de los pisos de madera.
(neh-seh-see-TAH-mos re-ah-lee-SAHR ehl ah-kah-BAH-doh deh lohs PEE-sohs deh mah-DEH-rah)

We need to sand the floors.
Necesitamos arenar los pisos.
(neh-seh-see-TAH-mos ah-reh-NAHR lohs PEE-sohs)

We need more sandpaper.
Necesitamos más papel de lija.
(neh-seh-see-TAH-mohs mahs pah-PEHL deh LEE-hah)

We need the edger.
Necesitamos el bordeador.
(neh-seh-see-TAH-mohs ehl bohr-deh-AH-door)

Use the edger to go around the perimeter of the room.
Utilice el bordeador para ir alrededor del perímetro de
la habitación.
(oo-tee-LEE-seh ehl bohr-de-AH-door PAH-rah eer ahl-reh-deh-DOOR
dehl peh-REE-meh-troh deh lah ah-bee-tah-see-ON)

We need clean rags.
Necesitamos trapos limpios.
(neh-seh-see-TAH-mohs TRAH-pohs LEEM-pee-ohs)

We need to wipe the floor down.
Necesitamos limpiar el piso.
(neh-seh-see-TAH-mos leem-pee-AHR ehl PEE-soh)

We need three coats of poly on the floors.
Necesitamos tres capas de poliuretano en los pisos.
(neh-seh-see-TAH-mohs trehs KAH-pahs deh poh-lee-oo-reh-TAH-noh
ehn lohs PEE-sohs)

We need a satin finish on the floors.
Necesitamos los pisos con una terminación satinada.
(neh-seh-see-TAH-mohs lohs PEE-sohs kohn OO-nah tehr-me-nah-see-ON
sah-tee-NAH-dah)

We need a high gloss finish on the floors.
Necesitamos los pisos con una terminación brillosa.
(neh-seh-see-TAH-mohs los PEE-sohs con OO-na tehr-mee-neh-see-ON
bree-YO-sa)

We need a clear coat finish on the floors.
Necesitamos los pisos con una terminación clara.
(neh-seh-see-TAH-mohs los PEE-sohs con OO-na tehr-mee-neh-see-ON
CLAH-rah)

We need a light coat finish on the floors.

Necesitamos los pisos con una terminación suave.

(neh-seh-see-TAH-mohs los PEE-sohs con OO-na tehr-mee-neh-see-ON
soo-AH-veh)

We need a dark coat finish on the floors.

Necesitamos los pisos con una terminación oscura.

(neh-seh-see-TAH-mohs los PEE-sohs con OO-na tehr-mee-neh-see-ON
ohs-KOO-rah)

We need to put paper down after the floor dries to protect it.

Una vez que el piso se seque, necesitamos colocar papel
para protegerlo.

(OO-nah vehs keh ehl PEE-soh seh SEH-keh, neh-seh-see-TAH-mos
koh-loh-CAR pah-PEHL PAH-rah proh-teh-HER-loh)

We can walk on the floors tomorrow.

Mañana podremos caminar sobre los pisos.

(Mahn-YAH-nah poh-DREH-mohs kah-me-nahr SOH-breh
lohs PEE-sohs)

We need to clean up the job site daily.

Necesitamos limpiar el área de trabajo a diario

(neh-seh-see-TAH-mos leem-pee-AHR ehl AH-reh-ah deh trah-BAH-hoh
ah dee-AH-ree-oh

Concrete

CONCRETE TERMS
Términos de Concreto

broom finish – acabado grueso / acabado con escoba
(ah-kah-BAH-doh grooh-EH-soh / kohn ehs-KOH-bah)
concrete [countertops] – mesones de concreto (meh-SOH-nehs
deh kohn-KREH-toh)
concrete [floors] – piso de concreto (PEE-soh deh kohn-KREH-toh)
curing – curado (kooh-RAH-doh)
etched – aguafuerte (AH-gwah-FWER-tay)
exposed aggregate – agregado al descubierto
(ah-greh-GAH-doh ahl dehs-kooh-bee-EHR-toh)
portland cement – cemento portland (seh-MEHN-toh POHR-lahnd)
screeding – acabado / capa (ah-kah-BAH-doh / KAH-pah)
smooth finish – acabado liso (ah-kah-BAH-doh LEEH-soh)
stained – teñido (teh-NYEE-doh)

CONCRETE TOOLS
Herramientas de Concreto

bull float – llana flotante / aplanador (YAH-nah floh-TAHN-teh /
Ah.plan.ah.DOOR)
concrete truck – camión de concreto (kah-meeh-OHN deh
kohn-KREH-toh)
edger – orillador (oh-reeh-yah-DOOR)
float – flotador (floh-tah-DOOR)
kicker – instalador de alfombras / rodillera (eehns-tah-lah-
DOHR deh ahl-FOHM-brahs / roh-deeh-YEH-rah)
lazer level – nivel láser (neeh-VEHL LAH-sehr)
level – nivel (neeh-VEHL)
power tamper – compactadora mecánica (kohm-pahk-tah-
DOH-rah meh-KAH-neeh-kah)
power trowel – alisador mecánico (ah-leeh-sah-DOOR
meh-KAH-neeh-koh)
pressure washer – lavadora de presión (lah-vah-DOH-rah deh
pray-see-ON)
shovel – pala (PAH-lah)
sledgehammer – mazo / mandarria (MAH-soh / mahn-DAH-ree-ah)
trowel – paleta / cuchara de albañil (pah-LEH-tah / kooh-CHAH-rah
deh ahl-bahn-YEEHL)
wheelbarrow – carretilla (kah-reh-TEEH-yah)

CONCRETE SUPPLIES
Provisiones de Concreto

2x4's – dos por cuatros (dohs pohr kooh-AH-trohs

acid stain – mancha de acido (MAHN-chah deh AH-see-doh

anchor bolts – pernos de anclaje (PEHR-nohs deh ahn-KLAH-heh

broom – escoba (ehs-KOH-bah

duplex nails – clavos en dúplex (CLAH-vohs enh DOOH-plex

hose – manguera (mahn-GEH-rah)

mortar – mortero (mohr-TEH-roh)

muriatic acid – acido muriático (AH-see-doh mooh-reeh-AH-teeh-koh

plastic sheet – pliego plástico / hoja plástica (plee-EH-goh PLAHS-teeh-koh / OH-hah PLAHS-teeh-kah)

plywood – plywood / madera terciada (plái uúd / mah-DEH-rah tehr-see-AH-dah)

rebar – barra de refuerzo (BAH-rah deh reh-fooh-EHR-soh)

retardant – retardador (reh-tahr-dah-DOOR)

rubber boots – botas de goma / botas de caucho (BOH-tahs deh GOH-mah / KAH-ooh-choh)

stakes – estacas (ehs-TAH-kahs)

tarp – lona impermeabilizada (LOH-nah eehm-pehr-meh-ah-bee-leeh-SAH-dah)

wire mesh – rejilla metálica (reh-HEEH-yah meh-TAH-leeh-kah)

wire ties – ataduras / amarres de alambre (ah-tah-DOOH-rahs / ah-MAH-rehs deh ah-LAHM-breh)

CONCRETE PHRASES
Frases de Concreto

See Page 32 for Basic Job Q & A's and Job Site Phrases

How long have you been working with concrete?
¿Cuánto hace que trabaja con concreto?
(koo-AHN-toh AH-seh keh trah-BAH-hah kohn kohn-KREH-toh?)

I have been working with concrete for _____ years.
Hace _____ años que trabajo con concreto.
(AH-seh _____ AHN-yohs keh trah-BAH-hoh kohn kohn-KREH-toh)

Where is the metal mesh?
¿Dónde está la tela metálica?
(DON-deh ehs-TAH lah TEH-lah meh-TAH-lee-kah?)

We need more rebar.
Necesitamos más barras de refuerzo.
(neh-seh-see-TAH-mohs mahs BAH-rrrahs deh reh-foo-EHR-soh)

Where is the rebar?
¿Dónde está la barra de refuerzo?
(DON-deh ehs-TAH lah BAH-rrrah deh reh-foo-EHR-soh?)

We need more rebar saddles and anchoring wire.
Necesitamos más barras de refuerzo y más alambre de anclaje.
(neh-seh-see-TAH-mohs mahs BAH-rahs deh reh-foo-EHR-soh
ee mahs ah-LAHM-breh deh ahn-KLAH-heh)

Where is the rake?
¿Dónde está el rastrillo?
(DON-deh ehs-TAH ehl rahs-TREE-yoh?)

Where is the shovel?
¿Dónde está la pala?
(DON-deh ehs-TAH lah PAH-lah?)

Where is the bull float?
¿Dónde está el llana flotante / aplanador?
(DON-deh ehs-TAH ehl YAH-nah floh-TAHN-teh / Ah.plan.ah.DOOR?)

Where is the caution tape?
¿Dónde está la cinta de precaución?
(DON-deh ehs-TAH lah SEEN-tah deh preh-kahw-see-ON?)

Where is the bench mark?
¿Dónde está la cota / el punto de referencia?
(DON-deh ehs-TAH lah KOH-tah / ehl POON-toh deh reh-feh-REHN-see-ah?)

How many yards of concrete will be needed?
¿Cuántas yardas de concreto se van a necesitar?
(koo-AHN-tahs YAHR-dahs deh kohn-KREH-toh seh vahn ah
neh-seh-SEE-tahr?)

We need more bags of concrete.
Necesitamos más bolsas de concreto.
(neh-seh-see-TAH-mohs mahs BOHL-sahs deh kohn-KREH-toh)

The concrete needs to be 3,000 psi / 5,000 psi.
El concreto debe ser de 3.000 libras por pulgada
cuadrada / 5.000 libras por pulgada cuadrada.
(ehl kohn-KREH-toh DEH-beh sehr deh trehs-MEEL LEE-bras pore pool-
GAH-dah kwah-DRAH-dah / SEEN-koh-MEEL LEE-bras pore pool-GAH-
dah kwah-DRAH-dah)

We need the fiberglass reinforced concrete.

Necesitamos el concreto que está reforzado con fibra
de vidrio.

(neh-seh-see-TAH-mohs ehl kohn-KREH-toh keh ehs-TAH
reh-fohr-SAH-doh kohn fee-BRAH deh VEE-dree-oh)

The truck will deliver _____ yards of concrete tomorrow.

El camión entregará _____ yardas de concreto mañana.

(ehl kah-me-ON ehn-treh-gah-RAH _____ YAHR-dahs deh kohn-KREH-
toh mahn-YAH-nah)

We need a level.

Necesitamos un nivel.

neh-seh-see-TAH-mohs oon NEE-vehl)

We need more stakes.

Necesitamos más estacas.

(neh-seh-see-TAH-mohs mahs ehs-TAH-kahs)

We need more lumber.

Necesitamos más madera.

(neh-seh-see-TAH-mohs mahs mah-DEH-rah)

We need more plywood.

Necesitamos más plywood / madera terciada.

(neh-seh-see-TAH-mohs mahs plái uúd / mah-DEH-rah tehr-see-AH-dah)

We need a straight edge.

Necesitamos un borde recto.

(neh-seh-see-TAH-mohs oon BOHR-deh REHK-toh)

We need to laser level.

Necesitamos nivelar con el nivel láser.

(neh-seh-see-TAH-mohs nee-veh-LAHR kohn ehl nee-VEHL LAH-sehr)

We need more wire mesh.

Necesitamos más tela metálica.

(neh-seh-see-TAH-mohs mahs TEH-lah meh-TAH-lee-kah)

We need to get the footings inspected before we pour the concrete.

Necesitamos inspeccionar el cimiento antes de volcar
el concreto.

(neh-seh-see-TAH-mohs eens-pek-see-oh-NAHR ehl see-me-EHN-toh
AHN-tehs deh vohl-KAHR ehl kohn-KREH-toh)

We need to build forms here.
Necesitamos construir encofrados aquí.
(neh-seh-see-TAH-mohs kohns-troo-EER ehn-koh-FRAH-dohs ah-KEY)

We will pour the concrete tomorrow.
Vaciaremos el concreto mañana.
(vah-see-ah-REH-mohs ehl kohn-KREH-toh mahn-YAH-nah)

We need to smooth out that spot in the concrete.
Necesitamos alisar ese punto en el concreto.
(neh-seh-see-TAH-mohs ah-lee-SAHR EH-seh poon-TOH ehn ehl kohn-KREH-toh)

We need to make this a smooth finish.
Necesitamos darle a esto una terminación lisa.
(neh-seh-see-TAH-mohs DAHR-leh ah EHS-toh OO-nah tehr-me-nah-see-ON LEE-sah)

We need to tamp this area down.
Necesitamos apisonar este área.
(neh-seh-see-TAH-mohs ah-pee-soh-NAHR EHS-teh AH-reh-ah)

We need to power wash the concrete.
Necesitamos lavar el concreto a presión.
(neh-seh-see-TAH-mohs lah-VAHR ehl kohn-KREH-toh ah preh-see-ON)

We need to let this set.
Necesitamos dejar esto fraguar.
(neh-seh-see-TAH-mohs deh-HAR es-toh frah-goo-AHR)

We need to cover the concrete with plastic.
Necesitamos cubrir el concreto con plástico.
(deh-BEH-mohs koo-BREER ehl kohn-KREH-toh kohn PLAHS-tee-koh)

We need to add stain to this.
Necesitamos agregarle tinte / tintura a esto.
(neh-seh-see-TAH-mohs ah-gray-GAHR-lay TEEN-tay / teen-TOO-rah ah es-toh)

We will use bricks for the border.
Vamos a usar ladrillos para el borde.
(VAH-mohs ah oo-SAR lah-DREE-yos pah-rah el BOOR-deh)

We will make a patio area here.

Construiremos un patio aquí.

(Con-stroo-eer-RAY-mohs oon pah-tee-oh ah-KEY)

These will be used for the countertops.

Usaremos esto para los mesones.

(oo-sah-REH-mohs EHS-to PAH-rah lohs meh-SOH-nehs)

These will be poured concrete walls.

Estas serán paredes vaciadas con concreto.

(ES-tahs sehr-AHN pah-RAY-days vah-see-AH-dahs con kohn-KREH-toh

Is it going to rain?

¿Lloverá?

(yoh-veh-RAH?)

We need to clean up the job site daily.

Necesitamos limpiar el área de trabajo a diario.

(neh-seh-see-TAH-mohs leem-peeAHR ehl AH-reh-ah deh trah-BAH-hoh ah dee-AH-ree-oh)

ALSO SEE MASONRY SECTION
TAMBÍEN VEA LA SECCIÓN DE MAMPOSTERÍA

Demolition

DEMOLITION TOOLS
Herramientas de Demolición

chisel – cinsel (seen-SEHL)
crow bar – pata de cabra / palanca (PAH-tah deh KAH-brah / pah-LAHN-kah)
dumpster – depósito de basura (deh-POH-see-toh deh bah-SOOH-rah)
dump truck – camión para botar basura (kah-meeh-OHN PAH-rah boh-TAHR bah-SOOH-rah)
hammer – martillo (mahr-TEEH-yoh)
magnetic sweeper – barredor magnético (bah-reh-DOHR mahg-NEH-teeh-koh)
nail puller – saca clavos (SAH-kah CLAH-vohs)
rake – rastrillo (rahs-TREE-yoh)
shovel – pala (PAH-lah)
sledge hammer – mazo / mandarria (MAH-soh / mahn-DAH-reeh-ah)
wrecking ball – bola de demolición (BOH-lah deh deh-moh-leeh-see-OHN)
wrecking bar – barra demoledora (BAH-rah deh-moh-leh-DOH-rah)

DEMOLITION SUPPLIES
Provisiones de Demolición

broom – escoba (ehs-KOH-bah)
caution tape – cinta de precaución (SEEN-tah deh preh-kah-ooh-see-OHN)
chalk – tiza / gis (TEEH-sah / heehs)
dust mask – careta de polvo (cah-RAY-tah deh POL-vo)
gloves – guantes (gooh-AHN-tehs)
hard hat – casco de seguridad (KAHS-koh deh seh-gooh-reeh-DAHD)
safety glasses – lentes de seguridad (lehn-tehs deh seh-gooh-reeh-DAHD)
spray paint – pintura en atomizador / pintura sprey (peehn-TOOH-rah ehn ah-toh-meeh-sah-DOHR / peehn-TOOH-rah spray)
tarp – lona impermeabilizada (LOH-nah eehm-pehr-meh-AH-bleh)
wheelbarrow – carretilla (kah-reh-TEEH-yah)

DEMOLITION & CLEAN-UP PHRASES

Frases de Demolición
y Limpieza de Obra

*See Page 32 for Basic Job Q & A's
and Job Site Phrases*

Have you ever done tear-out / demolition work before?
¿Ha hecho antes trabajos de remoción / demolición?
(ah EH-choh ahn-tehs trah-BAH-hohs deh reh-moh-see-ON / deh-moh-LEE-see-ON?)

I have been doing tear-out / demolition work for _____ years.
Hace _____ años que hago trabajos de remoción / demolición.
(AH-seh _____ AHN-yohs keh AH-goh trah-BAH-hohs deh reh-moh-see-ON / deh-moh-lee-see-ON)

Where is the hammer?
¿Dónde está el martillo?
(DON-deh ehs-TAH ehl mahr-TEE-yoh?)

Where is the broom?
¿Dónde está la escoba?
(DON-deh ehs-TAH lah ehs-KOH-bah?)

Where is the shovel?
¿Dónde está la pala?
(DON-deh ehs-TAH lah PAH-lah?)

Where is the sledgehammer?
¿Dónde está el marro / mazo?
(DON-deh ehs-TAH ehl MAH-roh / MAH-soh?)

Where is the crowbar?
¿Dónde está la pata de cabra / palanca?
(DON-deh ehs-TAH ehl lah PAH-tah deh KAH-brah / lah pah-LAHN-kah?)

Where is the wheelbarrow?
¿Dónde está la carretilla?
(DON-deh ehs-TAH lah kah-reh-TEE-yah?)

We need more gloves.
Necesitamos más guantes.
(neh-seh-see-TAH-mohs mahs goo-AHN-tehs)

Where are the gloves?
¿Adónde están los guantes?
(ah-DON-deh ehs-TAHN lohs goo-AHN-tehs?)

Where are the safety glasses?
¿Adónde están los lentes de seguridad?
(ah-DON-deh ehs-TAHN lohs LEHN-tehs deh seh-goo-ree-DAHD?)

We need to wear our safety glasses.
Necesitamos usar nuestros lentes de seguridad.
(neh-seh-see-TAH-mohs oo-sahr noo-EHS-trohs LEHN-tehs deh
seh-gooh-reeh-DAHD)

We need to wear our hard hats.
Necesitamos usar nuestros cascos de seguridad.
(neh-seh-see-TAH-mohs oo-sahr noo-EHS-trohs KAHS-kohs deh seh-gooh-
reeh-DAHD)

We need to tear out all the walls and ceilings marked with orange paint.
Necesitamos demoler todas las paredes y cielosrrasos
marcados con pintura anaranjada.
(neh-seh-see-TAH-mohs deh-moh-LEHR TOH-dahs lahs pah-REH-dehs
ee see-eh-loh-RAH-sohs mahr-KAH-dohs kohn peen-TOO-rah
ah-nah-rahn-HAH-dah)

We need to remove the old bricks.
Necesitamos quitar los ladrillos viejos.
(neh-seh-see-TAH-mohs key-TAHR lohs lah-DREE-yohs vee-EH-hohs)

We need to stack the bricks up after we get the old cement off of them.
Necesitamos apilar los ladrillos luego de retirarles el cemento
viejo.
(neh-seh-see-TAH-mohs ah-pee-LAHR lohs lah-DREE-yohs loo-EH-goh deh
reh-tee-RAHR-lehs ehl seh-MEHN-toh vee-EH-hoh)

We need to put all the rocks in one pile.
Necesitamos apilar todas las rocas.
(neh-seh-see-TAH-mohs ah-pee-LAHR TOH-dahs lahs ROH-kahs)

We need to stack all the debris in the dumpster neatly.
Necesitamos apilar todos los escombros en forma ordenada en
el basurero.
(neh-seh-see-TAH-mohs ah-pee-LAHR TOH-dohs lohs ehs-KOHM-brohs
ehn FOHR-mah orh-deh-NAH-dah ehn ehl bah-soo-REH-roh)

Is the dumpster full yet?
¿Ya está lleno el basurero?
(yah ehs-TAH YEH-noh ehl bah-soo-REH-roh?)

Let me know when the dumpster is almost full.
Avíseme cuando el basurero esté casi lleno.
(ah-VEE-seh-meh koo-AHN-doh ehl bah-soo-REH-roh
ehs-TEH KAH-see YEH-noh)

We need another dumpster.
Necesitamos otro basurero.
(neh-seh-see-TAH-mohs OH-troh bah-soo-REH-roh)

We need to clean up the yard.
Necesitamos limpiar el jardín.
(neh-seh-see-TAH-mohs leem-pee-AHR ehl hahr-DEEN)

We need to rake the yard.
Necesitamos rastrillar el jardín.
(neh-seh-see-TAH-mohs rahs-TREE-yahr ehl hahr-DEEN)

We need to sweep this up.
Necesitamos barrer esto.
(neh-seh-see-TAH-mohs bah-REHR EHS-toh)

We need to sweep the floors.
Necesitamos barrer los pisos.
(neh-seh-see-TAH-mohs bah-REHR lohs PEE-sohs)

We need to jackhammer this concrete out.
Necesitamos taladrar este concreto.
(neh-seh-see-TAH-mohs tah-LAH-drahr ehs-TEH kohn-KREH-toh)

We need to use the backhoe.
Necesitamos utilizar la retroexcavadora.
(neh-seh-see-TAH-mohs oo-tee-lee-SAHR lah reh-troh-ex-kah-vah-DOH-rah)

We need to cover this with a tarp.
Necesitamos cubrir esto con una lona impermeabilizada.
(neh-seh-see-TAH-mohs coo-BREER es-toh con oo-na LOH-na eehm-
pehr-meh-AH-bleh)

We need to tear this out.
Necesitamos demoler esto.
(neh-seh-see-TAH-mohs deh-moh-LEHR EHS-toh)

We need to remove this.
Necesitamos sacar esto.
(neh-seh-see-TAH-mohs sah-KAHR EHS-toh)

We need to remove the old siding.
Necesitamos quitar el revestimiento viejo.
(neh-seh-see-TAH-mohs key-TAHR ehl reh-vehs-tee-me-EHN-toh
vee-EH-hoh)

We need to remove this wood.
Necesitamos quitar esta madera.
(neh-seh-see-TAH-mohs key-TAHR ehs-TAH mah-DEH-rah)

We need to save the old window sashes.
Necesitamos salvar el marco de la ventana vieja.
(neh-seh-see-TAH-mohs sal-VAR ehl MAR-koh deh lah vehn-TAH-nah ve-
EH-ha)

We need to salvage that.
Necesitamos salvar eso.
(neh-seh-see-TAH-mohs sal-VAR EH-soh)

We need to leave this.
Necesitamos dejar esto.
(neh-seh-see-TAH-mohs deh-HAHR EHS-toh)

We need to clean up the job site daily.
Necesitamos limpiar el área de trabajo a diario.
(neh-seh-see-TAH-mohs leem-pee-AHR ehl AH-reh-ah deh trah-BAH-hoh
ah dee-AH-ree-oh)

Drywall

DRYWALL ■ Terms / Tools / Supplies

DRYWALL TERMS
Términos de Drywall

popcorn ceiling – techo de palomitas (TAY-choh deh
pah-loh-MEE-tas)
smooth finish – acabado liso (ah-kah-BAH-doh LEEH-soh)
spackled – spackled (spackled)
texture – textura (tehks-TOOH-rah)

DRYWALL TOOLS
Herramientas de Drywall

chalk line – línea de tiza / gis (LEE-neh-ah deh TEEH-sah / heehs)
drill – taladro (tah-LAH-droh)
drywall nailer – clavadora para drywall (klah-vah-DOH-rah
PAH-rah drái uól)
drywall square – escuadra para drywall (ehs-kooh-AH-drah
PAH-rah drái uól)
hammer – martillo (mahr-TEEH-yoh)
knife – cuchillo (kooh-CHEEH-yoh)
scaffold – andamio (ahn-DAH-meeh-oh)
screw gun – pistola para atornillar (peehs-TOH-lah PAH-rah
ah-tohr-neeh-YAHR)
stilts – zancos (SAHN-kohs)
trowel – paleta / cuchara de albañil (pah-LEH-tah / kooh-CHAH-rah
deh ahl-bahn-YEEHL)
walk board – tablero para caminar (tah-BLEH-roh PAH-rah kah-meeh-
NAHR)

DRYWALL SUPPLIES
Provisiones de Drywall

5 gallon bucket – balde de cinco galones (BAHL-deh deh SEEN-koh
gah-LOH-nehs)
corner bead – esquinero (ehs-keeh-NEH-roh)
flat tape – cinta plana (SEEN-tah PLAH-nah)
green board – drywall impermeable (drái uól eehm-pehr-meh-AH-bleh)
gypsum – yeso (YEH-soh)
mud – lodo / barro (LOH-doh / BAH-roh)
mud pan – bandeja / platón para el barro (bahn-DEH-hah /
plah-TOHN PAH-rah ehl BAH-roh)

nail – clavo (CLAH-voh)
pencil – lápiz (LAH-peez)
plaster – yeso / emplaste / plaster (YEH-soh / ehm-PLAHS-teh / plaster)
pull nails – clavos de extracción (CLAH-vohs deh ehks-trahk-see-OHN)
screws – tornillos (tohr-NEEH-yohs)
sheetrock – sheetrock / cartón piedra (chírrok / kahr-TOHN peeh-EH-drah)
tape – cinta (SEEN-tah)

DRYWALL AND SHEETROCK PHRASES
Frases de Drywall y Sheetrock

See Page 32 for Basic Job Q & A's and Job Site Phrases

How long have you been hanging drywall?
¿Cuánto hace que trabaja colocando drywall?
(koo-AHN-toh AH-seh keh trah-BAH-hah koh-loh-CAN-doh drái uól?)

How long have you been finishing drywall?
¿Cuánto hace que trabaja en la terminación de drywall?
(koo-AHN-toh AH-seh keh trah-BAH-hah ehn lah tehr-me-nah-see-ON deh drái uól?)

I have been working with drywall for _____ years.
Hace _____ años que trabajo con drywall.
(AH-she _____ AHN-yohs keh trah-BAH-hoh kohn drái uól)

When will the boards be delivered?
¿Cuándo entregarán las tablas?
(koo-AHN-doh ehn-treh-gah-RAHN lahs TAH-blahs?)

We need more boards.
Necesitamos más tablas.
(neh-seh-see-TAH-mohs mahs TAH-blahs)

How many boards will you need?
¿Cuántas tablas va a necesitar?
(koo-AHN-tahs TAH-blahs vah a neh-seh-SEE-tahr?)

We need to stack the boards there.
Necesitamos apilar las tablas allí.
(neh-seh-see-TAH-mohs ah-pee-LAHR lahs TAH-blahs ah-YEE)

Where are the finishing tools?
¿Dónde están las herramientas de terminación?
(DON-deh ehs-TAHN lahs eh-rah-me-EHN-tahs deh
tehr-me-nah-see-ON?)

We need more scaffolding.
Necesitamos más andamiaje.
(neh-seh-see-TAH-mohs mahs ahn-dah-me-AH-heh)

We need to use 2" screws / 1" screws.
Necesitamos utilizar tornillos de 2 / de 1 pulgadas.
(neh-seh-see-TAH-mohs oo-tee-lee-SAHR tohr-NEE-yohs deh dohs /
deh OO-nah pool-GAH-dahs)

We need to use 1/2" / 5/8" drywall.
Necesitamos utilizar drywall de 1/2 pulgada / de 5/8 de pulgada.
(neh-seh-see-TAH-mohs oo-tee-lee-SAHR drái uól deh MEH-dee-ah pool-
GAH-dah / deh SEEN-koh ohk-TAH-vohs deh pool-GAH-dah)

We need more mud.
Necesitamos más barro.
(neh-seh-see-TAH-mohs mahs BAH-roh)

Where is the mud?
¿Dónde está el barro?
(DON-deh ehs-TAH ehl BAH-roh?)

We need to use the 20-minute / 45-minute mud.
Necesitamos utilizar el barro de 20 minutos / 45 minutos.
(neh-seh-see-TAH-mohs oo-tee-lee-SAHR ehl BAH-roh deh VEIN-teh me-
NOO-tohs / kwah-rehn-TAH ee SEEN-koh me-NOO-tohs)

We need more tape.
Necesitamos más cinta.
(neh-seh-see-TAH-mohs mahs SEEN-tah)

Where is the tape?
¿Dónde está la cinta?
(DON-deh ehs-TAH lah SEEN-tah?)

We need to use mesh tape here.
Necesitamos utilizar cinta de tela aquí.
(neh-seh-see-TAH-mohs oo-tee-lee-SAHR SEEN-tah deh TEH-lah ah-KEY)

We need to flat tape this area.
Necesitamos cubrir esta área con cinta.
(neh-seh-see-TAH-mohs koo-BREER EHS-tah AH-reh-ah kohn SEEN-tah)

We need to use corner tape here.
Necesitamos colocar cinta esquinera aquí.
(neh-seh-see-TAH-mohs oo-tee-lee-SAHR SEEN-tah ehs-key-NEH-rah ah-KEY)

We need to use mesh tape for fixing cracks.
Necesitamos utilizar cinta de tela para arreglar las rajas / grietas.
(neh-seh-see-TAH-mohs oo-tee-lee-SAHR SEEN-tah deh TEH-lah PAH-rah
ah-reh-GLAHR lahs RAH-hahs / gree-EH-tahs)

How many corner beads will be needed?
¿Cuántos esquineros se necesitarán?
(koo-AHN-tohs ehs-key-NEH-rohs seh neh-seh-see-tah-RAHN?)

We need more corner bead.
Necesitamos más esquineros.
(neh-seh-see-TAH-mohs mahs ehs-key-NEH-rohs)

We need to repair this plaster.
Necesitamos reparar este yeso.
(neh-seh-see-TAH-mohs reh-pah-RAHR EHS-teh YEH-soh)

We need to fix the cracks in the wall.
Necesitamos arreglar las rajas / grietas en la pared.
(neh-seh-see-TAH-mohs ah-reh-GLAHR lahs RAH-hahs / gree-EH-tahs
ehn lah pah-REHD)

We need to finish this to a smooth finish.
Necesitamos darle a esto una terminación lisa.
(neh-seh-see-TAH-mohs DAHR-leh a EHS-toh OO-nah tehr-me-nah-see-ON
LEE-sah)

We need to sand this area more.
Necesitamos arenar más esta área.
(neh-seh-see-TAH-mohs ah-reh-NAHR mahs EHS-tah AH-reh-ah)

We need to skim this area one more time.
Necesitamos razar esta área una vez más.
(neh-seh-see-TAH-mohs rah-SAHR EHS-tah AH-reh-ah OO-nah
vehs mahs)

We need to hang the ceilings first.
Necesitamos colgar primero los cielosrrasos.
(neh-seh-see-TAH-mohs kohl-GAHR pree-MEH-roh lohs
see-eh-lohs-RAH-sohs)

We need to put the fan in here.
Necesitamos colocar el ventilador aquí.
(neh-seh-see-TAH-mohs koh-loh-CAR ehl vehn-tee-lah-DOOR ah-KEY)

We need to put scrap drywall in the dumpster.
Necesitamos colocar el drywall de desecho en el basurero.
(neh-seh-see-TAH-mohs koh-loh-CAR ehl drái uól deh deh-SEH-choh
ehn ehl bah-soo-REH-roh)

We need to clean up the job site daily.
Necesitamos limpiar el área de trabajo a diario.
(neh-seh-see-TAH-mohs leem-pee-AHR ehl AH-reh-ah deh trah-BAH-hoh
ah dee-AH-ree-oh)

Electrical

ELECTRICAL TERMS
Términos de Electricidad

12/14 wire – cable de doce / cable de catorce (KAH-bleh deh DOH-seh / deh kah-TOHR-seh)

alternating current – corriente alterna (koh-reeh-EHN-teh ahl-TEHR-nah)

ampere – amperio (ahm-PEH-reeh-oh)

automatic garage door openers – controles automáticos para abrir las puertas del garaje (kohn-TROH-lehs ah-ooh-toh MAH teeh-kohs PAH-rah ah-BREEHR lahs pooh-EHR-tahs dehl gah-RAH-HEH)

ballast – balasto (bah-LAS-toh)

breakers – interruptores / apagadores (eehn-teh-ROOHP-toh-rehs / ah-pah-gah-DOH-rehs)

buried box – caja enterrada / caja incrustada (KAH-hah ehn-teh-RAH-dah / KAH-hah eehn-kroohs-TAH-dah)

cable – cable (KAH-bleh)

circuit – circuito (seehr-kooh-EEH-toh)

circuit breaker – apagador / interruptor (ah-pah-gah-DOHR / eehn-teh-roohp-TOHR)

clips – pinzas / grapas (PEEHN-sahs / GRAH-pahs)

conductors – conductores (kohn-doohk-TOH-rehs)

conduit – tubo (TOOH-boh)

connector – conector (koh-nehk-TOHR)

corrosion proof – resistente a la corrosión (reh-sees-TEHN-teh ah lah koh-roh-see-OHN)

diffuser – difusor (deeh-fooh-SOHR)

dimmers – oscurecedores / regulador de voltage (ohs-kooh-reh-seh-DOH-rehs / reh-goo-lah-DOHR deh vol-TAH-heh)

diode – diodo (deeh-OH-doh)

direct current – corriente directa (koh-reeh-EHN-teh deeh-REHK-tah)

dual heating and cooling – combinación de calefacción y aire acondicionado (kohm-bee-nah-see-OHN deh kah-leh-fahk-see-OHN eeh AH-eeh-reh ah-kohn-deeh-see-oh-NAH-doh)

dumb waiters – transportadores de cargas (trahns-pohr-tah-DOH-rehs deh KAHR-gahs

electric motor for chandelier – motor eléctrico para la lámpara araña / candelabro (moh-TOHR eh-LEHK-tree-koh PAH-rah lah LAHM-pah-rah ah-RAHN-yah / can-deh-LAH-bro)

electric-eye switch – apagador fotoeléctrico (ah-pah-gah-DOHR FOH-toh-eh-LEHK-tree-koh)

elevator – elevador / ascensor (eh-leh-vah-DOOR / ahs-sehn-SOHR)

generator – generador (heh-neh-rah-DOOR)

G.F.I. – G.F.I. (heh eh-feh eeh)

G.F.I. box – caja G.F.I. / caja del interruptor de falla a tierra (KAH-hah heh EH-feh eeh / KAH-hah dehl eehn-teh-roohp-TOHR deh FAH-yah ah teeh-EH-rah

glare – resplandor / destello (rehs-plahn-DOHR / dehs-TEH-yoh)

ground fault interrupter – interruptor de falla de tierra (eehn-teh-roohp-TOHR deh FAH-yah deh teeh-EH-rah)

grounding – conexión a tierra (koh-nehk-see-OHN ah teeh-EH-rah)

heating cable – cable de calefacción (KAH-bleh deh kah-leh-fahk-see-OHN

heated floor – piso con calefacción (PEEH-soh kohn kah-leh-fahk-see-OHN)

H.I.D. (high intensity discharge) – descarga de alta intensidad (dehs-KAHR-gah deh AHL-tah een-ten-see-DAHD

high voltage – alto voltaje (AHL-toh vohl-TAH-heh)

illuminate – iluminar (eeh-looh-meeh-NAHR)

intercom system – sistema de intercomunicadores (sees-TEH-mah deh eehn-tehr-koh-mooh-neeh-kah-DOH-rehs)

kilowatt – kilovatio (keeh-loh-VAH-teeh-oh)

L.E.D. – L.E.D. (EH-leh eh deh)

line voltage – línea de voltaje (LEEH-neh-ah deh vohl-TAH-heh)

loop – lazada (LAH-sa-dah)

low voltage – voltaje bajo (vohl-TAH-heh BAH-hoh)

low voltage switch – apagador del voltaje bajo (ah-pah-gah-DOOR dehl vohl-TAH-heh BAH-hoh)

main electric panel – pánel principal de electricidad (PAH-nehl preehn-see-PAHL deh eh-lehk-tree-see-DAHD)

moisture-resistant – resistente a la humedad (reh-sees-TEHN-teh ah lah ooh-meh-DAHD)

parallel wiring – cables en paralelo (KAH-blehs ehn pah-rah-LEH-loh)

plastic insulation – aislamiento plástico (ah-eehs-lah-meeh-EHN-toh PLAHS-teeh-koh)

plastic-sheathed cable – cable con cobertura plástica (KAH-bleh kohn koh-behr-TOOH-rah PLAHS-teeh-kah)

power – energía (eh-nehr-HEEH-ah)

plug wiring – cables del enchufe (KAH-blehs del ehn-CHOOH-feh)

plugs – enchufes (ehn-CHOOH-fehs)

pre-wired cable – cable pre-embobinado (KAH-bleh preh-ehm-boh-bee-NAH-doh)

rapid start ballast – balasto de arranque rápido (bah-LAHS-toh deh ah-RAHN-keh RAH-peeh-doh)

receptacle – receptáculo (reh-sehp-TAH-kooh-loh)

reflector – reflector (reh-flehk-TOHR)

relay – relevo (reh-LEH-voh)

resistance – resistencia (reh-sees-TEHN-see-ah)

security system – sistema de seguridad (sees-TEH-mah deh seh-gooh-reeh-DAHD)

series wiring – cables en serie (KAH-blehs ehn SEH-reeh-eh)

service panel – tablero / pánel de servicio (tah-BLEH-roh / PAH-nehl deh sehr-VEEH-see-oh)

sprinkler system – sistema de riego (sees-TEH-mah deh reeh-EH-goh)

switch wiring – cables del interruptor / apagador (KAH-blehs del eehn-teh-roohp-TOHR / ah-pah-gah-DOOR)

switches – apagadores / interruptores (ah-pah-gah-DOH-rehs / eehn-teh-roohp-TOH-rehs)

socket – enchufe (enh-CHOOH-feh)

solar – solar (soh-LAHR)

template – plantilla / patrón (plahn-TEEH-yah / pah-TROHN)

thermostatically controlled roof ventilators – ventiladores de techo controlados termostáticamente (vehn-teeh-lah-DOH-rehs deh TEH-choh kohn-troh-LAH-dohs tehr-mohs-TAH-teeh-kah-mehn-teh)

thin-wall metal conduit – tubo de metal de pared fina (TOOH-boh deh meh-TAHL deh pah-REHD FEEH-nah)

TW wires – alambres TW / alambres tipo taiwan (ah-LAHM-brehs teh DOH-bleh veh / ah-LAHM-brehs TEEH-poh Taiwan)

UF cable – cable UF / cable de ultra frecuencia (KAH-bleh ooh-ef-eh/ deh OOHL-trah freh-kooh-EHN-see-ah)

ultraviolet – ultra violeta (OOHL-trah veeh-oh-LEH-tah)

vacuum system – sistema de aspiración / vacío (sees-TEH-mah deh ahs-peeh-rah-see-OHN / vah-SEE-oh)

voltage – voltaje (vohl-TAH-heh)

volts – voltios (VOHL-teeh-ohs)

wall mounted receptacle – receptáculo montado en la pared (reh-sehp-TAH-kooh-loh mohn-TAH-doh ehn lah pah-REHD)

water heater [electric] – calentador de agua eléctrico (kah-lehn-TAH-door deh AH-gwa eh-lehk-tree-koh)

water heater [gas] – calentador de agua de gas (kah-lehn-TAH-door deh AH-gwa deh gas)

weatherproof fixtures – dispositivos resistentes al clima (deehs-poh-see-TEEH-vohs reh-sees-TEHN-tehs ahl KLEEH-mah)

wire size – tamaño del alambre / cable (tah-MAHN-yoh dehl ah-LAHM-breh / KAH-bleh)

ELECTRICAL TOOLS
Herramientas de Electricidad

wire cutters – cortadores de cable / alambre (kohr-tah-DOH-rehs deh KAH-bleh / ah-LAHM-breh)

screwdriver – destornillador / desarmador (dehs-tohr-neeh-yeeh-ah-DOHR / dehs-ahr-mah-DOHR)

drill – taladro (tah-LAH-droh)

hammer – martillo (mahr-TEEH-yoh)

OHM meter – medidor de ohmnios (meh-deeh-DOHR deh OHM-neeh-ohs)

wire strippers – protectores para pisar sobre los cables (proh-tehk-TOH-rehs PAH-rah PEEH-sahr SOH-breh lohs KAH-blehs)

side cutters – cortadores para laterales (kohr-tah-DOH-rehs PAH-rah lah-teh-RAH-lehs)

strippers – pinzas pelacables (PEEN-sahs PEH-lah KAH-blehs)

ELECTRICAL SUPPLIES
Provisiones de Electricidad

covers – cubiertas (coo-bee-EHR-tas)

extention cord – cable de extensión (CAH-blay deh eks-ten-see-ON)

faceplates – tapas de los enchufes (TAH-pahs deh lohs en-CHEW-fays)

gloves – guantes (gooh-AHN-tehs)

ground wire nuts – casquillos para empalmes de cables a tierra (kahs-KEEH-yohs PAH-rah ehm-PAHL-mehs deh KAH-blehs ah teeh-EH-rah)

light bulb – bombilla / foco (bohm-BEE-ya / FOH-coh)

nails – clavos (KLAH-vohs)

outlet box – toma de corriente (TOH-mah deh cohr-ee-EN-tay)

power strip – tira de la energía (TEE-rah deh la en-ehr-HEE-ah)

screws – tornillos (tohr-NEEH-yohs)

switchplates – placa interruptora (PLAH-cah en-tehr-oop-TOHR-ah)

tape measure – cinta para medir (SEEN-tah PAH-rah meh-DEEHR)

wire nuts – casquillos para empalmes de cables (kahs-KEEH-yohs PAH-rah ehm-PAHL-mehs deh KAH-blehs)

wire staples – grapa de metal (GRAH-pah deh meh-TAHL)

LIGHTING STYLES AND FIXTURES
Estilos de Luces y Accesorios

accent lighting – iluminación de ambientación (ee-loo-me-nah-see-ON deh ahm-bee-ehn-tah-see-OHN)

architectural lighting – iluminación arquitectónica
(ee-loo-me-nah-see-ON ahr-keeh-tehk-TOH-neeh-kah)
bullet light – bombilla (bohm-BEE-yah)
can light – plafón (plah-FOHN)
ceiling fan with light kit – ventilador de techo con luz
incorporada (vehn-teeh-lah-DOHR deh teh-choh kohn loohs
eehn-kohr-poh-RAH-dah)
chandelier – lámpara araña / candelabro (LAMH-pah-rah
ah-RAHN-yah / can-deh-LAH-broh)
copper fixture – accesorios de cobre (ahk-seh-SOH-reeh-ohs
deh KOH-breh)
deck light – iluminación del balcón (ee-loo-me-nah-see-ON
dehl bahl-KOHN)
down light – luz que alumbra hacia abajo (loohs keh
ah-LOOHM-brah AH-see-ah ah-BAH-hoh)
floodlight – luz industrial / reflector (loohs ehn-doohs-tree-AHL /
reh-flehk-TOHR)
fluorescent – fluorescente (floh-reh-SEHN-teh)
garden lighting – iluminación para el jardín (ee-loo-me-nah-see-
ON PAH-rah ehl hahr-DEEHN)
halogen – halógeno (ah-LOH-heh-noh)
lamp – lámpara (LAMH-pah-rah)
lamp post – poste de luz (POHS-teh deh loos)
landscape lighting – iluminación de paisaje (ee-loo-me-nah-see-ON
deh pah-eeh-SAH-heh)
lanterns – faroles / linternas (fah-ROH-lehs / leehn-TEHR-nahs)
pathway light – luz de sendero / de pasillo (loohs deh sehn-DEH-roh
/ deh pah-SEEH-yoh)
post lantern – farol (fah-ROHL)
recessed – incrustado (eehn-kroohs-TAH-doh)
sconces – lámparas / candelabros de muro (LAHM-pah-rahs / kahn-
deh-LAH-brohs deh MOO-roh)
spotlights – luz direccional (loohs deeh-rehk-see-oh-NAHL)
stake – estaca (ehs-TAH-kah)
step light – luz de paso (loohs deh PAH-soh)
task lighting – iluminación para el sitio de trabajo (ee-loo-me-nah-
see-ON PAH-rah el SEE-teeh-oh deh trah-BAH-hoh)
task lights – luces de trabajo (LOOH-sehs deh trah-BAH-hoh)
torches – antorchas (ahn-TOHR-chahs)
track – trayecto / riel (trah-YEHK-toh / ree-EHL)
under counter lights – luces que alumbran debajo del mesón
(LOOH-sehs keh ah-LOOHM-brahn deh-BAH-hoh del meh-SOHN)
uplight – luz que alumbra hacia arriba (loohs keh ah-LOOHM-brah
AH-see-ah ah-REEH-bah)

valance light – luces del entrecortinado (LOOH-sehs dehl ehn-treh-kohr-teeh-NAH-doh)

wall washing – iluminación para la pared (ee-loo-me-nah-see-ON PAH-rah lah pah-REHD)

well light – luz del pozo (loohs dehl POH-soh)

ELECTRICAL PHRASES
Frases de Electricidad

See Page 32 for Basic Job Q & A's and Job Site Phrases

How long have you been an electrician?
¿Cuánto hace que es electricista?
(koo-AHN-toh AH-seh keh ehs eh-lek-tree-SEES-tah?)

I have been an electrician for _____ years.
Hace _____ años que soy electricista.
(AH-seh _____ AHN-yohs keh SOH-ee eh-lek-tree-SEES-tah)

We need to get the electricity turned on.
Necesitamos conectar la electricidad.
(neh-seh-see-TAH-mohs koh-nek-TAHR lah eh-lek-tree-see-DAHD)

We need to get the electricity turned off.
Necesitamos desconectar la electricidad.
(neh-seh-see-TAH-mohs dehs-koh-nek-TAHR lah eh-lek-tree-see-DAHD)

Is it on or off?
¿Está prendido o apagado?
(es-TAH pren-DEED-oh oh ah-pah-GAHD-oh?)

We need to get the temporary pole installed.
Necesitamos instalar el poste provisional.
(neh-seh-see-TAH-mohs eens-tah-LAHR ehl POHS-teh proh-vee-see-oh-NAHL)

Where are the wire cutters?
¿Dónde está el cortacables?
(DON-deh ehs-TAH ehl KOHR-tah KAH-blehs?)

Where is the screwdriver?
¿Dónde está el destornillador / desarmador?
(DON-deh ehs-TAH ehl dehs-tohr-nee-YAH-door / dehs-ahr-mah-DOOR?)

Where is the hammer?
¿Dónde está el martillo?
(DON-deh ehs-TAH ehl mahr-TEE-yoh?)

Where is the fuse box?
¿Dónde está la caja de fusibles?
(DON-deh ehs-TAH lah KAH-hah deh foo-SEE-blehs?)

Where is the conduit bender?
¿Dónde está el dobla conducto / tubo?
DON-deh ehs-TAH ehl DOH-blah koh-DOOK-toh / TOO-boh?)

We need the conduit bender.
Necesitamos el dobla conducto / tubo.
(neh-seh-see-TAH-mohs ehl DOH-blah koh-DOOK-toh / TOO-boh)

We need more conduit.
Necesitamos más conductos / tubos.
(neh-seh-see-TAH-mohs mahs kohn-DOOK-tohs / TOO-bohs)

We need more Romax.
Necesitamos más cable Romax.
(neh-seh-see-TAH-mohs mahs KAH-bleh Romax)

We need speaker wires in the house.
Necesitamos cables para parlantes en la casa.
(neh-seh-see-TAH-mohs KAH-blehs PAH-rah pahr-LAHN-tehs ehn lah KAH-sah)

We are using fiber-optic in this house.
En esta casa estamos usando fibra óptica.
(en ES-tah CAH-sah es-TAH-mos ooh-SAHN-doh fee-brah OHP-tee-ca)

How many plugs / switches are in that room?
¿Cuántos enchufes / interruptores hay en esa habitación?
(koo-AHN-tohs ehn-CHOO-fehs / een-teh-roop-TOH-rehs AH-ee ehn EH-sah ah-bee-tah-see-ON?)

We need to put the faceplates on the plugs and switches.
Necesitamos colocarle las tapas a los enchufes y a los interruptores.
(neh-seh-see-TAH-mohs koh-loh-CAR-leh lahs TAH-pahs ah lohs ehn-CHOO-fehs ee ah lohs een-teh-roop-TOH-rehs)

We need to rough-in the house.
Necesitamos hacer las conexiones de tubería y de electricidad a la casa.
(neh-seh-see-TAH-mohs ah-SEHR lahs koh-nehx-see-OH-nehs deh to-beh-REE-ah ee deh eh-lehk-tree-see-DAHD ah lah KAH-sah)

We need a two-gang box here.
Necesitamos una caja metálica para dos enchufes / interruptores aquí.
(neh-seh-see-TAH-mohs OO-nah KAH-hah meh-TAH-lee-kah PAH-rah dohs ehn-CHOO-fehs/een-teh-roop-TOH-rehs ah-KEY)

We need a three-gang box here.
Necesitamos una caja metálica para tres enchufes / interruptores aquí.
(neh-seh-see-TAH-mohs OO-nah KAH-hah meh-TAH-lee-kah PAH-rah trehs ehn-CHOO-fehs / een-teh-roop-TOH-rehs ah-KEY)

We need a three-way from here to here.
Necesitamos un tres vías desde aquí hasta allí.
(neh-seh-see-TAH-mohs oohn trehs VEE-ahs DEHS-deh ah-KEY AHS-tah ah-YEE)

We need 110 volts here.
Necesitamos 110 voltios aquí.
(neh-seh-see-TAH-mohs see-EHN-toh dee-EHS VOL-tee-ohs ah-KEY)

We need 220 volts here.
Necesitamos 220 voltios aquí.
(neh-seh-see-TAH-mohs dohs-see-EHN-tohs VEH-in-teh VOL-tee-ohs ah-KEY)

We need to wire the laundry room for 220 volts.
Necesitamos cablear el lavadero con electricidad de 220 voltios.
(neh-seh-see-TAH-mohs kah-bleh-AHR ehl lah-vah-DEH-roh kohn eh-lek-tree-see-DAHD deh dohs-see-EHN-tohs VOL-tee-ohs)

We need to wire for under-cabinet lights in the kitchen.
Necesitamos cablear para luces debajo de la alacena en la cocina.
(neh-seh-see-TAH-mohs kah-bleh-AHR PAH-rah LOO-sehs deh-BAH-hoh deh lah ah-lah-sehn-ah ehn lah koh-SEE-nah)

Are the fixtures in yet?
¿Llegaron ya los accesorios?
(yeh-GAH-rohn yah lohs ahk-sehs-OHR-ee-ohs?)

We need to install can lights in this room.
Necesitamos instalar los plafones en esta habitación.
(neh-seh-see-TAH-mohs eens-tah-LAHR lohs plah-FOH-nehs ehn
EHS-tah ah-bee-tah-see-ON)

We need to put can lights here, center first.
Necesitamos colocar los plafones aquí, los del centro primero.
(neh-seh-see-TAH-mohs koh-loh-CAR lohs plah-FOH-nehs ah KEY, lohs
dehl SEHN-troh preeh-MEH-roh)

We need to install the light fixtures.
Necesitamos instalar los accesorios de iluminación.
(neh-seh-see-TAH-mohs eens-tah-LAHR lohs ahk-sehs-OHR-ee-ohs deh
ee-loo-me-nah-see-ON)

We need to put this light in the bedroom / bathroom / kitchen.
Necesitamos colocar esta luz en el dormitorio / baño / la
cocina.
(neh-seh-see-TAH-mohs koh-loh-CAR EHS-tah loose ehn ehl door-me-
TOH-reeoh / BAH-nee-oh / lah koh-SEE-nah)

We need to put this chandelier in the dining room / foyer.
Necesitamos colocar esta lámpara araña / candelabro en el
comedor / vestíbulo.
(neh-seh-see-TAH-mohs koh-loh-CAR EHS-tah LAHM-pah-rah ah-RAH-
neeah / can-deh-LAH-bro ehn ehl koh-meh-DOOR / vehs-TEE-boo-loh)

We need to put the ceiling fan in this room.
Necesitamos colocar el ventilador de techo en esta habitación.
(neh-seh-see-TAH-mohs koh-loh-CAR ehl vehn-tee-lah-DOOR deh TEH-
choh ehn EHS-tah ah-bee-tah-see-ON)

Pull the wire thru the wall.
Jale el cable a través de la pared.
(HAH-leh ehl KAH-bleh ah trah-VEHS deh lah pah-REHD)

Don't touch the shiny red button.
No toque el botón rojo brillante.
(noh TOH-keh ehl boh-TOHN roh-HOH bree-YAHN-teh)

We need to run cable.
Necesitamos poner cable.
(neh-seh-see-TAH-mohs poh-NEHR KAH-bleh)

We need to get an inspection.
Necesitamos obtener una inspección.
(neh-seh-see-TAH-mohs ohb-teh-NEHR OO-nah eens-pek-see-ON)

We need to do a final check.
Necesitamos hacer un chequeo final.
(neh-seh-see-TAH-mos AH-sehr oon che-KAY-oh fee-NAL)

We need to put the debris in the dumpster.
Necesitamos colocar los escombros en el basurero.
(neh-seh-see-TAH-mohs koh-loh-CAR lohs ehs-KOHM-brohs ehn ehl bah-soo-REH-roh)

We need to clean up the job site daily.
Necesitamos limpiar el área de trabajo a diario.
(neh-seh-see-TAH-mohs leem-pee-AHR ehl AH-reh-ah deh trah-BAH-hoh ah dee-AH-ree-oh)

HVAC

HVAC TERMS
Términos de HVAC

barometer – barómetro (bah-ROH-meh-troh)
BTU – BTU (beh teh ooh)
damper – válvula reguladora de aire (VAHL-vooh-lah reh-gooh-lah-DOH-rah deh AH-eeh-reh)
down flow – flujo hacia abajo (FLOOH-hoh AH-see-ah ah-BAH-hoh)
electric – eléctrico(a) (eh-LEHK-treeh-koh)
forced air – aire forzado (AH-eeh-reh fohr-SAH-doh)
furnace – horno (OR-noh)
gas pack – sistema de gas compacto de calefacción y aire acondicionado / gas pack (sees-TEH-mah deh gas kohm-PAHK-toh deh kah-leh-fahk-see-OHN eeh AH-eeh-reh ah-kohn-deeh-see-oh-NAH-doh / gas pack)
heat pump – bomba de calefacción (BOHM-bah deh kah-leh-fahk-see-OHN)
kelvin – kelvin (Kelvin)
natural gas – gas natural (gas nah-tooh-RAHL)
oil – aceite / petróleo (ah-SEH-eeh-te / peh-TROH-leoh)
propane – propano (proh-PAH-noh)
radiant floor heat – calor por radiación através del piso (kah-LOHR pohr rah-deeh-ah-see-OHN ah-trah-VEHS dehl PEEH-soh)
radiation – radiación (rah-deeh-ah-see-OHN)
radon – radón (rah-DOHN)
rankin – rankin (Rankin)
return – retorno (reh-TOHR-noh)
R-factor – factor R (FAHK-tohr EH-reh)
thermostat – termostato (tehr-mohs-TAH-toh)
water heater [electric] – calentador de agua elèctrico (kah-lehn-TAH-door deh AH-gwa eh-LEHK-tree-koh)
water heater [gas] – calentador de agua de gas (kah-lehn-TAH-door deh AH-gwa deh gas)

HVAC TOOLS
Herramientas de HVAC

carbon monoxide detector – detector de monóxido de carbono (deh-tehk-TOHR deh moh-NOHK-see-doh deh kahr-BOH-noh)
drill – taladro (tah-LAH-droh)

laser temperature gauge – indicador láser de temperatura
(een-dee-cah-DOHR LAH-sehr de tehm-peh-rah-TOOH-rah)

pliers – alicates (ah-leeh-KAH-tehs)

pressure gauge – manómetro de presión (mah-NOH-meh-troh deh
preh-see-OHN)

screw drivers – destornilladores / desarmadores (dehs-tohr-neeh-
yah-DOH-rehs / dehs-ahr-mah-DOH-rehs)

snips – tijeras para metal (teeh-HEH-rahs PAH-rah meh-TAHL)

staple gun – pistola para engrapar (peehs-TOH-lah PAH-rah ehn-
grah-PAHR)

HVAC SUPPLIES
Provisiones de HVAC

air filter – filtro de aire (FEEHL-troh deh AH-eeh-reh)

flexible ducting – conductos flexibles (kohn-DOOHK-tohs
flehk-SEE-blehs)

insulation – aislamiento (ah-eehs-lah-meeh-EHN-toh)

metal ducting – conductos de metal (kohn-DOOHK-tohs deh
meh-TAHL)

metal hangers – colgadores de metal (kohl-gah-DOH-rehs
deh meh-TAHL)

nails – clavos (CLAH-vohs)

register covers – rejillas cobertoras (reh-HEEH-yahs koh-behr-TOH-rahs)

screws – tornillos (tohr-NEEH-yohs)

HVAC PHRASES
Frases de HVAC

*See Page 32 for Basic Job Q & A's
and Job Site Phrases*

How long have you been working with heating and air?
¿Cuánto hace que trabaja con calefacción y aire acondicionado?
(koo-AHN-toh AH-seh keh trah-BAH-hah kohn kah-leh-fahk-see-ON ee
EYE-reh ah-kohn-dee-see-oh-NAH-doh?)

I have been working with heating and air for ____ years.
Hace ____ años que trabajo con calefacción y aire
acondicionado.
(AH-seh ____ AHN-yohs keh trah-BAH-hoh kohn kah-leh-fahk-seeON
ee EYE-reh ah-kohn-dee-seeoh-NAH-doh)

Where is the thermometer?
¿Dónde está el termómetro?
(DON-deh ehs-TAH ehl tehr-MOH-meh-troh?)

We need more sheet metal.
Necesitamos más planchas de metal.
(neh-seh-see-TAH-mohs mahs PLAHN-chahs deh meh-TAHL)

Where is the flex duct?
¿Dónde está el conducto flexible?
(DON-deh ehs-TAH ehl kohn-DOOK-toh flehx-SEE-bleh?)

We need flex duct in the attic / basement.
Necesitamos un conducto flexible en el ático / sótano.
(neh-seh-see-TAH-mohs oon kohn-DOOK-toh flehx-SEE-bleh ehn
ehl AH-tee-koh / SOH-tah-noh)

We need floor grills.
Necesitamos rejillas para el piso
(neh-seh-see-TAH-mohs reh-HEE-yahs pah-rah ehl PEE-soh)

We need to remove the old unit from the house.
Necesitamos quitar la unidad / el equipo viejo de la casa.
(neh-seh-see-TAH-mohs key-TAHR lah oo-nee-DAHD / ehl eh-KEY-poh
vee-EH-hoh deh lah KAH-sah)

How big of an HVAC unit is needed for this house?
¿Qué tamaño de unidad / equipo de calefacción y aire
acondicionado se necesita para esta casa?
(keh tah-MAHN-yoh deh oo-nee-DAHD / eh-KEY-poh deh kah-leh-fahk-
see-ON ee EYE-reh ah-kohn-dee-see-oh-NAH-doh seh neh-seh-SEE-tah
PAH-rah EHS-tah KAH-sah?)

We need a split heating and cooling system.
Necesitamos una unidad que tenga el sistema combinado de
calefacción y aire acondicionado.
(neh-seh-see-TAH-mohs ooh-nah oo-neeh-DAHD kay TEHN-gah ehl sees-
TEH-mah cohm-beeh-NAH-doh deh kah-leh-fahk-see-ON ee EYE-reh ah-
kohn-DEE-see-oh-NAH-doh)

We need the number of units to be used.
Necesitamos saber cuántas unidades se van a usar.
(neh-seh-see-TAH-mohs sah-behr KWAN-tahs ooh-neeh-DAH-dehs seh
vahn ah ooh-SAHR)

We need the size of the unit.
Necesitamos saber el tamaño de la unidad.
(neh-seh-see-TAH-mohs sah-behr el tah-MAHN-yo deh la oo-neeh-DAHD)

We need to put in a heat pump.
Necesitamos instalar una bomba de calefacción.
(neh-seh-see-TAH-mohs eens-tah-LAHR OO-nah BOHM-bah deh
kah-leh-fahk-see-ON)

We need to put in a gas unit.
Necesitamos instalar una unidad / un equipo de gas.
(neh-seh-see-TAH-mohs eens-tah-LAHR OO-nah oo-nee-DAHD / oon
eh-KEY-poh deh gas)

The unit will be ready to hook up tomorrow.
La unidad / el equipo estará lista/o mañana para conexión.
(lah oo-nee-DAHD / ehl eh-KEY-poh ehs-tah-RAH LEES-toh / tah PAH-
rah koh-nehx-see-ON mahn-YAH-nah)

We need to set the unit here.
Necesitamos instalar la unidad aquí.
(neh-seh-see-TAH-mohs eens-tah-LAHR lah oo-nee-DAHD ah-KEY)

We need to install the rain guard on the unit.
Necesitamos instalar el protector contra la lluvia a la unidad
/ el equipo.
(neh-seh-see-TAH-mohs eens-tah-LAHR ehl proh-TECH-tohr KOHN-trah
lah YOO-vee-ah ah lah oo-nee-DAHD/ehl eh-KEY-poh)

How many feeds come off the unit?
¿Cuántas porciones salen de cada unidad / equipo?
(koo-AHN-tahs pohr-see-OH-nehs SAH-lehn deh KAH-dah oo-nee-
DAHD / eh-KEY-poh?

We need an overflow pan under the unit.
Necesitamos una bandeja recolectora debajo de la unidad /
el equipo.
(neh-seh-see-TAH-mohs OO-nah bahn-DEH-hah reh-koh-lek-TOH-rah
deh-BAH-hoh deh lah oo-nee-DAHD / ehl eh-KEY-poh)

What is the warranty of the unit?
¿Cuál es el período de garantía de la unidad / el equipo?
(koo-AHL ehs ehl peh-REE-oh-doh deh gah-rahn-TEE-ah deh lah oo-
nee-DAHD / ehl eh-KEY-poh?)

We need a concrete pad this big.
Necesitamos una tableta de concreto así de grande
(neh-seh-see-TAH-mohs oo-nah tah-BLAY-tah deh kohn-KREH-toh
ah-SEE deh GRAN-deh)

We need to install a vent pipe thru there.
Necesitamos instalar un tubo de ventilación a través de allí.
(neh-seh-see-TAH-mohs eens-tah-LAHR oon TOO-boh deh
vehn-tee-lah-see-ON ah TRAH-vehs deh ah-YEE)

We need to run the duct work thru the house.
Necesitamos instalar los conductos de aire en la casa.
(neh-seh-see-TAH-mohs eens-tah-LAHR lohs kohn-dook-TOHS deh
EYE-reh ehn lah KAH-sah)

We need to insulate and staple all hard ducting.
Necesitamos aislar y engrapar todos los ductos duros.
(neh-seh-see-TAH-mohs eyes-LAHR ee ehn-GRAH-pahr TOH-dohs lohs
DOOK-tohs DO-rohs)

We need to hook up the stove for gas.
Necesitamos conectar el gas a la estufa.
(neh-seh-see-TAH-mohs koh-NEHK-tahr ehl gas ah lah es-TOO-fa)

We need to install diverters here.
Necesitamos instalar desviadores aquí.
(neh-seh-see-TAH-mohs eens-tah-LAHR dehs-vee-ah-DOH-rehs ah-KEY)

We need vent fans in all bathrooms.
Necesitamos ventilaciones en todos los baños.
(neh-seh-see-TAH-mohs vehn-tee-lah-see-OH-nehs ehn TOH-dohs lohs
BAHN-yohs)

Check the circuit breaker.
Chequee el interruptor de circuito.
(cheh-KEH-eh ehl een-teh-roop-TOHR deh seer-koo-EEH-toh)

We need to turn the circuit breaker on / off.
Necesitamos colocar el interruptor de circuito en encendido /
apagado.
(neh-seh-see-TAH-mohs koh-loh-CAR ehl een-teh-roop-TOHR deh seer-
koo-EEH-toh ehn ehn-sehn-DEE-doh / ah-pah-GAH-doh)

We need to put the thermostat here.

Necesitamos colocar el termostato aquí.

(neh-seh-see-TAH-mohs koh-loh-CAR ehl tehr-mohs-TAH-toh ah-KEY)

We need to get an inspection.

Necesitamos obtener una inspección.

(neh-seh-see-TAH-mohs ohb-teh-NEHR OO-nah eens-pek-see-ON)

We need to clean up the job site daily.

Necesitamos limpiar el área de trabajo a diario.

(neh-seh-see-TAH-mohs leem-pee-AHR ehl AH-reh-ah deh trah-BAH-hoh ah dee-AH-ree-oh)

ALSO SEE ELECTRICAL SECTION
TAMBIÉN VEA LA SECCIÓN DE ELÉCTRICO

MASONRY

MASONRY & STONE TERMS
Términos de Mampostería y Piedras

aggregate – agregado / en bruto (ah-greh-GAH-doh / ehn BROOH-toh)

asphalt – asfalto (ahs-FAHL-toh)

brick – ladrillo (lah-DREEH-yoh)

brick patio – patio de ladrillo (patio deh lah-DREEH-yo)

brick wall – pared de ladrillo (pah-REHD deh lah-DREEH-yoh)

concrete – concreto (kohn-KREH-toh)

driveway – entrada (enh-TRAH-dah)

dry stack – apilado en seco (ah-peeh-LAH-doh ehn SEH-koh)

fire pit – fogón / fosa de fuego (foh-GOHN / FOH-sah deh foo-EH-goh)

gravel – grava / granzón (GRAH-vah / grahn-SOHN)

patio – patio (patio)

paver bricks – ladrillos para pavimentar (lah-DREEH-yohs PAH-rah pah-veeh-mehn-TAHR)

stone – piedra (peeh-EH-drah)

stone and mortar – piedra y mortero (peeh-EH-drah eeh mohr-TEH-roh)

stone wall – pared de piedra (PAH-rehd deh peeh-EH-drah)

thin set – equipo delgado (eh-KEEH-poh dehl-GAH-doh)

walkway – pasillo / sendero (pah-SEE-yoh / sehn-DEH-roh)

MASONRY TOOLS
Herramientas de Mampostería

chisel – cincel (seen-SEHL)

concrete saw – sierra para concreto (see-EH-rah PAH-rah kohn-KREH-toh)

concrete trowel – cuchara / paleta de concreto (kooh-CHAH-rah / pah-LEH-tah deh kohn-KREH-toh)

edger – orillador (oh-reeh-yah-DOHR)

float – flotador (floh-tah-DOHR)

groover – canalizador (kah-nah-leeh-sah-DOHR)

hammer – martillo (mahr-TEEH-yoh)

inside corner tool – instrumento para la orilla interna (eehns-trooh-MEHN-toh PAH-rah lah oh-REEH-yah eehn-TEHR-nah)

jointer – ensamblador (ehn-sahm-blah-DOHR)

laser level – nivel láser (neeh-VEHL LAH-sehr)

level – nivel (neeh-VEHL)

lintels – dinteles (deen-TEH-lehs)

mason hammer – martillo para masonería (mahr-TEEH-yoh PAH-rah Mah-soan-air-EE-ah)

mason line – línea del albañil (LEEH-neeh-ah dehl ahl-bahn-YEEHL)

mason's folding rule – regla doblable para el albañil (REH-glah doh-BLAH-bleh PAH-rah ehl ahl-bahn-YEEHL)

mixer – mezcladora (mehs-clah-DOH-rah)

mixing tub – cubeta para mezclar (kooh-BEH-tah PAH-rah mehs-KLAHR)

outside corner tool – instrumento para la orilla externa (eehns-trooh-MEHN-toh PAH-rah lah oh-REEH-yah ehks-TEHR-nah)

pointing trowel – cuchara puntuda (kooh-CHAH-rah poohn-TOOH-dah)

shovel – pala (PAH-lah)

tamper – compactadora (kohm-pahk-tah-DOH-rah)

trowel – paleta / cuchara de albañil / espátula (pah-LEH-tah / kooh-CHAH-rah deh ahl-bahn-YEEHL / ehs-PAH-too-lah)

vibrator – vibrador (veeh-brah-DOHR)

MASONRY SUPPLIES
Provisiones de Mampostería

2x4 – dos por cuatro (dohs pohr kooh-AH-troh)

accelerator – acelerador (ah-seh-leh-rah-DOHR)

anchor bolts – pernos de anclaje (PEHR-nohs deh ahn-KLAH- heh)

block – bloque (bloh-keh)

brick – ladrillo (lah-DREEH-yoh)

broom – escoba (ehs-KOH-bah)

buckets – baldes (BAHL-dehs)

cement mixer – mezcladora de cemento (mehs-klah-DOH-rah deh seh-MEHN-toh)

concrete – concreto (kohn-KREH-toh)

flashing – resguardo (rehs-gooh-AHR-doh)

forms – encofrados (enh-koh-FRAH-dohs)

gravel – grava / granzón (GRAH-vah / grahn-SOHN)

lintels – dinteles (deehn-TEH-lehs)

mesh – malla / red (MAH-yah / red)

mortar – mortero / argamasa (mohr-TEH-roh / AR-gah-MAH-sah)

plastic – plástico (PLAHS-teeh-koh)

retardant – retardador (reh-tahr-dah-DOHR)

rubber boots – botas de goma / caucho (BOH-tahs deh GOH-mah / KAH-ooh-choh)

sand – arena (ah-REH-nah)

sill plastic – plástico de soporte (PLAHS-teeh-koh deh soh-POHR-teh)

stakes – estacas (ehs-TAH-kahs)
treated lumber – madera tratada (mah-DEH-rah trah-TAH-dah)
wall ties – refuerzos para paredes (reh-fooh-EHR-sohs PAH-rah pah-REH-dehs)
water – agua (AH-gwah)
waterproofing – impermeabilización (eehm-pehr-meh-ah-bee-leeh-sah-see-OHN)
wheelbarrow – carretilla (kah-reh-TEEH-yah)

STONE NAMES
Nombres de Piedras

architectural cut limestone – piedra caliza de corte arquitectónico (peeh-EH-drah kah-LEEH-sah deh KOHR-teh ahr-keeh-tehk-TOH-neeh-koh)
bluestone – piedra azul (peeh-EH-drah ah-SOOHL)
brick – ladrillo (lah-DREEH-yoh)
cast stone – piedra de desecho (peeh-EH-drah deh deh-SEH-choh)
cobble – adoquíne / guijarro (ah-doh-KEE-neh / gweeh-HAH-roh)
fieldstone – piedra de campo (peeh-EH-drah deh KAHM-poh)
flagstone – laja (LAH-hah)
granite – granito (grah-NEEH-toh)
gravel – grava / granzón (GRAH-vah / gran-SOHN)
lava rock – piedra de lava (peeh-EH-drah deh LAH-vah)
limestone – piedra caliza (peeh-EH-drah kah-LEEH-sah)
man-made stone – piedra artificial (peeh-EH-drah ahr-teeh-fee-see-AHL)
marble – mármol (MAHR-mohl)
natural stone – piedra natural (peeh-EH-drah nah-tooh-RAHL)
old brick – ladrillo viejo (lah-DREEH-yoh veeh-EH-hoh)
pavers – piedra para pavimentar (peeh-EH-drah PAH-rah pah-veeh-mehn-TAHR)
pebbles – piedrita / guijarro (peeh-eh-DREEH-tah / gweeh-HAH-roh)
quartzite – cuarzita (kooh-ahr-SEE-tah)
rock – roca (ROH-kah)
salvaged brick – ladrillo rescatado / recuperado (lah-DREEH-yoh rehs-kah-TAH-doh / reh-kooh-peh-RAH-doh)
sandstone – arenisca (ah-reh-NEEHS-kah)
slate – pizarra (peeh-SAH-rah)
soapstone – esteatita / talco natural (ehs-teh-ah-TEEH-tah / TAHL-koh nah-tooh-RAHL)
stone – piedra (peeh-EH-drah)
travertine – mármol travertino (MAHR-mohl trah-vehr-TEEH-noh)

MASONRY – BRICK & STONE PHRASES

Frases de Mampostería
– Ladrillo y Piedra

*See Page 32 for Basic Job Q & A's
and Job Site Phrases*

How long have you been working with brick / stone?
¿Cuánto hace que trabaja con ladrillo / piedra?
(koo-AHN-toh AH-seh keh trah-BAH-hah kohn lah-DREE-yoh /
peeh-EH-drah?)

I have been working with brick / stone for _____ years.
Hace _____ años que trabajo con ladrillo / piedra.
(AH-seh _____ AHN-yohs keh trah-BAH-hoh kohn lah-DREE-yoh /
peeh-EH-drah)

Where is the level?
¿Dónde está el nivel?
(DON-deh ehs-TAH ehl nee-VEHL?)

Where is the laser level?
¿Dónde está el nivel láser?
(DON-deh ehs-TAH ehl nee-VEHL LAH-sehr?)

Where is the mortar?
¿Dónde está el mortero / argamasa?
(DON-deh ehs-TAH ehl more-TEH-roh / ahr-gah-MAH-sah?)

How many more bags of mortar will be needed?
¿Cuántas bolsas más de mortero / argamasa se necesitarán?
(koo-AHN-tahs BOHL-sahs mahs dehmore-TEH-roh / ahr-gah-MAH-sah
seh neh-seh-see-tah-RAHN?)

We need to mix more mortar.
Necesitamos mezclar más mortero / argamasa.
(neh-seh-see-TAH-mohs mehs-KLAHR mahs more-TEH-roh / ahr-gah-
MAH-sah)

We need the motor to be a rough finish.
Necesitamos que el acabado de el mortero / la argamasa sea
áspero.
(neh-seh-see-TAH-mohs kay el ah-ka-BAH-doh deh ehl more-TEH-roh /
la ahr-gah-MAH-sah say-ah AHS-pehr-oh)

We need to clean the mortar off the brick.
Necesitamos quitarle el mortero / la argamasa al ladrillo.
(neh-seh-see-TAH-mohs key-TAHR-leh ehl more-TEH-roh / la ahr-gah-
MAH-sah ahl lah-DREE-yoh)

Where is the trowel?
¿Dónde está la paleta?
(DON-deh ehs-TAH lah pah-LEH-tah?)

Where is the wheelbarrow?
¿Dónde está la carretilla?
(DON-deh ehs-TAH lah kah-reh-TEE-yah?)

We need more scaffolding.
Necesitamos más andamiaje.
(neh-seh-see-TAH-mohs mahs ahn-dah-me-AH-heh)

Please bring me more brick / stone.
Por favor, tráigame más ladrillos / piedras.
(pore fah-VOHR, TRAH-ee-gah-meh mahs lah-DREE-yohs /
peeh-EH-drahs)

How many more bricks are needed?
¿Cuántos ladrillos más se necesitan?
(koo-AHN-tohs lah-DREE-yohs mahs seh neh-seh-SEE-tahn?)

The bricks will be delivered tomorrow.
Mañana entregarán los ladrillos.
(Mahn-YAH-nah ehn-treh-gah-RAHN lohs lah-DREE-yohs)

We need to stack the bricks here.
Necesitamos apilar los ladrillos aquí.
(neh-seh-see-TAH-mohs ah-PEE-lahr lohs lah-DREE-yohs ah-KEY)

We need to brick this side of the house.
Necesitamos colocar ladrillo en este lado de la casa.
(neh-seh-see-TAH-mohs koh-loh-CAR lah-DREE-yoh ehn EHS-teh
LAH-doh deh lah KAH-sah)

We need to clean the grout joints.
Necesitamos limpiar las juntas de lechada.
(neh-seh-see-TAH-mohs leem-pee-AHR lahs HOON-tahs deh leh-CHAH-dah)

How many more stones are needed?
¿Cuántas piedras más se necesitan?
(koo-AHN-tahs peeh-EH-drahs mahs seh neh-seh-SEE-tahn?)

We need to stack the stones here.
Necesitamos apilar las piedras aquí.
(neh-seh-see-TAH-mohs ah-PEE-lahr lahs peeh-EH-drahs ah-KEY)

We need to build a stone wall.
Necesitamos construir una pared de piedra.
(neh-seh-see-TAH-mohs kohns-troo-EER OO-nah pah-REHD deh peeh-EH-drah)

We need to chip the sides off the stones.
Necesitamos emparejar los bordes de las piedras.
(neh-seh-see-TAH-mohs em-pah-ray-HAR los BOOR-days deh las
peeh-EH-drahs0

We need to level this wall.
Necesitamos nivelar esta pared.
(neh-seh-see-TAH-mohs nee-veh-LAHR EHS-tah pah-REHD)

We need a 5-gallon bucket.
Necesitamos un balde de 5 galones.
(neh-seh-see-TAH-mohs oon BAHL-deh deh SEEN-koh gah-LOH-nehs)

We need clean water.
Necesitamos agua limpia.
(neh-seh-see-TAH-mohs AH-gwah LEEM-pee-ah)

Pull the string across the top for a straight line.
Tense el hilo por encima para formar una línea recta.
(TEHN-seh ehl EE-loh pore ehn-SEE-mah PAH-rah fohr-MAHR
OO-nah LEE-neh-ah REK-tah)

We need to dry stack a wall here.
Necesitamos instalar / levantar una pared aquí.
(neh-seh-see-TAH-mohs eens-TAH-lahr / leh-VAN-tahr OO-nah
pah-REHD ah-KEY)

We need to get an inspection.
Necesitamos obtener una inspección.
(neh-seh-see-TAH-mohs ohb-teh-NEHR OO-nah eens-pek-see-ON)

We will use bricks for this part of the driveway.
Usaremos ladrillos para esta parte de la entrada.
(oo-sah-RAY-mohs lah-DREE-yos pah-rah ehs-tah PAHR-tay deh la een-TRAH-dah)

We need to use these bricks for the chimney.
Necesitamos usar estos ladrillos para la chimenea.
(neh-seh-see-TAH-mohs oo-SAHR ehs-tos lah-DREE-yos pah-rah la chee-meh-NAY-ah)

We need to put the _____ above the window.
Necesitamos poner el / la _____ por encima de la ventana.
(neh-seh-see-TAH-mohs poh-NEHR el / la _____ poor en-SEE-ma deh la ven-TAH-na)

We need three rows of block for the foundation.
Necesitamos tres hileras de bloques para la fundación / la base.
(neh-seh-see-TAH-mohs trays ee-LEH-rahs deh BLO-cays pah-ra la foon-day-see-ON/la BAH-say)

We need to seal the foundation.
Necesitamos sellar la fundación / la base.
(neh-seh-see-TAH-mohs say-YAR la foon-dah-see-ON/ la BAH-say)

We need to stucco that area.
Necesitamos poner estuco en esa área.
(neh-seh-see-TAH-mohs poh-NEHR es-TOO-coh en eh-sah AH-ree-ah)

We need to build a retaining wall.
Necesitamos construir una pared de contención.
(neh-seh-see-TAH-mohs cons-troo-EER oo-na pah-REHD deh con-ten-see-ON)

We need to build a stone mailbox.
Necesitamos construir un buzón de piedra.
(neh-seh-see-TAH-mohs cons-troo-EER oon boo-ZON deh peeh-EH-drah)

We need to build a stone entrance.
Necesitamos construir una entrada de piedra.
(neh-seh-see-TAH-mohs cons-troo-EER oo-na en-TRAH-da deh peeh-EH-drah)

We need to clean up the job site daily.

Necesitamos limpiar el área de trabajo a diario.

(neh-seh-see-TAH-mohs leem-pee-AHR ehl AH-reh-ah deh trah-BAH-hoh ah dee-AH-ree-oh)

ALSO SEE CONCRETE SECTION
TAMBIÉN VEA LA SECCIÓN DE CONCRETO

PAINTING

PAINITNG TERMS
Términos de Pintura

cut-in – recortar / cortar (reh-kohr-TAHR / kohr-TAHR)
dark – oscuro (ohs-KOOH-roh)
exterior – exterior (ehks-teh-reeh-OR)
latex – látex (latex)
light – suave / liviano / claro (soo-ah-vay / lee-vee-AH-noh / KLAH-roh)
mildew resistant – resistente al moho (reh-sees-TEHN-teh ahl MOH-oh)
mural – mural (mooh-RAHL)
oil – aceite (ah-SEH-eeh-teh)
pastel – pastel (pahs-TEHL)
primary colors – colores primarios (koh-LOH-rehs preeh-MAH-reeh-ohs) [See Basics Section]
primer – imprimador / pintura base (eemh-preeh-mah-DOHR / peehn-TOOH-rah BAH-seh)
secondary colors – colores secundarios (koh-LOH-rehs seh-koohn-DAH-reeh-ohs)
spray paint – pintura en atomizador / pintura sprey (peehn-TOOH-rah enh ah-toh-meeh-sah-DOHR / peehn-TOOH-rah spray)
stain – mancha / broncear (MAHN-chah / bron-say-ar)
texture paint – pintura con textura (peehn-TOOH-rah kohn tehks-TOOH-rah)
touch-up – retocar (reh-toh-KAHR)

PAINTING TOOLS
Herramientas de Pintura

brush – pincel / brocha / cepillo (peehn-SEHL / BROH-chah / seh-PEEH-yoh)
can opener – abre latas (ah-breh LAH-tahs)
china bristle – cerda china (SEHR-dah CHEEH-nah)
chisel – cincel (seen-SEHL)
edger – orillador (oh-reeh-yah-DOOR)
extension pole – poste de extensión (POHS-teh deh ehks-tehn-see-OHN)
latex brush – pincel / brocha de latex (peehn-SEHL / BROH-chah deh latex)

nozzle – boquilla (boh-KEEH-yah)
razor blade – hojilla / navaja (oh-HEEH-yah / nah-VAH-ha)
roller – rodillo (roh-DEEH-yoh)
spackling – masilla (mah-SEE-yah)
sprayer – rociador / atomizador (roh-see-ah-DOHR / ah-toh-meeh-sah-DOHR)

PAINTING SUPPLIES
Provisiones para Pintura

bucket – balde / cubo / cubeta (BAHL-deh / KOOH-boh / kooh-BEH-tah)
caulk – masilla (mah-SEE-yah)
drop cloths – trapos de limpieza (TRAH-pohs deh leehm-peeh-EH-sah)
glue – goma / pegamento / cola (GOH-mah / peh-gah-MEHN-toh / KOH-lah)
linseed oil – aceite de linaza (ah-SEH-eeh-teh deh leeh-NAH-sah)
mineral spirits – aguarrás (ah-goo-ah-RAHS)
paint chart – carta de pinturas (KAHR-tah deh peehn-TOOH-rahs)
painter's putty – masilla de pintor (mah-SEE-yah deh peehn-TOHR)
paint remover – removedor de pintura (reh-moh-veh-DOOR deh peehn-TOOH-rah)
paint tray – bandeja / platón de pintura (bahn-DEH-hah / plah-TOHN deh peehn-TOOH-rah)
sandpaper – lija (LEEH-hah)
sponge – esponja (ehs-POHN-hah)
stir stick – palo / barilla para revolver (PAH-loh / bah-REEH-yah PAH-rah reh-vohl-VEHR)
tape – cinta (SEEN-tah
wire brush – cepillo de alambre (seh-PEEH-yoh deh ahl-AM-breh)
wood filler – relleno para madera (reh-YEH-noh PAH-rah mah-DEH-rah)

PAINTING FINISHES
Acabados de Pintura

antiqued – antiguo (ahn-TEEH-gooh-oh)
brushed – cepillado (seh-peeh-YAH-doh)
crackling – estallido (es-ta-YEE-doh)
distressed – envejecido / maltratado (enh-veh-heh-SEE-doh / mahl-trah-TAH-doh)
faux – simulacro / falso (see-mooh-LAH-kroh / FAHL-soh)
glaze – glaseado (glah-say-AH-doh)

oil rubbed – embadurnado en aceite / embarrado de aceite
(ehm-bah-doohr-NAH-doh enh ah-SEH-eeh-teh / ehm-bah-RAH-doh
deh ah-SEH-eeh-teh)
paint – pintura (peehn-TOOH-rah)
polished – pulido (pooh-LEEH-doh)
rag rolling – acabado con rodillo forrado con trapo
(ah-kah-BAH-doh kohn roh-DEEH-yoh foh-RAH-doh kohn TRAH-poh)
sponging – esponjado (ehs-ponh-HAH-doh)
stain – mancha (MAHN-chah)
stenciling – esténsil (ehs-TEHN-seehl)
texturing – texturizado (tehks-tooh-reeh-SAH-doh)

PAINTING PHRASES
Frases de Pintura

See Page 32 for Basic Job Q & A's and Job Site Phrases

How long have you been painting?
¿Cuánto hace que pinta?
(koo-AHN-toh AH-seh keh PEEHN-tah?)

I have been painting for _____ years.
Hace _____ años que pinto.
(AH-seh _____ AHN-yohs keh PEEHN-toh)

The paint and supplies will be delivered tomorrow.
La pintura y las provisiones seràn enviadas mañana.
(Lah peehn-TOOH-rah ee lahs pro-vis-ee-OH-nehs seh-RAHN en-vee-AH-
dahs mahn-YAH-nah)

Where are the mineral spirits?
¿Dónde está el aguarrás?
(DON-deh ehs-TAH ehl ah-gwah-RAHS?)

We need more rags.
Necesitamos más trapos.
(neh-seh-see-TAH-mohs mahs TRAH-pohs)

Where are the rollers?
¿Dónde están los rodillos?
(DON-deh ehs-TAHN lohs roh-DEE-yohs?)

We need more rollers.
Necesitamos más rodillos.
(neh-seh-see-TAH-mohs mahs roh-DEE-yohs)

Where are the brushes?
¿Dónde están los pinceles / las brochas?
(DON-deh ehs-TAHN lohs peen-SEH-lehs / lahs BROH-chahs?)

We need more brushes.
Necesitamos más pinceles / brochas.
(neh-seh-see-TAH-mohs mahs peen-SEH-lehs / BROH-chahs)

We need to clean the brushes over here.
Necesitamos limpiar los pinceles / las brochas aquí.
(neh-seh-see-TAH-mohs leem-peeAHR lohs peen-SEH-lehs / lahs BROH-chah
ah-KEY)

We need to store the brushes here.
Necesitamos guardar los pinceles / las brochas aquí.
(neh-se-see-TAH-mohs gwar-DAR lohs peehn-SEHL-ehs)/ lahs
BROH-chas ah-KEY)

We need more tape.
Necesitamos más cinta.
(neh-seh-see-TAH-mohs mahs SEEN-tah)

We need more drop cloths.
Necesitamos más trapos para limpiar.
(neh-seh-see-TAH-mohs mahs TRAH-pohs PAH-rah leem-pee-AHR)

We need the extension pole.
Necesitamos el poste de extensión.
(neh-seh-see-TAH-mohs ehl POHS-teh deh ex-tehn-see-ON)

Where is the extension pole?
¿Dónde está el poste de extensión?
(DON-deh ehs-TAH ehl POHS-teh deh ex-tehn-see-ON?)

We need the ladder.
Necesitamos la escalera.
(neh-seh-see-TAH-mohs lah ehs-kah-LEH-rah)

We need a bucket of water.
Necesitamos un balde de agua.
(neh-seh-see-TAH-mohs oon BAHL-deh deh AH-gwah)

We need to store the paint buckets here.
Necesitamos guardar los baldes de pintura aquí.
(neh-seh-see-TAH-mohs gwar-DAR lohs BAHL-dehs deh
peehn-TOOH-rah ah-KEY)

We need more paint.
Necesitamos más pintura.
(neh-seh-see-TAH-mohs MAHS peehn-TOOH-rah)

We need interior / exterior paint.
Necesitamos pintura para el interior / exterior.
(neh-seh-see-TAH-mohs peehn-TOOH-rah pah-rah in-teh-ree-OR /
ex-teh-ree-OR)

We need oil base paint for the trim.
Necesitamos pintura con base de aceite para las molduras.
(neh-seh-see-TAH-mohs peehn-TOOH-rah kohn BAH-se deh ah-SAY-the
pah-rah las mol-DOO-rahs)

We need latex paint.
Necesitamos pintura de látex.
(neh-she-see-TAH-mohs peehn-TOOH-rah deh latex)

We need to scrape and do the prep work.
Necesitamos raspar / rasquetear y realizar el trabajo preparativo.
(neh-seh-see-TAH-mohs rahs-PAHR / rahs-keh-teh-AHR ee reh-ah-LEE-sahr
ehl trah-BAH-hoh preh-pah-rah-TEE-voh)

We need to strip the old paint off.
Necesitamos raspar la pintura vieja.
(neh-seh-see-TAH-mohs rahs-PAHR lah peen-TOO-rah vee-EH-hah)

We need to scrape the windows.
Necesitamos raspar / rasquetear las ventanas.
(neh-seh-see-TAH-mohs rahs-PAHR / rahs-keh-teh-AHR lahs vehn-TAH-nahs)

We need to sand.
Necesitamos arenar / lijar.
(neh-seh-see-TAH-mohs ah-reh-NAHR / lee-HAHR)

We need to caulk.
Necesitamos enmasillar.
(neh-seh-see-TAH-mohs ehn-mah-see-YAHR)

We need to prime this before installing.
Necesitamos colocarle una capa de protector a esto antes de instalarlo.
(neh-seh-see-TAH-mohs koh-loh-CAR-leh OO-nah KAH-pah deh proh-tech-TOHR ah EHS-toh AHN-tehs deh eens-tah-LAHR-loh)

We need to sand this before the final coat of paint.
Necesitamos arenar esto antes de colocar la capa final de pintura.
(neh-seh-see-TAH-mohs ah-reh-NAHR EHS-toh AHN-tehs deh koh-loh-CAR lah KAH-pah fee-NAHL deh peen-TOO-rah)

We need to caulk here.
Necesitamos enmasillar aquí.
(neh-seh-see-TAH-mohs ehn-mah-see-YAHR ah-KEY)

We need to touch-up here.
Necesitamos retocar aquí.
(neh-seh-see-TAH-mohs reh-toh-CAR ah-KEY)

We need one coat of primer and two coats of base.
Necesitamos una capa de protector y dos capas de base.
(neh-seh-see-TAH-mohs OO-nah KAH-pah deh proh-tech-TOHR ee dohs KAH-pahs deh BAH-seh)

Where is the paint for this room?
¿Dónde está la pintura para esta habitación?
(DON-deh ehs-TAH lah peen-TOO-rah PAH-rah EHS-tah ah-bee-tah-see-ON?)

We need to get the first coat of paint on the walls and ceilings.
Necesitamos colocar la primera capa de pintura en las paredes y en los cielosrrasos.
(neh-seh-see-TAH-mohs koh-loh-CAR lah pree-MEH-rah KAH-pah deh peen-TOO-rah ehn lahs pah-REH-dehs ee ehn lohs see-eh-lohs-RAH-sohs)

We need to put the body color here.
Necesitamos colocar el color principal aquí.
(neh-seh-see-TAH-mohs koh-loh-CAR ehl koh-LOHR preen-see-PAHL ah-KEY)

We need to put the trim color here.
Necesitamos colocar el color para la madera moldeada aquí.
(neh-seh-see-TAH-mohs koh-loh-CAR ehl koh-LOHR PAH-rah lah mah-DEH-rah mohl-dehAH-dah ah-KEY)

We need to put the 3rd color here.
Necesitamos colocar el tercer color aquí.
(neh-seh-see-TAH-mohs koh-loh-CAR ehl tehr-SEHR koh-LOHR ah-KEY)

We need to stain / paint the kick plates.
Necesitamos tintar / pintar los zócalos.
(neh-seh-see-TAH-mohs teen-TAHR / peen-TAHR lohs SOH-cah-lohs)

We need to stain / paint the stair treads.
Necesitamos tintar / pintar los peldoños de las escaleras.
(neh-seh-see-TAH-mohs teen-TAHR / peehn-TAHR lohs pel-DAHN-yos deh lahs es-cah-LAY-rahs)

We need to stain / paint the front door.
Necesitamos tintar / pintar la puerta principal.
neh-seh-see-TAH-mohs teen-TAHR / peehn-TAHR lah pooh-EHR-tah prin-seeh-PAHL)

We need to stain / paint the mantel.
Necesitamos tintar / pintar la repisa de la chimenea.
(neh-seh-see-TAH-mohs teen-TAHR / peehn-TAHR lah ray-PEE-sah deh lah chi-meh-NEH-ahl)

We need to paint the bedroom / kitchen / bathroom.
Necesitamos pintar la habitación / la cocina / el baño.
(neh-seh-see-TAH-mohs peen-TAHR lah ah-bee-tah-see-ON / lah koh-SEE-nah / ehl BAH-nee-oh)

We need to paint the shutters.
Necesitamos pintar las contraventanas.
(neh-seh-see-TAH-mohs peehn-TAHR lahs con-trah-ven-TAH-nahs)

We need to clean up the job site daily.
Necesitamos limpiar el área de trabajo a diario.
(neh-seh-see-TAH-mohs leem-pee-AHR ehl AH-reh-ah deh trah-BAH-hoh ah dee-AH-ree-oh)

PLUMBING

PLUMBING TERMS
Términos de Plomería

access panel – panel / tablero de acceso (pah-NEHL / tah-BLEH-roh deh ahk-SEH-soh)

adaptor – adaptador (ah-dahp-tah-DOOR)

aerator – aireador (ah-eh-reh-ah-DOOR)

air chamber – cámara de aire (KAH-mah-rah deh AH-eeh-reh)

air check – punto de chequeo de aire (POOHN-toh deh cheh-KEH-oh deh AH-eeh-reh)

apron – delantal (deh-lahn-TAHL)

back flow preventor – preventor de reflujo (preh-vehn-TOHR deh reh-FLOOH-hoh)

backflow – reflujo (reh-FLOOH-hoh)

backwash – flujo en reverso (FLOOH-hoh ehn reh-VEHR-soh)

baffle – deflector (deh-flehk-TOHR)

ball cock – válvula de cierre automático (VAHL-vooh-lah deh see-EH-reh ah-ooh-toh-MAH-teeh-koh)

base – base (BAH-seh)

black water – agua negra (AH-goo-ah NEH-grah)

casing – caja / estuche / recinto (KAH-hah / ehs-TOOH-cheh / reh-SEEN-toh)

cast iron – hierro colado / fundido (eeh-EH-roh koh-LAH-doh / foon-DEE-doh)

circuit vent – circuito de ventilación (seehr-kooh-EEH-toh deh vehn-teeh-lah-see-OHN)

common vent – ventilación común (vehn-teeh-lah-see-OHN koh-MOON)

condensation – condensación (kohn-dehn-sah-see-OHN)

copper pipe – tubería de cobre (tooh-beh-REEH-ah deh KOH-breh)

coupling – acoplar (ah-koh-PLAR)

crow's foot – pata de cuervo / cabra (PAH-tah deh kooh-EHR-voh / KAH-brah)

culvert –tubería subterránea de agua (tooh-beh-REEH-ah soob-tehr-AHN-ee-ah deh AH-goo-ah)

diverter – desviador (dehs-veeh-ah-DOOR)

drain – desaguadero / escurridero (deh-sah-gooh-ah-DEH-roh / ehs-kooh-reeh-DEH-roh)

elbow – codo (KOH-doh)

end drain – desaguadero final (deh-sah-gooh-ah-DEH-roh fee-NAHL)

female threads – rosca hembra (ROHS-kah EHM-brah)

fixture – accesorio / artículo (ahk-seh-SOH-reeh-oh / ahr-TEEH-kooh-loh)

fixture unit – unidad de accesorio (ooh-neeh-DAHD deh ahk-seh-SOH-reeh-oh)

flapper – colgador (kohl-gah-DOHR)

flex – flexionar (flehk-see-oh-NAHR)

flue – tubo de escape (TOOH-boh deh ehs-KAH-peh)

foam insulation – espuma de aislamiento (ehs-POO-mah deh ah-eehs-lah-meeh-EHN-toh)

gasket – empacadura (ehm-pah-kah-DOOH-rah)

handles – manijas (mah-NEEH-hahs)

input – entrada / aporte (ehn-TRAH-dah / ah-POHR-teh)

joint – unión / empalme / junta (ooh-neeh-OHN / ehm-PAHL-meh / HOOHN-tah)

knock-out plug – tapón de vaciado total (tah-POHN deh vah-see-AH-doh toh-TAHL)

L tubing – tubería L (tooh-beh-REEH-ah EH-leh)

leach field – terreno percolado (teh-REH-noh pehr-koh-LAH-doh)

leach lines – líneas de percolación (LEEH-neh-ahs deh pehr-koh-lah-see-OHN)

lock nut – tuerca de traba (tooh-EHR-kah deh trah-BAH)

M tubing – tubería M (tooh-beh-REEH-ah EH-meh)

main – principal / madre (preehn-see-PAHL / MAH-dreh)

manhole – boca de acceso / tapa de alcantarilla (BOH-kah deh ahk-SEH-soh / TAH-pah deh al-can-tah-REE-yah)

mission coupling – abrazadera metálica (ah-brah-sah-DEH-rah meh-TAH-leeh-kah)

nipple – tetilla (teh-TEEH-yah)

O ring – empacadura de anillo / O-ring (ehm-pah-kah-DOOH-rah deh ah-NEEH-yoh / oh ring)

outlet / discharge – salida / descarga (sah-LEEH-dah / dehs-KAHR-gah)

overflow hood – recolector de rebalse (reh-koh-lehk-TOHR deh reh-BAHL-seh)

overflow tube – tubería para el rebalse (tooh-beh-REEH-ah PAH-rah ehl reh-BAHL-seh)

packing – empacado (emh-pah-KAH-doh)

PEX pipe – tubería de PEX (tooh-beh-REE-ah deh PEX)

plug – tapón (tah-POHN)

PVC pipe – tubería de PVC / tubería plástica (tooh-beh-REEH-ah deh peh veh seh / tooh-beh-REEH-ah PLAHS-teeh-kah)

riser – tubo vertical (TOOH boh vehr-teeh-KAHL)

safety shut off valve – válvula de seguridad de cierre (VAHL-vooh-lah deh seh-gooh-reeh-DAHD deh see-EH-reh)

septic – pozo séptico (POH-soh SEHP-teeh-koh)
service entrance – entrada para los servicios (ehn-TRAH-dah PAH-rah lohs sehr-VEEH-see-ohs)
sewer – cloaca / alcantarilla (kloh-AH-kah / ahl-kan-tah-REE-yah)
sill caulk – sellador (seh-YAH-dohr)
sleeve – manga (MAHN-gah)
slip joint – unión / empalme / junta de presión (ooh-neeh-OHN / ehm-PAHL-meh / HOOHN-tah deh preh-see-OHN)
solder – soldadura (sohl-dah-DOOH-rah)
solvent weld – solvente para soldar (sohl-VEHN-teh PAH-rah sohl-DAHR)
spigot – llave / grifo / canilla (YAH-veh / GREEH-foh / kah-NEEH-yah)
stem – boca de la tubería (BOH-kah deh lah tooh-beh-REEH-ah)
storm drain – desagüe para las tormentas (deh-SAH-gooh-eh PAH-rah lahs tohr-MEHN-tahs)
stub-out – fragmento de tubería (frahg-MEHN-toh deh tooh-beh-REEH-ah)
sump – colector de rebalse (koh-lehk-TOHR deh rehBAHL-seh)
tee – te (teh)
trap – trampa (TRAHM-pah)
uniflex – uniflex (ooh-neeh-FLEKS)
union – unión (ooh-neeh-OHN)
valve – válvula (VAHL-vooh-lah)
vent – ventilación (vehn-teeh-lah-see-OHN)
water meter – medidor de agua (meh-deeh-DOHR deh AH-goo-ah)
water service pipe – tubería de agua (tooh-beh-REEH-ah deh AH-goo-ah)
water table – mesa de agua subterránea (MEH-sah deh AH-gooh-ah soohb-teh-RAH-neh-ah)
water tap – caño / llave de agua (KAHN-yoh / YAH-veh deh AH-goo-ah)
weld – soldar (sohl-DAHR)

PLUMBING TOOLS
Herramientas de Plomeria

adjustable wrench – llave de tubo ajustable (YAH-veh deh TOOH-boh ah-hoohs-TAH-bleh)
allen wrench – llave alen (YAH-veh Allen)
blowtorch – soplete (soh-PLEH-teh)
channel pliers – alicates de presión (ah-leeh-KAH-tehs deh preh-see-OHN)
circular saw – sierra circular (see-EH-rah seehr-kooh-LAHR)
drill – taladro (tah-LAH-droh)

hole saw bit – agujereador (ah-gooh-heh-reh-ah-DOHR)
keyhole saw – serrucho para drywall (seh-ROOH-choh PAH-rah drái uól)
level – nivel (neeh-VEHL)
needle nose pliers – alicate puntudo (ah-leeh-KAH-teh poohn-TOOH-doh)
pipe cutter – cortador de tubos (kohr-tah-DOHR deh TOOH-bohs)
pipe wrench – llave de tubo (YAH-veh deh TOOH-boh)
plumber's snake – culebra destapa cañerías (kooh-LEH-brah dehs-TAH-pah kahn-yeh-REEH-ahs)
square – escuadra (ehs-kooh-AH-drah)
stud finder – stud finder / busca montantes (stud finder / boohs-kah mohn-TAHN-tehs)
tape measure – cinta para medir (SEEN-tah PAH-rah meh-DEEHR)
torch – antorcha (anh-TOHR-chah)
utility knife – cortapluma (kohr-tah-PLOOH-mah)
wrench – llave (YAH-veh)

PLUMBING SUPPLIES
Provisiones de Plomería

caps – tapas (TAH-pahs)
copper pipe – tubería de cobre (tooh-beh-REEH-ah deh KOH-breh)
couplings – acoplados (ah-koh-PLAH-dohs)
elbows – codos (KOH-dohs)
faucets – llaves / grifos (YAH-vehs / GREEH-fohs)
female fittings – conexiones hembras (koh-nehk-see-OH-nehs EHM-brahs)
gas pipe – tubería de gas (tooh-beh-REEH-ah deh gas)
handles – manijas (mah-NEEH-hahs)
male fittings – conexiones machos (koh-nehk-see-OH-nehs MAH-chohs)
plastic PVC pipe – tubería de PVC / tubería plástica (tooh-beh-REEH-ah PLAHS-teeh-kah)
plumber putty – masilla de plomero (mah-SEE-yah deh ploh-MEH-roh)
plumber tape – cinta de plomero (SEEN-tah deh ploh-MEH-roh)
plunger – sopapo / destapa cañerías (soh-PAH-poh / dehs-TAH-pah kahn-yeh-REEH-ahs)
shower valve – válvula de regadera (VAHL-vooh-lah deh reh-gah-DEH-rah)
silicone caulk – masilla de silicón (mah-SEE-yah deh see-leeh-KOHN)
tees – tes (tehs)

teflon tape – cinta de teflón / teflón (SEEN-tah deh teh-FLOHN / teh-FLOHN)

wall-mount valve – válvula montada en la pared (VAHL-vooh-lah mohn-TAH-dah ehn lah pah-REHD)

washers – arandelas (ah-rahn-DEH-lahs)

PLUMBING FIXTURES
Accesorios de Plomería

bathtub – bañera (bahn-YEH-rah)

bidet – bidet (bidet)

body spray – aerosol para el cuerpo (ah-EH-roh-sohl PAH-rah ehl kooh-EHR-poh)

ceramic sink – lavamanos de cerámica (lah-vah-MAH-nohs deh seh-RAH-meeh-kah)

claw foot tub – bañera con patas (bahn-YEH-rah kohn PAH-tahs)

commode – poceta (poh-SEH-tah)

composting toilet – poceta sin cloaca o pozo séptico (poh-seh-tah seen kloh-AH-kah oh POH-soh SEHP-teeh-koh)

copper sink – lavamanos de cobre (lah-vah-MAH-nohs deh KOH-breh)

farmhouse sink – lavamanos de granja (lah-vah-MAH-nohs deh GRAHN-jah)

jacuzzi® – jacuzzi (jacuzzi)

kitchen faucet – llave de agua de la cocina (YAH-veh deh AH-goo-ah deh lah koh-SEE-nah)

laundry sink – lavamanos de la lavandería (lah-vah-MAH-nohs deh lah lah-vahn-deh-REEH-ah)

low consumption toilet – poceta de consumo bajo (poh-SEH-tah deh kohn-SOOH-moh BAH-hoh)

master bath faucet – llave de agua del baño principal (YAH-veh deh AH-goo-ah dehl BAHN-yoh preehn-see-PAHL)

outdoor shower – regadera fuera de la casa (reh-gah-DEH-rah fooh-EH-rah deh lah KAH-sah)

pedestal sink – lavamanos con pedestal (lah-vah-MAH-nohs kohn peh-dehs-TAHL)

recessed tub – bañera incrustada (bahn-YEH-rah eehn-kroohs-TAH-dah)

sauna – sauna (SAH-ooh-nah)

shower – regadera / ducha (reh-gah-DEH-rah / DOOH-chah)

sink – lavamanos (lah-vah-MAH-nohs)

stainless steel sink – lavamanos de acero inoxidable (lah-vah-MAH-nohs deh ah-SEH-roh eeh-nohk-see-DAH-bleh)

steam shower – regadera con vapor (reh-gah-DEH-rah kohn vah-POHR)

tankless water heater – calentador de agua sin tanque
(kah-lehn-tah-DOHR deh AH-goo-ah seen TAHN-keh)

toilet – poceta / excusado / retrete (poh-SEH-tah / eks-kooh-SAH-doh
/ reh-TREH-teh)

touchless faucet – llave de agua automática (YAH-veh deh AH-goo-
ah ah-ooh-toh-MAH-teeh-kah)

under mount sink – lavamanos de pie (lah-vah-MAH-nohs deh
peeh-EH)

urinal – urinal / urinario (ooh-reeh-NAHL / ooh-reeh-NAH-reeh-oh)

utility sink – lavamanos con gabinete (lah-vah-MAH-nohs kohn gah-
bee-NEH-teh)

vegetable sink – batea (bah-TEH-ah)

water heater [electric] – calentador de agua eléctrico (cah-lehn-tah-
DOHR deh AH-goo-ah eh-LEK-tree-coh)

water heater [gas] – calentador de agua de gas (cah-lehn-tah-DOHR
deh AH-goo-ah deh gahs)

whirlpool bath – bañera de hidromasajes (bahn-YEH-rah
deh eeh-droh-mah-SAH-hehs)

PLUMBING PHRASES
Frases de Plomería

*See Page 32 for Basic Job Q & A's
and Job Site Phrases*

How long have you been a plumber?
¿Cuánto hace que es plomero?
(koo-AHN-toh AH-seh keh ehs ploh-MEH-roh?)

I have been a plumber for _____ years.
Hace _____ años que soy plomero.
(AH-seh _____ AHN-yohs keh SOH-ee ploh-MEH-roh)

We need to get the water turned on.
Necesitamos conectar el agua.
(neh-seh-see-TAH-mohs koh-nehk-TAHR ehl AH-gwah)

We need to get the water turned off.
Necesitamos desconectar el agua.
(neh-seh-see-TAH-mohs dehs-koh-nehk-TAHR ehl AH-gwah)

Where is the pipe wrench?
¿Donde esta la llave de tubo?
(DON-deh ehs-TAH lah YAH-veh deh TOO-boh?)

Where is the shovel?
¿Dónde está la pala?
(DON-deh ehs-TAH lah PAH-lah?)

Where is the hammer?
¿Dónde está el martillo?
(DON-deh ehs-TAH ehl mahr-TEE-yoh?)

Where is the propane torch?
¿Dónde está la antorcha de propano?
(DON-deh ehs-TAH lah ahn-TOHR-chah deh proh-PAH-noh?)

Where is the glue?
¿Dónde está el pegamento / la goma / la cola?
(DON-deh ehs-TAH ehl peh-gah-MEHN-toh / lah GOH-mah /
lah KOH-lah?)

Where is the septic system?
¿Dónde está el pozo séptico?
(DON-deh ehs-TAH ehl POH-soh SEHP-tee-koh?)

Where is the pump?
¿Dónde está la bomba?
(DON-deh ehs-TAH lah BOHM-bah?)

We need more copper pipe.
Necesitamos más cañería de cobre.
(neh-seh-see-TAH-mohs mahs kahn-yeh-REE-ah deh KOH-breh)

We need more PVC pipe.
Necesitamos más cañería de plástico / PVC.
(neh-seh-see-TAH-mohs mahs kahn-yeh-REE-ah deh PLAHS-tee-koh /
PVC)

We need more PEX pipe.
Necesitamos más cañería de PEX.
(neh-seh-see-TAH-mohs mahs kahn-yeh-REE-ah deh PEX)

We need to pull this piping out.
Necesitamos retirar esta cañería.
(neh-seh-see-TAH-mohs reh-tee-RAHR EHS-tah kahn-yeh-REE-ah)

We need to solder that pipe.
Necesitamos soldar ese caño.
(neh-seh-see-TAH-mohs sohl-DAR EH-seh KAHN-yoh)

We need to rough in the house.
Necesitamos hacer las conexiones de tubería y de plomería a la casa.
(neh-seh-see-TAH-mohs ah-SEHR lahs koh-nehx-see-OH-nehs deh to-beh-REE-ah ee deh ploh-meh-REE-ah ah lah KAH-sah)

We need to trim out the house.
Necesitmos sacarle los detalles a la casa.
(neh-seh-see-TAH-mohs sah-CAR-leh los deh-TAH-yehs a la CAH-sah)

We need to dig a new water line in the front yard.
Necesitamos excavar una nueva línea de agua en el jardín del frente.
(neh-seh-see-TAH-mohs ex-kah-VAHR OO-nah noo-EH-vah LEEN-eh-ah deh AH-gwah ehn ehl hahr-DEEN dehl FREHN-teh)

We need to tap into the street line.
Necesitamos conectar con la tubería de la calle.
(neh-seh-see-TAH-mohs co-nek-TAHR con la too-beh-REE-ah deh la CAH-yeh)

We need to turn the water off at the street.
Necesitamos desconectar el agua de la calle.
(neh-seh-see-TAH-mohs dehs-koh-nehk-TAHR ehl AH-gwah deh lah KAH-yeh)

We need to put a drain pan here.
Necesitamos colocar una bandeja de desagüe / drenaje aquí.
(neh-seh-see-TAH-mohs koh-loh-CAR OO-nah bahn-DEH-hah deh deh-SAH-gweh / dreh-NAH-heh ah-KEY)

We need to check the water pressure.
Necesitamos chequear la presión del agua.
(neh-seh-see-TAH-mohs cheh-kay-AHR la pray-see-ON del AH-gwah)

We need to fix the clog.
Necesitamos destapar la obstrucción.
(neh-seh-see-TAH-mohs dehs-tah-PAHR lah ohbs-trook-see-ON)

We need to install the sprinkler system.
Necesitamos instalar el sistema de riego.
(neh-seh-see-TAH-mohs een-sta-LAHR el sees-TEM-ah day ree-EH-go)

We need to install a sump pump.
Necesitamos instalar una bomba extractora.
(neh-seh-see-TAH-mohs een-sta-LAHR OO-na BOM-bah
eks-trak-TOHR-ah)

We need to install the septic system.
Necesitamos instalar el pozo séptico.
(neh-seh-see-TAH-mohs een-sta-LAHR el POH-zoh SEHP-tee-co)

We need to get the soil tested.
Necesitamos hacer un examen de tierra.
(neh-seh-see-TAH-mohs ah-SEHR oon eks-AH-meen deh tee-EH-rah)

We need to mark off the leach field.
Necesitamos demarcar el terreno percolado.
(neh-seh-see-TAH-mohs day-mar-KAR el tehr-EH-no per-coh-LAH-do)

Have you found the leak?
¿Ha encontrado el escape?
(ah ehn-kohn-TRAH-doh ehl es-CAH-peh?)

How many faucets will there be in the house?
¿Cuántos grifos habrán en la casa?
(koo-AHN-tohs GREE-fohs ah-BRAHN ehn lah KAH-sah?)

We need to put this faucet in the kitchen / bathroom / laundry room.
Necesitamos colocar este grifo en la cocina / el baño /
la lavandería.
(neh-seh-see-TAH-mohs koh-loh-CAR EHS-teh GREE-foh ehn lah koh-SEE-
nah / ehl BAH-neeoh / lah lah-vahn-deh-REE-ah)

Are the fixtures in yet?
¿Llegaron ya los accesorios?
(yeh-GAH-rohn yah lohs ahk-sehs-OR-ee-ohs?)

We need to install the fixtures.
Necesitamos instalar los accesorios.
(neh-seh-see-TAH-mohs een-sta-LAHR los ak-sehs-OOR-ee-ohs)

We need to get an inspection.
Necesitamos obtener una inspección.
(neh-seh-see-TAH-mohs ohb-teh-NEHR OO-nah eens-pek-see-ON)

We need to clean up the job site daily.
Necesitamos limpiar el área de trabajo a diario.
(neh-seh-see-TAH-mohs leem-pee-AHR ehl AH-reh-ah deh trah-BAH-hoh ah dee-AH-ree-oh)

ROOFING

ROOFING TERMS
Términos de Techado

asphalt – asfalto (ahs-FAHL-toh)
built-up roof – techo levantado (TEH-choh leh-vahn-TAH-doh)
course – curso (KOOHR-soh)
deck – balcón (bahl-KOHN)
drip edge – canaleta (kah-nah-LEH-tah)
dormer – ventanilla sobresaliente / dórmer (vehn-tah-NEEH-yah soh-breh-sah-leeh-EHN-teh / dormer)
eave – alero (ah-LEH-roh)
end lap – revestimiento con tablas al final (reh-vehs-teeh-meeh-EHN-toh kohn TAH-blahs ahl fee-NAHL)
flashing – resguardo (rehs-gooh-AHR-doh)
flat – plano (PLAH-noh)
gable – hastial / gable (ahs-teeh-AHL / gueibol)
gambrel – techo con hastiales / gambrel (TEH-choh kohn ahs-teeh-AH-lehs / gambrel)
grade – declive / nivelar (deh-CLEEH-veh / neeh-veh-LAHR)
hip – caballete / vértice (kah-bah-YEH-teh / VEHR-teeh-se)
pitch – alquitrán (ahl-keeh-TRAHN)
ridge – caballete / cumbrera (cah-bah-YEH-tay / koohm-BREH-rah)
rise – tubo vertical (TOOH-boh vehr-teeh-KAHL)
roof vents – ventilaciones del techo (vehn-teeh-lah-see-OH-nehs dehl TEH-choh)
rubber roof – techo de caucho (TEH-choh deh KAH-ooh-choh)
shed – cobertizo (koh-behr-TEEH-soh)
side lap – revestimiento con tablas en los lados (reh-vehs-teeh-meeh-EHN-toh kohn TAH-blahs ehn lohs LAH-dohs)
skylight – tragaluz (trah-gah-LOOS)
slope – inclinación (eehn-kleeh-nah-see-OHN)

ROOFING TOOLS
Herramientas para Techado

crowbar – palanca / pata de cabra / cuervo (pah-LAHN-kah / PAH-tah deh KAH-brah / kooh-EHR-voh)
extension ladder – escalera de extensión (ehs-kah-LEH-rah deh ehks-tehn-see-OHN)
fork – horquilla (ohr-KEEH-yah)

hammer – martillo (marh-TEEH-yoh)
hatchet – hacha (AH-chah)
knife – cuchillo (kooh-CHEEH-yoh)
ladder lift – levantador de escalera (leh-vahn-TAH-dohr deh ehs-kah-LEH-rah)
nail pullers – extractor de clavos (ehks-trahk-TOHR deh KLAH-vohs)
pry bar – palanca de fuerza (pah-LAHN-kah deh fooh-EHR-sah)
rake – rastrillo (rahs-TREE-yoh)
shears – tijeras para cortar metal (teeh-HEH-rahs PAH-rah kohr-TAHR meh-TAHL)
shovel – pala (PAH-lah)
snips – tijeras (teeh-HEH-rahs)
tape measure – cinta para medir (SEEN-tah PAH-rah meh-DEEHR)

ROOFING SUPPLIES
Provisiones para Techado

brackets – soportes (soh-POHR-tehs)
chalk line – línea de tiza / gis (LEEH-neh-ah deh TEEH-sah / heehs)
cleats – abrazaderas (ah-brah-sah-DEH-ras)
felt – fieltro (fee-EHL-troh)
flashing – resguardo (rehs-gooh-AHR-doh)
knee pads – protectores de rodillas / rodilleras (proh-tehk-TOH-rehs deh roh-DEEH-yahs / roh-dee-YEH-rahs)
magnetic sweeper – barredor magnético (bah-reh-DOHR mahg-NEH-teeh-koh)
nail bag – bolsa de clavos (bohl-sah deh CLAH-vohs)
nails – clavos (CLAH-vohs)
plastic cement – cemento plástico (seh-MEHN-toh PLAHS-teeh-koh)
plywood – plywood / madera terciada (plái uúd / mah-DEH-rah tehr-see-AH-dah)
power vent – extractor a motor (eks-trahk-TOHR ah moh-TOHR)
ridge vent – caballete de ventilación (cah-bah-YEH-tay deh vehn-teeh-lah-see-OHN)
spray paint – pintura en atomizador / pintura sprey (peehn-TOOH-rah enh ah-toh-meeh-sah-DOHR / peehn-TOOH-rah spray)
tar – brea (BREH-ah)
tarp – lona impermeabilizada (LOH-nah eem-pehr-meh-AH-bleh)
wheelbarrow – carretilla (kah-reh-TEEH-yah)

ROOFING PHRASES
Frases de Techado

See Page 32 for Basic Job Q & A's and Job Site Phrases

How long have you been roofing?
¿Cuánto hace que es techista?
(koo-AHN-toh AH-seh keh ehs teh-CHEESE-tah?)

I have been roofing for _____ years.
Hace _____ años que soy techista.
(AH-seh _____ AHN-yohs keh SOH-ee teh-CHEESE-tah)

Can you do metal roofs?
¿Sabe trabajar con techos de metal?
(SAH-beh trah-bah-HAHR kohn TEH-chohs deh meh-TAHL?)

Can you do copper roofs?
¿Sabe trabajar con techos de cobre?
(SAH-beh trah-bah-HAHR kohn TEH-chohs deh KOH-breh?)

We need to tear off and dispose of the old roof.
Necesitamos arrancar y desechar el techo viejo.
(neh-seh-see-TAH-mohs ah-rahn-CAR y deh-seh-CHAHR ehl TEH-choh vee-EH-hoh)

We need to tear off shingles first.
Necesitamos primero arrancar las tejas.
(neh-seh-see-TAH-mohs pree-MEH-roh ah-rahn-CAR lahs TEH-hahs)

We need to use a tarp to catch shingles.
Necesitamos utilizar una lona para atajar las tejas.
(neh-seh-see-TAH-mohs oo-tee-lee-SAHR OO-nah LOH-nah PAH-rah ah-tah-HAHR lahs TEH-hahs)

We need to put shingles and debris in the dumpster.
Necesitamos colocar las tejas y los escombros en el basurero.
(neh-seh-see-TAH-mohs koh-loh-CAR lahs TEH-hahs ee lohs ehs-KOHM-brohs ehn ehl bah-soo-REH-roh)

We need a dumpster.
Necesitamos un basurero.
(neh-seh-see-TAH-mohs oon bah-soo-REH-roh)

Where are the shingles?
¿Dónde están las tejas?
(DON-deh ehs-TAHN lahs TEH-hahs?)

We need more shingles.
Necesitamos más tejas.
(neh-seh-see-TAH-mohs mahs TEH-hahs)

The shingles will be delivered tomorrow.
Mañana entregarán las tejas.
(Mahn-YAH-nah ehn-treh-gah-RAHN lahs TEH-hahs)

Where is the felt?
¿Dónde está el fieltro?
(DON-deh ehs-TAH ehl fee-EHL-troh?)

We need more felt.
Necesitamos más fieltro.
(neh-seh-see-TAH-mohs mahs fee-EHL-troh)

Where are the nails?
¿Dónde están los clavos?
(DON-deh ehs-TAHN lohs KLAH-vohs?)

We need more nails.
Necesitamos más clavos.
(neh-seh-see-TAH-mohs mahs KLAH-vohs)

We need more scaffolding.
Necesitamos más andamiaje.
(neh-seh-see-TAH-mohs mahs ahn-dah-mee-AH-heh)

Where is the hammer?
¿Dónde está el martillo?
(DON-deh ehs-TAH ehl mahr-TEE-yoh?)

Where is the saw?
¿Dónde está el serrucho?
(DON-deh ehs-TAH ehl seh-ROO-choh?)

Where is the roofing fork?
¿Dónde están las tenazas para techar?
(DON-deh ehs-TAHN lahs teh-NAH-sahs PAH-rah teh-CHAHR?)

Where is the coil nailer?

¿Dónde está la pistola para clavos enrollados en tiras / pistola de clavos con tambor?

(DON-deh ehs-TAH lah pees-TOH-lah PAH-rah KLAH-vohs ehn-roh-YAH-dohs ehn TEE-rahs / pees-TOH-lah deh KLAH-vohs kohn tam-BOHR?)

We need to flash this.

Necesitamos colocarle cubrejuntas a esto.

(neh-seh-see-TAH-mohs koh-loh-CAR-leh koo-breh-HOON-tahs ah EHS-toh)

We need to flash around the chimney.

Necesitamos colocar cubrejuntas alrededor de la chimenea.

(neh-seh-see-TAH-mohs koh-loh-CAR koo-breh-HOON-tahs ahl-reh-deh-DOOR deh lah chee-meh-NEH-ah)

We need to flash around the skylights.

Necesitamos colocar cubrejuntas alrededor de los tragaluces / las claraboyas.

(neh-seh-see-TAH-mohs koh-loh-CAR koo-breh-HOON-tahs ahl-reh-deh-DOOR deh lohs trah-gah-LOO-sehs / lahs klah-rah-BOH-yahs)

We need to flash the chimney in copper.

Necesitamos colocarle cubrejuntas de cobre a la chimenea.

(neh-seh-see-TAH-mohs koh-loh-CAR-leh koo-breh-HOON-tahs deh KOH-breh ah lah chee-meh-NEH-ah)

We need to use shake shingles on this roof.

Necesitamos utilizar tejas de madera / ripias en este techo.

(neh-seh-see-TAH-mohs oo-tee-lee-SAHR TEH-hahs deh mah-DEH-rah / REE-pee-ahs ehn EHS-teh TEH-choh)

We need to use 30-year architectural shingles on this roof.

Necesitamos utilizar tejas arquitectónicas de 30 años de durabilidad en éste techo.

(neh-seh-see-TAH-mohs oo-tee-lee-SAHR TEH-hahs ahr-key-tech-TOH-nee-kahs deh TREH-in-tah AHN-yohs deh do-rah-be-lee-DAHD ehn EHS-teh TEH-choh)

We need to use slate on this roof.

Necesitamos utilizar pizarras en este techo.

(neh-seh-see-TAH-mohs oo-tee-lee-SAHR pee-SAH-rahs ehn EHS-teh TEH-choh)

We need to use metal on this roof.
Necesitamos utilizar metal en este techo.
(neh-seh-see-TAH-mohs oo-tee-lee-SAHR meh-TAHL ehn EHS-teh TEH-choh)

We need to use ridge-venting here.
Necesitamos utilizar un canal de ventilación aquí.
(neh-seh-see-TAH-mohs oo-tee-lee-SAHR oohn kah-NAHL deh vehn-tee-lah-see-ON ah-KEY)

We need to use rubber roofing.
Necesitamos utilizar techo de caucho.
(neh-seh-see-TAH-mohs oo-tee-lee-SAHR TEH-choh deh KAH-ooh-choh)

We need to use rubber here.
Necesitamos utilizar caucho aquí.
(neh-seh-see-TAH-mohs oo-tee-lee-SAHR KAH-ooh-choh ah-KEY)

We need to glue the roof down.
Necesitamos pegar / adherir el techo.
(neh-seh-see-TAH-mohs pay-HAR / ahd-hair-ehr el TEH-choh)

We need to put skylights here.
Necesitamos colocar tragaluces / claraboyas aquí.
(neh-seh-see-TAH-mohs koh-loh-CAR trah-gah-LOO-sehs / klah-rah-BOH-yahs ah-KEY)

We need new decking.
Necesitamos una cubierta nueva / un balcón nuevo aquí.
(neh-seh-see-TAH-mohs OO-nah koo-bee-EHR-tah noo-EH-vah / oon bahl-KOHN noo-EH-voh ah-KEY)

We need to replace the decking here.
Necesitamos reemplazar la cubierta / el balcón aquí.
(neh-seh-see-TAH-mohs rehm-plah-SAHR lah koo-bee-EHR-tah / ehl bahl-KOHN ah-KEY)

We need to use drip edge.
Necesitamos utilizar un canalete de desagüe.
(neh-seh-see-TAH-mohs oo-tee-lee-SAHR oohn kah-nah-LEH-teh deh deh-SAH-gweh)

We need to install roof vents here.
Necesitamos instalar ventilaciones de techo aquí.
(neh-seh-see-TAH-mohs eens-tah-LAHR vehn-tee-lah-see-OH-nehs deh TEH-choh ah-KEY)

We need to caulk here.
Necesitamos enmasillar aquí.
(neh-seh-see-TAH-mohs ehn-mah-see-YAHR ah-KEY)

We need to get an inspection.
Necesitamos obtener una inspección.
(neh-seh-see-TAH-mohs ohb-teh-NEHR OO-nah eens-pek-see-ON)

We need to clean up the job site daily.
Necesitamos limpiar el área de trabajo a diario.
(neh-seh-see-TAH-mohs leem-pee-AHR ehl AH-reh-ah deh trah-BAH-hoh ah dee-AH-ree-oh)

ALSO SEE FRAMING IN THE CARPENTRY SECTION
TAMBIEN VEA ENMARCAR EN LA SECCIÓN DE CARPINTERIA

Techado – Frases

Necesitamos utilizar un canalete de desagüe.
We need to use drip edge.
(Ui nid tu ius drip ech)

Necesitamos instalar ventilaciones de techo aquí.
We need to install roof vents here.
(Ui nid tu instol ruf vents jiar)

Necesitamos utilizar techo de caucho.
We need to use rubber roofing.
(Ui nid tu ius raber rúfin)

Necesitamos pegar / adherir el techo.
We need to glue the roof down.
(Ui nid tu glú de ruf dáun)

Necesitamos enmasillar aquí.
We need to caulk here.
(Ui nid tu cok jiar)

Necesitamos obtener una inspección.
We need to get an inspection.
(Ui nid tu guet an inspekshon)

Necesitamos limpiar el área de trabajo a diario.
We need to clean up the job site daily.
(Ui nid tu clin ap de llob-sáit déili)

TAMBIEN VEA ENMARCAR EN LA SECCIÓN DE CARPINTERIA
ALSO SEE FRAMING IN THE CARPENTRY SECTION

Mañana entregarán las tejas.
The shingles will be delivered tomorrow.
(De shíngols uil bi dilíverd tumórrou)

Necesitamos utilizar tejas de madera / ripias en este techo.
We need to use shake shingles on this roof.
(Ui nid tu ius shéik shíngols on dis ruf)

Necesitamos utilizar tejas arquitectónicas de 30 años de durabilidad en éste techo.
We need to use 30-yr. architectural shingles on this roof.
(Ui nid tu ius zérti-iér, arquitékchural shíngols on dis ruf)

Necesitamos utilizar pizarras en este techo.
We need to use slate on this roof.
(Ui nid tu ius sléit on dis ruf)

Necesitamos utilizar metal en este techo.
We need to use metal on this roof.
(Ui nid tu ius métal on dis ruf)

Necesitamos utilizar un canal de ventilación aquí.
We need to use ridge-venting here.
(Ui nid tu ius rich-véntin jíar)

Necesitamos utilizar caucho aquí.
We need to use rubber here.
(Ui nid tu ius ráber jíar)

Necesitamos colocar tragaluces / claraboyas aquí.
We need to put skylights here.
(Ui nid tu put skái láits jíar)

Necesitamos una cubierta nueva / un balcón nuevo aquí.
We need new decking.
(Ui nid níu dékin)

Necesitamos reemplazar la cubierta / el balcón aquí.
We need to replace the decking here.
(Ui nid tu ripléis de dékin jíar)

The Lingo Guide
Para Constructores

*Cubre todos los tópicos de construcción
desde la demolición hasta el techado y todo lo demás*

Dedicated to David, Caleb and Silas with love.

Published by:
The Lingo Guide®
Nashville, TN

Contact:
info@thelingoguide.com
www.thelingoguide.com

The Lingo Guide for Builders is meant solely as a tool to assist in advancing communications between English and Spanish speakers. It is not meant to be used for any legally binding communications nor is the editor, publisher, or author responsible for any errors, omissions, or damages resulting from the use of information contained in *The Lingo Guide for Builders*.

CONTENIDOS

Básicas

TÉRMINOS BÁSICOS
Basic Terms

A

abanico / ventilador – fan (fan)
abertura – opening (óupenin)
acabado – finish (fínish)
acceso – access (ácces)
accesorio / conexión – fitting (fítin)
accesorio – fixture (fíxcher)
accesorio de iluminación – light fixture (láit fíxcher)
acera – sidewalk (sáid uók)
acero – steel (stil)
adición – addition (adíshon)
aguas negras / cloacas – sewage (súech)
aire libre – open air (óupen éar)
aislamiento – insulation (insuléishon)
aislante – insulating (insuléiting)
alambre / cable – wire (uáier)
alambre de paca / alambre para empacar / alambre para amarrar – wire tie (uáier tai)
albañil – mason (méison)
alcance – scope (skóup)
ancla – anchor (ánkor)
andamio – scaffold (scáfold)
apoyo / soporte – support (sapórt)
aprendíz – apprentice (apréntis)
arandela / empaque / junta – gasket (gásket)
arandela / ojal / hembra – grommet (grómet)
arandela / planchuela de perno – washer (uásher)
arenisca – sandstone (sánd stoun)
armado – framed (fréimd)
armazón – framework (fréim uérk)
ático / desván – attic (átic)
auto cierre – self-closing (self clóusin)
azotado / enjarre / enlucido / yeso – plaster (plaster)
azulejo / baldosa – floor tile (flor táil)

B

baldosas cerámicas – ceramic tile (serámic táil)
bañera – bathtub (baz tab)

baño – bathroom (baz rum)
baño / sanitario – restroom (rest rum)
baranda / pasamanos – railing (réilin)
barra de refuerzo – rebar (ríbar)
base de tejado – subroof (sab ruf)
bastidores de madera – wood framing (uúd fréiming)
bisagra – hinge (jinch)
boca de acceso / pozo de entrada / tapa de alcantarilla – manhole (mán jóul)
bomba – pump (pámp)
bombilla – lightbulb (láit balb)
borde / orilla – rim (rim / ech)
bordillo / guarnición / borde de acera – curb (kerb)
buzón de correos – mailbox (méil box)

C

cabecera / cabezal – header (jéder)
cable a tierra – ground wire (gráund uáier)
cable de extensión – extension cord (exténshon córd)
cabria / viga – rafter (ráfter)
caja de fusible – fuse box (fiús box)
calefacción – heating (jítin)
calefactor / calentador – heater (jíter)
calentador de agua – water heater (uóter jíter)
caliber / grosor – gauge [thickness] (guéich)
calibrador / indicador / medidor – gauge [instrument] (guéich)
camino / pasillo – walkway (uók uéi / paz)
campanario – steeple (stípol)
canal / canalete – gutter (gáter)
canaleta / museca – chase (chéis)
candado / cerradura / cerrojo – lock (lok)
cañería / caño / tubería / tubo – pipe, piping (páip / páipin)
cañería principal de gas – gas main (gas méin)
capa base / bajo piso – underlayment (ánder léiment)
capacidad / ocupación / cupo – occupancy (ókiupansi)
carpintero – carpenter (cárpinter)
carril / baranda – rail (réil)
cerca / medianera – fence (fens)
cercha / reticulado / armadura / cabreada / caballete – truss (tras)
cerramiento – enclosure (enclóusher)
césped / pasto / grama / chipica / zacate – lawn (lon)
chimenea – chimney (chímni)
clavo – nail (néil)
clavo con fuste corrugado – ring shank nail (rín shánk néil)

clavo para madera – spike (spáik)
clavo sin cabeza – finishing nail (fínishin néil)
cloaca / alcantarilla – sewer (súer)
código – code (cóud)
columna – column (kólum)
combustible – fuel (fiúl)
compuerta – hatch (jach)
concreto – concrete (cónkrit)
conducto – duct / conduit (dact / kónduit)
conducto / portacables flexible – flex conduit (flex kónduit)
conductos de humo – flue (flu)
conector – connector (conéctor)
conexión / unión – connection (conékshon)
contracción / encogimiento / reducción – shrinkage (shrínkesh)
contrahuella [escalera] – riser [stair] (ráiser)
contratista – contractor (contráctor)
contrapiso / bajopiso / piso subterráneo – subfloor (sab flor)
corona – crown (cráun)
costilla – rib (ríb)
cremallera / tarima – rack (rák)
cresta / cumbrera – ridge (rich)
croquis / diseño / diagramación – layout (léi áut)
cuadro de tejado / cubierta de tejado – roofing square (rúfing scuéar)
cuarto / sala / habitación – room (rum)
cuarto interior – interior room (intírior rum)
cubierta / balcón – deck, decking (dék, dékin)
cubrejuntas / tapajuntas – flashing (fláshin)

D

descarga / liberación / desenganche – release (rilís)
declive / inclinación / pendiente / inclinar / ladear – incline (incláin)
desagüe / drenaje – drain / drainage (dréin / dréinech)
desagüe de tejado – roof drain (ruf dréin)
desempeño / comportamiento / rendimiento – performance (perfórmans)
desplazamiento / pieza en "S"/ pieza de inflexión / desvío / desnivel – offset (of set)
diesel – diesel (Dísel)
dintel – lintel (líntel)
dispositivo de traba – latching device (láchin diváis)
drywall / muro en seco – drywall (drái uól)
ducha – shower stall (sháuer stol)

E

edificio / edificación – building (bíldin)
electricidad – electricity (electríciti)

electricista – electrician (electríshan)
elevador / ascensor – elevator (elevéitor)
eliminación / remoción – removal (rimúval)
empalme / unión – junction (llánkshon)
empalme / traslape / junta / union – splice (spláis)
empanelado – paneling (páneling)
empaque / empacadura de cera – wax seal (uáx sil)
encerrado – enclosed (enclóust)
enchufe / toma corriente – electrical outlet (eléctrical áutlet)
enclavamiento / entrelazado – interlocking (ínter lókin)
encofrado – formwork (form uérk)
encofrados – forms [concrete] (fórms [cónkrit])
enlace / tirante / conexión – link / linkage (link / línkech)
enmasillado – caulking (cóking)
enrasado – furred out, furring (férd áut / férin)
entablado – sheathing (shízin)
entarimado de tejado – roof sheeting (ruf shíting)
entrada – doorway (dór uéi)
escaleras – stairs (sters)
escalera – ladder (láder)
escalones – steps (steps)
escape – exhaust (exóst)
escombro – rubble (rábol)
esfuerzo – stress (stres)
estante / tarima / plataforma – pallet (pálet)
estribo para vigueta – joist hangers (llóist jánguers)
estructura – structure (strákcher)
excavar – dig (dig)

F

fachada – façade (faséid)
fieltro – felt (felt)
fluorescente – fluorescent (florésent)
fontanero / plomero – plumber (plámer)
fregadero / lavaplatos – kitchen sink (kíchen sink)
friso / alfarje / revestimiento – wainscot, wainscotting (uéinscot / uéinscotin)
fundación – foundation (faundéishon)
fusible – fuse (fiús)

G

ganchos / colgadores – hangers (jánguers)
garaje / cochera – garage (garách)
gas – gas (gas)

gases / emanaciones – fumes (fiúms)
generador – generator (yeneréitor)
grava / gravilla / granzón – gravel (grávol)
grueso / áspero – coarse (cors)

H

hastial – gable (guéibol)
herramienta – tool (tul)
hoyo / agujero / boquete / hueco – hole (jóul)
humo – smoke (smóuk)

I

iluminación industrial / luz de faro – floodlight (flad láit)
imprimado – primed (práimd)
imprimador – primer (práimer)
ingeniero – engineer (énllenir)
nterruptor de circuito – circuit breaker (sérkit bréiker)
interruptor / fusible de seguridad a tierra – ground fault circuit (gráund folt sérkit)
interruptor principal – main breaker (méin bréiker)

L

ladrillo cerámico – masonry tile (méisonry táil)
ladrillo frontal – facing brick (féisin brik)
lamina / chapa / metálica / laminado – sheet metal (shit métal)
larguero – runner (ráner)
lavabo – sink (sínk)
lavadora y secadora – washer and dryer (uásher and dráier)
lechada / mortero de cemento – grout (gráut)
levantamiento / alzada – lift (líft)
línea / límite de propiedad / deslinde – property line (próperti láin)
línea de marcar, tendel / línea de gis / línea de demarcación / línea de tiza – chalk line (chók láin)
linterna / lámpara / faro – flashlight (flásh láit)
listón – strip (strip)
listón para clavar – nailing strip (néilin strip)
llave / grifo – faucet (fóset)
llave / grifo / canilla / espiga – spigot (spígot)
local / sitio – premises (prémises)
losa – slab (slab)
lugar de la obra – job site (llob sait)
luz – light (láit)

M

machihembrado – tongue and groove (tan and gruv)

madera – timber (tímber)
madera aglomerada / madera contraenchapada – particle board (párticol bórd)
madera de construcción – lumber (lámber)
madera tratada – treated wood (tríted uúd)
manija / mango / agarradera – handle (jándol)
mampostería – masonry (méisonri)
mampostería reforzada – reinforced masonry (rienfórst méisonri)
manga – sleeve (slív)
manguera – hose (jóus)
marco / estructura / armazón – frame (fréim)
mastique – mastic (mastíc)
medidor – meter (míter)
moldura – molding (móulding)
montante / parante / barrote – stud (stad)
morsa / prensa – vise (váis)
mortero / argamasa – mortar (mórtar)
muro / pared – wall (uól)
muro con montante / parante – stud bearing wall (stad bérin uól)
muro de fundación – foundation wall (faundéishon uól)
muro / pared exterior – exterior wall (extírior uól)

N
nivel de terreno – grade (gréid)

O
oxidantes – oxidizers (Oksi-dáisers)

P
papel de brea – tar paper (tár péipar)
paredes agrietadas – cracked walls (crákt uóls)
pasamano – handrail (jánd réil)
pasillo – passageway / hallway (pásech uéi / jól uéi)
pasta de muro – joint compound (llóint cómpaund)
pavimento – pavement (péivment)
pendiente / talud / declive – slope (slóup)
permiso [de construcción] – permit (pérmit)
perno de seguridad – lock bolt (lok bolt)
piedra / roca – stone (stoun)
piedra caliza – limestone (láim stóun)
pintor – painter (péinter)
piso – floor (flor)
placa de interruptor / apagador – switch plate (suích pléit)
plancha de yeso / cartón de yeso – wallboard (uól bord)

planos – blueprints (blúprints)
planos de diseño – design drawings (disáin dróins)
planos de casa – house plans (Jáus plans)
planta baja – ground level (gráund level)
plataforma – floor deck (flor dek)
plataforma metálica – metal deck (métal dek)
pliego / chapa / plancha / lámina – sheet (shit)
plomería / cañería / tubería – plumbing (plámin)
portátil – portable (pórtabol)
postes – poles / posts (póuls / póusts)
presión – pressure (préshor)
principal / matriz – main (méin)
proporción – rate (réit)
provisional – temporary (témporari
puerta – door (dor)
puerta de ducha – shower door (sháuer dór)
puerta pivotante / puerta giratoria – swinging door (súinguin dor)

R

rajas / grietas – cracks (craks)
recinto – shaft (shaft)
refuerzo – bracing (bréicin)
refuerzo / armadura – reinforcement (rienfórsment)
regadera – shower head (sháuer jed)
regulador – damper/ regulator (damper / reguiuléitor)
rejilla / registro – register (réllister)
relleno – backfill (bak fil)
relleno / rellenado – filled (fíld)
remache – rivet (rívet)
reparación – repair (ripéar)
repisa – shelf (shelf)
residencia – residence (résidens)
resistol / pegamento / goma / cola – glue (glu)
respiradero / ventilación – vent (vent)
retraso – setback (set bak)
revestimiento de tejado – roof covering (ruf cáverin)
revestimiento de vinilo – vinyl siding (váinol sáidin)
revestimiento para pisos / material para pisos – flooring (flórin)
revoque / enlucido / estuco – stucco (stúko)
revoque / enlucido / repello / forjado – plastering (plásterin)
roca / piedra – rock (rók)
rociador – sprinkler (sprínkler)

S

salida – exit (éxit)
sanitario / excusado / retrete / baño – toilet (tóilet)
seguro – insurance (Inchurans)
selladores – sealants (sílants)
sensor de humo / detector de humo – smoke detector (smóuk ditéctor)
sheetrock – sheetrock (shít-rok)
sitio – site (sáit)
sofito – soffit (sófit)
soldadura – welding (uéldin)
solera doble – double plate (dábol pléit)
solera inferior – sill plate (síl pléit)
soporte de ventana / repisa – window sill (uíndou sil)
sótano – basement (béisment)
stud finder / busca montantes – stud finder (stad fáinder)
supervisor / inspector – supervisor (superváisor)

T

tabique / separación / division – partition (partíshon)
tabla de cumbrera – ridge board (rich bord)
tablero duro – hardboard (járd bórd)
tableros de madera contrachapada / plywood – plywood (plái uúd)
tablón – plank (plánk)
tejado – roofing (rúfin)
techo interno / cielorraso – ceiling (sílin)
tejado a dos aguas – gable roof (géibol ruf)
tejado a cuatro aguas – hip roof (jíp ruf)
tejado plano – flat roof (flat ruf)
teja / tejamanil – shingle (shíngol)
teja de asfalto – asphalt shingle (ásfalt shíngol)
teja de madera / ripio – wood shingle (uúd shíngol)
termita – termite (térmait)
terreno / lote – lot (lot)
tiras metálicas – stripping (strípin)
tomacorriente / enchufe – power outlet (páuer áut let)
tornillo – screw (scru)
traba / trabar / bloque / bloquear – block, blocking (blok, blókin)
trabajo – work (uérk)
traslape / rebajo a media madera – shiplap (shíp lap)
traslape / sobresolape / superposición – overlap (óuver lap)
tubería principal / matriz – water main (uóter méin)

U

umbral / entrada – threshold (zres jóuld)
unión – joint (llóint)
urinal / urinario / mingitorio – urinal (iúrinal)
uso / usar / utilizar – use (iús)

V

vacío / aspiradora – vacuum (vákium)
válvula / llave de alivio – relief valve (relíf valv)
válvula de cierre – shut-off valve (shat of valv)
vano / claro / espacio – span (span)
ventana – window (uíndou)
ventanilla sobresaliente / dórmer – dormer (dórmer)
ventilación principal – main vent (méin vent)
vestíbulo – vestibule (véstibiul)
vidriado / encristalado – glazed / glazing (gléist / gléisin)
viga de carga – load bearing joist (lóud bérin llóist)
viga maestra / jácena – girder (guérder)
vigueta – joist (llóist)
vigueta de piso – floor joist (flor llóist)
vivienda / residencia – dwelling (duélin)
voladizo / vuelo / saledizo – overhang (óuver jan)
voltaje – voltage (vóltech)
voltios – volts (volts)
vuelos – nosings (nóusin)

Y

yerbas / yerbajos / malezas / paja / yuyos – weeds (uíds)

Z

zapatilla eléctrica – power strip (páuer strip)
zócalo – baseboard (béis bord)

HERRAMIENTAS BÁSICAS
Basic Tools

alicates / pinzas – pliers (pláiers)
antorcha – torch (torch)
aplanadora / rodillo – roller (róuler)
azadón – hoe (jóu)
barreta – bar (bar)
bomba – pump (pamp)
barreno – drill bit (dríl bít)
burro – sawhorse (so jors)
caja de corte en ángulos – mitre box (máiter box)

caja de herramientas – toolbox (tul box)
carretilla – wheelbarrow (uíl bárrou)
cepillo de carpintero – plane (pléin)
cepillo automático – joiner (llóiner)
clavadora automática – nail gun (néil gan)
destornillador / desarmador – screwdriver (scru dráiver)
desarmador / destornillador de paleta – flathead screwdriver (flát jed scru dráiver)
desarmador / destornillador de punta en cruz – phillips screwdriver (fílips scru dráiver)
doblador de varilla – rebar bender (ríbar bénder)
embudo – funnel (fánol)
engrapadora – stapler (stéipler)
engrapadora auotomática – staple gun (stéipl gan)
escalera [de mano] – ladder (láder)
escoba – broom (brum)
escuadra
 – square (scuéar)
 – framing square (fréimin scuéar)
 – de carpintero– carpenter's square (cárpinters scuéar)
fresadora – router (ráuter)
gafas / lentes de seguridad – safety glasses (séifty gágols gláses)
hacha – axe (ax)
hilo de plomada – plumb line (plám láin)
lámpara de trabajo – work light (uérk láit)
lavado apresiòn – power washer (Páuer uácher)
linterna / lámpara / faro – flashlight (flash láit)
llave – wrench (rench)
llave francesa – adjustible wrench (Ayástabol rench)
llave inglesa perico – plumber's wrench (Plóm-mers rench)
llave de cadena – chain pipe wrench (chéin páip rench)
llijadora – sander (sánder)
lima – file (fáil)
mandil de carpintero – carpenter's apron (cárpinters éipron)
manguera – hose (jóus)
marro / mazo – sledgehammer (slech jámer)
martillo – hammer (jámer)
mazo – mallet (Málet)
navaja – utility knife (iutílity náif)
nivel – level (lével)
pala – shovel (shávol)
pico – pick (pík)
pincel / brocheta / brocha – brush (brash)

prensa – clamp (clamp)
prensa de "C" – C-clamp (clamp)
rastrillo – rake (Réik)
regla "T" – T square (tí scuéar)
mezcladora / revolvedora – mixer (míxer)
serrucho – hand saw (jánd so)
sierra / serrucho – saw (so)
sierra alternante – reciprocating saw (resiprokéitin so)
sierra fija / sierra de mesa – table saw (téibol so)
sierra circular de mano – circular saw (sérkiular so)
sierra fija – radial saw (réidial so)
sierra de cadena – chainsaw (chéin so)
sierra de corte angular – compound mitre saw (cómpaun máiter so)
sierra de retroceso – mitre saw (máiter so)
sierra de vaivén – jigsaw (llíg so)
sopladora – blower (blóuer)
soplete – soldering torch (sólderin torch)
taladradora [eléctrica] – electric drill (eléctrik dríl)
taladro – drill (dríl)
tijeras para metal – sheet metal shears (shít métal shíars)
zapapico – pickaxe (pik ax)

PROVISIONES BÁSICAS
Basic Supplies

arena – sand (sand)
baldes / cubetas / cubos – buckets (bákets)
banderines – flags (flags)
casco de seguridad – hard hat (jard jat)
césped / pasto – sod (sod)
cinta de precaución – caution tape (cóshon téip)
cinta para demarcar – marking tape (márkin téip)
cinta para medir – tape measure (téip mésher)
clavos – nails (néils)
corta pluma – utility knife (iutíliti náif)
goma / pega / cola – glue (glu)
grava / granzón – gravel (grávol)
guantes – gloves (glavs)
lapicera / bolígrafo / lápiz – pen / pencil (pen / pénsol)
lentes de seguridad – safety glasses (gágols)
linterna / faro – flashlight (flash láit)
marcador negrol – magic marker (Madzik markr)
masilla – caulk (cok)

pintura en atomizador / pintura sprey – spray paint (spréi péint)
paja – straw (stro)
protectores de rodillas – knee pads (ni pads)
pintura para demarcar – marking paint (márkin péint)
papel – paper (péiper)
semillas y paja – seed & straw (sid and stro)
tiza / gis – chalk (chok)
tornillos – screws (scrus)
trapos – rags (rags)
zacate / semilla de pasto / grama / chipica – grass seed (gras sid)

ESTILOS ARQUITECTÓNICOS
Architectural Styles

artesano – craftsman (crafts man)
bungalow – bungalow (bángalou)
cabaña – cottage (cótech)
cabaña – cabin (cábin)
campestre – country estate (cántri estéit)
casa a orillas de la playa – waterfront house (uóter front jáus)
casa de playa – beach house (bich jáus)
casa sin terreno – zero lot line (zíro lot láin)
chalet – chalet (shalé)
clásico americano – American classic (américan clásic)
contemporáneo – contemporary (contémporeri)
cuatro cuadrado – four-square (for scuéar)
desván – loft (loft)
dúplex – duplex (dúplex)
estilo antiguo / viejo mundo – old-world style (óuld uórld stáil)
estilo francés – French country (French cántri)
estilo mediterráneo – Mediterranean style (mediteréinien stáil)
granja – farm house (farm jáus)
marco en A – A-frame (éi fréim)
residencia – estate home (estéit jóum)
rancho – ranch (ranch)
victoriano – victorian (victórian)

ELECTRODOMÉSTICOS
Appliances

aostador – toaster (tóuster)
bandeja de calentamiento – warming tray (uórmin tréi)
batidora – mixer (míkser)

cafetera – coffee pot (cófi pot)
calentador de agua – hot water heater (jot uóter jíter)
campana de la estufa – vent hood (vent jud)
congelador / frízer – freezer (frízer)
deshumidificador – dehumidifier (di jiumídifaier)
dispensador de basura – garbage disposal (gárbech dispóusal)
estufa de gas / horno de gas – gas stove / oven (gas stóuv / óven)
estufa eléctrica / horno eléctrico – electric stove / oven (eléctric stóuv / óven)
exprimidor – juicer (llúcer)
fabricador de hielo – ice maker (áis méiker)
filtro de agua – water filter (uóter fílter)
horno – convection oven (convékshon óven)
lavadora de platos – dishwasher (dish uásher)
lavadora – washing machine (uáshin machín)
licuadora – blender (blénder)
microondas – microwave (máicro uéiv)
purificador de aire – air purifier (éar piúrifaier)
refrigerador / nevera / heladera – refrigerator (refríllereitor)
secadora – dryer (dráier)

TÉRMINOS DE CASA & ACCESORIOS
House Terms & Accessories

acres de terreno – acreage (éicrech)
ático / desván / tapanco – attic (átic)
buzón de correo – mailbox (méil box)
carpa – tent (tent)
casita de árbol – tree house (tri jáus)
casa de juego / casa de muñecas – play house (pléi jáus)
casa de piscina / pileta / alberca – pool house (pul jáus)
cerca de privacidad – privacy fence (práivaci fens)
cerca de hierro / reja – wrought iron fence (rot áirn fens)
choza para colgar hamaca – hammock hut (jámak jot)
cobertizo para jardinería – gardening shed (gárdenin shed)
construcción fuera de la casa / construcción aparte – out building (áut bíldin)
columpio de porche – porch swing (porch suín)
comedero de pájaros – bird feeder (berd fíder)
computadora – computer (compiúter)
contraventanas / postigos – shutters (sháters)
cópula – copula (cópiula)

cortinas – curtains (kértens)
cuarto para herramientas – tool shed (tul shed)
encercado – fenced (fenst)
enramada / cobertizo para carros – carport (car port)
espejos – mirrors (mírrors)
fogón / fosa de fuego – fire pit (fáier pit)
hierro colado – wrought iron (rot áirn)
garaje – garage (garách)
jardineras / canteros de ventana – window boxes (uíndou bókses)
mesa de planchar Incrustada – built-in ironing board
(bilt in áirnin bord)
muebles de patio – patio furniture (pátio férnacher)
persianas – shades (shéids)
piscina / pileta / alberca – pool (pul)
primer piso – 1st floor (ferst flor)
remolque / traila – trailer (tréiler)
segundo piso – 2nd floor (sécond flor)
sendero / camino de piedras – stepping stones (stépin stóuns)
sótano – basement (béisment)
sótano iluminado – full-light basement (ful láit béisment)
tapa de chimenea – chimney cap (chímni cap)
teléfonos – telephones (télefouns)
tercer piso – 3rd floor (zerd flor)
terreno de cinco acres – five-acre track (fáiv éiker trak)
toldos – awnings (ónins)
veleta – weather vane (uéder véin)
vidrios ahumados para ventanas – stained glass windows
(stéind glas uíndous)
un acre – one acre (uán éiker)
televisión plana – flat panel TV (Flat panel ti vi)
sistema recíproco de comunicacion – intercom systems (Intercom
sístems)
televisión de plasma – plasma screen TV (plasma scrin ti vi)
estéreo – stereo / audio speaker (stéreo / audio spiker)
conección al internet sin cable – WI-FI (Uái-fái)

HABITACIONES
Room Types

balcón – deck (dek)
baño – bathroom (baz rum)
baño del cuarto matrimonial – master bath (máster baz)
biblioteca – library (láibreri)

casa de invitados – guest house (guest jáus)
cocina – kitchen (kíchen)
cocina exterior – outside kitchen (aút sáid kíchen)
cocina comedor – eat-in kitchen (it in kíchen)
comedor – dining room (dáinin rum)
cuarto de ejercicios – exercise room (éksersais rum)
cuarto / dormitorio / recámara matrimonial – master bedroom (máster bed rum)
cuarto para desayunar – breakfast room (brékfast rum)
cuarto para invitados – guest room (guest rum)
despensa – pantry (pántri)
dormitorio / recámara / cuarto – bedroom (bed rum)
estudio – study (stádi)
medio baño – half bath (jaf baz)
oficina – office (ófis)
patio – patio (pátio)
porche encubierto – screened-in porch (scrind in porch)
suit matrimonial – master suite (máster suít)
sala – living room (lívin rum)
salón de billar – billiards room (bíliards rum)
salón de computadora – media room (mídia rum)
salón de estar – den (den)
salón de juegos – play room (pléi rum)
salón de lavandería – laundry room (lóndri rum)
salón estilo florida – Florida room (flórida rum)
salón familiar – family room (fámili rum)
salón para pasatiempo – hobby room (jóbi rum)
salón para sacudirse los pies – mud room (mad rum)
salón para vinos – wine room (uáin rum
solar – solarium (solériom)
solar / salón iluminado por el sol – sunroom (san rum)
tocador – powder room (páuder rum)
vestíbulo – foyer (fóier)

INSECTOS
Insects

abeja – bee (bi)
afídido – aphid (éifid)
avispa – wasp (uásp)
babosa – slug (slog)
caracol – snail (snéil)
chicharra / libélula – dragonfly (drágon flái)
chinche de calabaza – squash bug (skuásh bog)
enrollador de hojas – leaf roller (lif róler)
escarabajo – beetle (bítol)
escarabajo de hoja de rosa – rose leaf beetle (róus lif bítol)
escarabajo de rosa – rose chafer (róus cháfer)
escarabajo japonés – Japanese beetle (llápanis bítol)
gorgojo / coco – weevil (uívol)
gusano – caterpillar (cáterpilar)
grillo – cricket (críket)
hormigas – ants (ants)
hormiga de fuego – fire ant (fáiar ant)
huevos de araña – spider mites (spáider máits)
lombriz excavadora – grub worm (grob uórm)
lombriz / gusano de bolsa – bagworm (bag uórm)
mantis religiosa – praying mantis (préin mántis)
mariposa – butterfly (báter flái)
mariquita – ladybug (léidi bog)
mosca blanca – whitefly (uáit flái)
mosca de agua – midge (mich)
mosquito / zancudo – mosquito (moskíto)
nematodo – nematode (nimatóud)
oruga de cabaña – tent caterpillar (tent cáterpilar)
perforador de tallos – stem borer (stem bórer)
salta hojas – leafhopper (lif jóper)
saltamontes – grasshopper (gras jóper)

REINO ANIMAL
Wildlife

armadillo / cachicamo / quirquincho – armadillo (ármadilo)
ardilla listada – chipmunk (chípmank)
ardilla – squirrel (skuérl)
castor – beaver (bíver)
conejo – rabbit (rábit)

coyote – coyote (cáioti)
culebra / víbora / serpiente – snake (snéik)
gato – cat (cat)
lagartija – lizard (lízard)
marmota – groundhog (gráund jog)
mapache – raccoon (racún)
musaraña – shrew (shru)
perro – dog (dog)
rana – frog (frag)
ratón / ratones – mouse / mice (máus, máis)
ratón de campo – vole (vóul)
sapo – toad (tóud)
topo – mole (móul)
venado / siervo – deer (díar)
zorro – fox (fox)
zarigüeya / rabipelado / faro – opossum (pásom)
zorrillo / zorrino / mofeta – skunk (skank)

LOS COLORES
Colors

amarillo – yellow (iélou)
anaranjado – orange (órench)
azul – blue (blú)
blanco – white (wáit)
marrón / café – brown (bráun)
negro – black (blák)
púrpura / morado – purple (pérpl)
rojo – red (rrréd)
rosado – pink (pínk)
verde – green (grín)

LOS MESES DEL AÑO
Months

enero – January (llánueri)
febrero – February (fébruari)
marzo – March (march)
abril – April (éiprol)
mayo – May (méi)
junio – June (llun)
julio – July (llulái)
agosto – August (ógost)

septiembre – September (septémber)
octubre – October (octóber)
noviembre – November (novémber)
diciembre – December (dicémber)

LOS DIAS DE LA SEMANA
Days

lunes – Monday (mándei)
martes – Tuesday (tiúsdei)
miércoles – Wednesday (uénsdei)
jueves – Thursday (zérsdei)
viernes – Friday (fráidei)
sábado – Saturday (sáterdei)
domingo – Sunday (sándei)

DESCRIPCIONES DEL TIEMPO Y ESTACIONES
Seasons & Weather Descriptions

primavera – spring (spring)
verano – summer (sámer)
otono – fall (fol)
invierno – winter (uínter)
caliente – hot (jot)
frio – cold (could)
lluvia / lloviendo – rain / raining (rein / réinin)
luz del sol / soleado – sunshine / sunny (sanchain / sani)
nieve / nevando – snow / snowing (snou / snó-uin)
sequía / seco – drought / dry (dráut / drai)
hielo – ice (áis)
congelado / congelando – freeze / freezing (friis / friisin)

LOS NUMEROS
Numbers

1 – one (uán)
2 – two (tu)
3 – three (zri)
4 – four (for)
5 – five (fáiv)
6 – six (six)
7 – seven (séven)
8 – eight (éit)
9 – nine (náin)
10 – ten (ten)

11 – eleven (iléven)
12 – twelve (tuélv)
13 – thirteen (zertín)
14 – fourteen (fortín)
15 – fifteen (fiftín)
16 – sixteen (sixtín)
17 – seventeen (seventín)
18 – eighteen (eitín)
19 – nineteen (naintín)
20 – twenty (tuénti)
21 – twenty-one (tuénti-uán)
30 – thirty (zérti)
40 – forty (fórti)
50 – fifty (fífti)
60 – sixty (síxti)
70 – seventy (séventi)
80 – eighty (éiti)
90 – ninety (náinti)
100 – one hundred (uán jándred)
200 – two hundred (tu jándred)
500 – five hundred (fáiv jándred)
1,000 – one thousand (uán záusand)

FRASES BÁSICAS EN CONVERSACIÓN
Basic Conversational Phrases

¿Habla inglés?
Do you speak English?
(¿Du iú spik ínglish?)

¿Habla español?
Do you speak Spanish?
(¿Du iú spik spánish?)

Hola. – Hello. (Jeló)

Adiós. – Good-bye (Gudbái)

Sí. – Yes. (iés)

No. – No. (nóu)

Por favor. – Please. (plis)

Gracias. – Thank you. (zéink iú)

¿Cuál es su nombre / Cómo se llama?
What is your name?
(¿Uát is iór néim?)

Mi nombre es _____ / Me llamo _____.
My name is _____.
(Mái néim is _____)

¿Cómo está usted hoy / Cómo le va?
How are you today?
¿(Jáu ar iú tudéi?)

¿Cómo está su familia?
How is your family?
¿(Jáu is iór fámili?)

Muy bien, gracias.
Very well, thank you.
(Véri uel, zéink iú)

No estoy bièn hoy
I am not well today.
(Ai am not uél tudei)

Necesito ayuda
I need help.
(Ai nid jelp)

Nos vemos mañana.
I will see you tomorrow.
(Ái uíl si iú tumórrou)

No estaré aquí mañana.
I will not be here tomorrow.
(Ái uíl not bi jíar tumórrou)

¿Pasó un buen fin de semana?
Did you have a good weekend?
(Did iú jav a gud uík end?)

Sí, pasé un muy buen fin de semana.
Yes, I had a very good weekend.
(Iés, ái jad a véri gud uík end)

¿Voy a la tienda, necesita algo?
I am going to the store, do you need anything?
(Ái am góin tu de stor, du iú nid éni zin?)

¿Qué hora es?
What time is it?
(¿Uát táim is it?)

¿Adónde? – Where? (¿Uéar?)

Adónde está? – Where is? (Uéar is)

Adónde están? – Where are? (Uéar ar.)

Qué es eso? – What is that?

¡Felicitaciones!
Congratulations!
(Congratu-léichons)

¡Feliz Cumpleaños!
Happy Birthday!
(Japi bérdei)

¡Feliz Navidad!
Merry Christmas!
(Meri krismas!)

¡Feliz Año Nuevo!
Happy New Year!
(Japi niú yiar!)

¡Feliz Semana Santa!
Happy Easter!
(Japi íster!)

¡Feliz Aniversario!
Happy Anniversary!
(Japi anivérsari!)

¡No se preocupe. Sea feliz!
Don't worry. Be happy!
(Don uári. Bi japi!)

La vida es buena.
Life is good!
(Láif is gud!)

PREGUNTAS Y RESPUESTAS BÁSICAS EN EL TRABAJO
Basic Job Q & A's

¿Tiene referencias?
Do you have references?
¿(Dú iú jav réferences?)

Sí, tengo referencias.
Yes, I have references.
(Iés, ái jav réferences)

No, no tengo referencias.
No, I do not have references.
(Nóu, ái du not jav réferences)

Necesitamos una copia de su licencia de conducir.
We need a copy of your driver's license.
(Uí nid ei copi of yur dráivers láisens)

Necesitamos una copia de su tarjeta de residencia.
We need a copy of your green card
(Uí nid ei copi of yur grin card

Necesitamos una copia de su permiso de trabajo.
We need a copy of your work permit.
(Uí nid ei copi of yur uork permit)

Necesitamos una copia de su tarjeta de seguro social.
We need a copy of your social security card.
(Uí nid ei copi of yur sochal securiti card)

Necesitamos una copia de su seguro.
We need a copy of your insurance.
(Uí nid ei copi of yur inchurans)

Necesitamos que firme los formatos.
We need you to sign the forms.
(Uí nid yu tu sáin de forms)

¿Cuál es su número de teléfono?
What is your phone number?
¿(Uát is iór fóun námber?)

Mi número es _____.
My phone number is _____.
(Mái fóun námber is _____)

Sígame hasta el sitio de trabajo.
Follow me to the job site.
(Folou mi tu de chob sáit)

¿Cuántos hombres tiene para ayudarlo/a?
How many men do you have to help you?
(¿Jáu méni men du iú jav tu jelp iú?)

¿Cuán grande es su cuadrilla / equipo?
How big is your crew?
(¿Jáu big is iór cru?)

Mi cuadrilla / equipo tiene _____ hombres.
My crew has _____ men.
(Mái cru jas _____ men)

Tiene un buen equipo de hombres.
You have a good crew of men.
(Iú jav a gud cru ov men)

¿Tiene sus propias herramientas?
Do you have your own tools?
(¿Du iú jav iór óun tuls?)

¿Cuándo puede comenzar con el trabajo?
When can you start the job?
(¿Uén can iú start de llob?)

Puedo comenzar el trabajo la semana que viene.
I can begin the job next week.
(Ái can biguín de llob next uík)

¿Cuánto le tomará completar este trabajo?
How long will it take you to complete this job?
(¿Jáu long uíl it téik iú tu complít dis llob?)

Tomará un mes / una semana / un día para terminar el trabajo.
It will take a month / week / day to do the job.
(It uíl téik a monz / uík / déi tu fínish)

Necesitamos un estimado por el trabajo.
We need an estimate for the job.
(Uí nid an éstimet for de chob)

¿Puede darme un cotizado para hacer otro trabajo?
Can you give me a bid to do another job?
(Can yu guif mi ei bid tu du anoser chob)

Podemos darle un cotizado para hacer otro trabajo.
We can give you a bid to do another job.
(Uí can guív iú a bid tu du anóder llob?)

¿Puede trabajar mañana?
Can you work tomorrow?
(¿Can iú uérk tumórrou?)

Puedo trabajar todos los días.
I can work every day.
(Ái can uérk évri déi)

No, no puedo trabajar mañana
No I cannot work tomorrow.
(No. Ai canot uork tumórou)

¿Cuánto paga este trabajo?
How much does this job pay?
(¿Jáu mach das dis llob péi?)

Su paga será $_____ la hora.
Your pay is going to be $_____ per hour.
(Iór péi is góin tu bi _____ dólars per áuer)

¿Cuándo es el día de pago?
When is pay day?
(¿Uén is péi déi?)

Le pagaré al final de la semana / del día / del trabajo.
I will pay you at the end of the week / day / job.
(Ái uíl péi iú at di end ov de uík / déi / llob)

FRASES BÁSICAS EN EL LUGAR DE TRABAJO
Basic Job Site Phrases

No se permite el uso de drogas.
Drug use is not tolerated.
(Drag iús is not toleréitid)

No consumimos alcohol en el lugar de trabajo.
We do not drink on the job site.
(Uí du not drink on de chob sáit)

Su trabajo se ve bien.
Your work looks good.
(Iór uérk luks gud)

Sosténgalo allí mientras lo clavo.
Hold it there while I nail it.
(Jold it déar uáil ái néil it)

Recoja esto.
Pick this up. (pik dis ap)

Levántelo un poco.
Raise it a little. (réis it a lítol)

Bájelo un poco.
Lower it a little. (lóuer it a lítol)

Martille esto.
Hammer this. (jámer dis)

Consiga a alguien que lo ayude.
Get someone to help you.
(Guet sam uán tu jelp iú)

Déjeme ayudarle con eso.
Let me help you with that.
(Let mi jélp iú uíz dat)

Ayúdeme a cargar esto.
Help me carry this.
(Jelp mi cárri dis)

La llave estará escondida aquí.
The key will be hidden here.
(De ki uíl bi jíden jíar)

Por favor cierre la puerta con llave antes de irse.
Please lock the door when you leave.
(Plís lok de dor uén iú liv)

El baño portable está allí atrás.
The port-a-pot is out back.
(De port-a-pot is áut bak)

El basurero está allá.
The dumpster is over there.
(De dámpster is óuver déar)

¡Tenga cuidado!
Be careful! (¡Bi kérful!)

Sígame.
Follow me. (fólou mi)

Empuje.
Push. (push)

Jale.
Pull. (pul)

¡Cuidado!
Watch out! (¡Uách áut!)

Necesitamos organizar las herramientas.
We need to organize the tools.
(Uí nid tu órganais de tuls)

Mire en la camioneta.
Look in the truck.
(Luk in de trak)

Buèn cinturòn de herramientas.
Nice tool belt.
(Náis tul belt)

Necesitamos los planos de la casa.
We need the house plans.
(Uí nid de haus plans)

¿Quiere tomar un descanso para almorzar?
Do you want to take a lunch break?
(¿Du iú uánt tu téik a lonch bréik?)

¿Adónde está el hospital / una clínica?
Where is the hospital / clinic?
(¿Uéar is de jóspital / clínic?)

Carpintería

TÉRMINOS DE CARPINTERÍA

ESTILOS DE GABINETES Y TÉRMINOS
Cabinet Styles & Terms

cartón de aglomerado / contraenchapado – particle board (párticol bord)

catedral – cathedral (cazídral)

chapa de madera – wood veneer (uud veníer)

con arco / arqueado – arched (archt)

culata / caja / surtido / reservas – stock (stok)

deslizantes de las gavetas / los cajones – drawer slides (dror sláids)

enmarcado – framed (fréimd)

empalme angular – mitered joint (míterd llóint)

ensamblamiento – joinery (llóineri)

en toda su extensión – full extension (ful exténshon)

escuadra – square (skúear)

ferretería / herrería – hardware (jard uéar)

hacer a la medida – custom (cóstom)

herramientas track and roller – track & roller (trak and róler)

junta de acoplamiento machihembrado – coping joint (cóup and pátern llóint)

madera maciza – solid wood (sólid uud)

madera manufacturada – engineered wood (enllenírd uud)

panel levantado / elevado [sólido] – raised panel solid (réist pánel sólid)

panel plano incrustado – recessed flat panel (rísest flat pánel)

páneles superiores – top panels (top pánels)

paneles / tableros laterales – side panels (sáid pánels)

páneles inferiores – bottom panels (bótom pánols)

paneles traseros – back panels (bak pánels)

plywood / madera prensada – plywood (plái uud)

puerta enmarcada – framed door (fréimd dor)

puerta de panel plano – flat panel door (flat pánel dor)

puerta / gaveta sin marcos – full overlay door / drawer (ful óuver léi dor / dror)

puerta / gaveta con tope – traditional overlay (tradíshonal óuver léi)

puerta / gaveta incrustada – inset door / drawer (in set dor / dror)

puerta / gaveta con canalete y manija – lipped door / drawer (lipt dor / dror)

puertas con vidrios insertados – glass insert doors (glas ínsert dors)
puertas con travesaños – mullion doors (múlion dors)
refuerzo para el gabinete – cabinet bracing (cábinet bréicin)
rolinera / rodamiento – ball bearing (bol bérin)
sin marco – frameless (fréim les)
sobresale de su marco – door / drawer (dor / dror)
tablero para rodapies / zócalo – toe kick board (tóu kik bord)
tira de clavos – nail rail (néil réil)
tocador – vanities (vánitis)
vidrio biselado – beveled glass (béveld glas)
vidrio templado – tempered glass (témperd glas)

TÉRMINOS DE CIELOS RASOS / TECHOS INTERNOS
Ceiling Terms

acabado liso – smooth finish (smuz fínish)
bandeja / platón – tray (tréi)
con bóveda / cúpula – vaulted (válted)
moteado – speckled (spékold)
ocho / nueve / diez / doce pies de alto – 8 / 9 / 10 / 12 feet high (éit / náin / ten / tuélv fit jái)
tablero para paredes – bead board (bid bord)
tragaluces / claraboyas – skylights (skái láits)
vigas al descubierto – exposed beams (éxpoust bims)

TÉRMINOS DE MESADAS / MEZONES
Countertop Terms

acero inoxidable – stainless steel (stéin les stil)
afilado – honed (jond)
arenisca – sandstone (sand stóun)
baldoza – tile (táil)
color de la lechada / cemento – grout color (gráut cólor)
concreto – concrete (cónkrit)
cuarzo – quartz (kuárz)
esteatita / talco natural – soapstone (sóup stóun)
granito – granite (gránit)
laminado – laminate (lámineit)
mármol – marble (márbol)
mármol travertino – travertine (trávertin)
metales – metals (métal)
mezón para cortar / tablón carnicero – butcher block (búcher blok)
pizarra – slate (sléit)

piedra – stone (stóun)
piedra cultivada – cultured stone (cólcherd stóun)
piedra natural – natural stone (náchural stóu)
piedra sintética – synthetic stone (sinzétic stóun)
salpicado – backsplash (bak splash)
superficie sólida – solid surface (sólid sérfes)
vidrio – glass (glas)

TÉRMINOS DE PUERTAS Y VENTANAS
Door & Window Terms

aluminio – aluminum (alúminom)
bahía – bay (béi)
bóveda de ventana – casement window (kéisment uíndou)
colgado doble – double-hung (dábol jang)
con aislamiento – insulated (ínsuleited)
contapesos de las ventanas – window weights (uíndou uéits)
cuadro – picture (píkcher)
decorativo – decorative (decórativ)
herramientas paladín – paladin (paládin)
madera – wood (uud)
pánel de vidrio – pane glass (péin glas)
puerta antigua – antique door (antík dor)
puerta de rejilla – screen door (scrin dor)
puertas de centro hueco – hollow core door (jálou cor dors)
puertas del garaje – garage door (garách dors)
puertas de metal – metal door (métal dors)
puertas francesas – French door (french dors)
puertas laminadas – laminated door (lámineited dors)
puertas macizas – solid core door (sólid cor dors)
tamaño jamba – jamb size (llamb sáis)
tragaluces / claraboyas – skylights (skái láits)
travesaños – mullions (múlions)
ventana de rejilla – screen window (scrin uíndou)
ventanas con toldo – awning window (ónin uíndous)
ventana con protección para las tormentas – storm window
 (storm uíndou)
vidrio – glass (glas)
vidrio ahumado – stained glass (stéin glas)
vidrio para ventana – window glass (uíndou glas)
travesaño – transoms (tránsoms)

TÉRMINOS DE MATERIALES PARA EXTERIORES
Exterior Materials Terms

bloque – block (blok)
concreto – concrete (cónkrit)
canaleta y cañerías de cobre – copper gutters and downspouts (cóper gáters and dáun spáuts
canaleta y cañerías – gutters and downspouts (gáters and dáun spáuts)
estuco – stucco (stáco)
ladrillo – brick (brik)
páneles solares – solar panels (sólar pánels)
papel protector para la casa en construcción – house wrap (jáus rap)
piedra – stone (stóun) [ver nombres relacionados con piedra]
revestimiento de aluminio – aluminum siding (alúminom sáidin)
revestimieno de vinilo – vinyl siding (váinol sáidin
revestimiento – siding (sáidin)
tejas de baldoza – tile roofing shingles (táil rúfin shíngols)
tejas de pizarra – slate roofing shingles (sléit ruf shíngols)
tejas de ripia / madera – shake shingles (shéik shíngols)

TÉRMINOS DE PISOS
Floor Terms

alfombra – carpet (cárpet)
baldoza – tile (táil)
concreto – concrete (cónkrit)
ladrillo – brick (brik)
laminado – laminate (láminat)
madera – hardwood (jard uud)
piedra – stone (stóun) [ver nombres relacionados con piedra]
vinilo – vinyl (váinol)
bambú – bamboo (bambú)

TÉRMINOS DE FERRETERÍA / HERRERÍA
Hardware Terms

arrastres / tirantes – pulls (puls)
barras para las toallas – towel bars (tóuel bars)
bisagra – hinges (jínlles)
bronce – bronze (brons)
cerradura sin manija con cilindro doble – double cylinder deadbolt (dábol cílinder ded bolt)

cerraduras sin manijas – deadbolt locks (ded bolt loks)
cerámica – ceramic (cerámic)
cobre – copper (cóper)
cromo – chrome (cróum)
cristal – crystal (crístal)
ganchos – hooks (juks)
hierro forjado – wrought iron (rot áirn)
juegos de cerraduras – locksets (slok sets)
latón – brass (bras)
manijas de las puertas – door knobs (dor nabs)
madera – wood (uud)
manijas – knobs (nabs)
niquel – nickel (níkol)
peltre – pewter (piúter)
placas traseras – back plates (bak pléits)
plástico – plastic (plástic)
plata – silver (sílver)
porcelana – porcelain (pórcelan)
sostenedor de papel – paper holder (péiper jóulder)
sujetador de puerta – door stop (dor stop)
trabas / cerrojos de las ventanas – window locks (uíndou loks)
vidrio – glass (glas)

TÉRMINOS DE MOLDURAS
Trim Terms

altura de los peldaños – stair risers (ster ráisers)
barandas del balcón – deck railing (dek réilin)
cavidad de la puerta – door casing (dor kéisin)
chimeneas – hearths (jarzs)
columnas – columns (cóloms)
empanelado de madera – wood paneling (uud pánelin)
escaleras de atrás – rear staircase (ríer ster kéis)
escaleras [en curva] – curved staircase (kervd ster kéis)
estantes / entrepaños del closet – closet shelves (clóset shelvs)
estantes para libros incrustados – built-in bookshelves
  (bilt in buk shelvs)
estantería – shelving (shélvin)
facia – facia (féisha)
gabinetes fabricados a la medida – custom cabinets (cóstom cábinets)
mezón separado en la cocina – kitchen work island (?)
moldura de caja para cuadros – picture box molding
  (píkcher box móldin)

moldura decorativa – decorative molding (decórativ móldin)
moldeadura del pasamanos de la silla – chair rail molding
 (chéar réil móuldin)
moldura en relieve – crown molding (cráun móldin)
molenillo fabricado a la medida – custom millwork (cóstom mil uérk)
pasamanos de las escaleras – stair handrails (ster jand réils)
peldaños de las escaleras – stair treads (ster treds)
tableros para paredes – bead board (bid bord)
trabajo especial en madera – special woodwork (spéshial uud uérk)
revestimiento – wainscoting (uéinscotin)
repisa de la chimenea – fireplace mantel (fáier pléis mántel)
repisas – mantels (mántols)
rodapiés – shoe mold (shu móuld)
sofito – soffit (sófit)
ventana estilo balcón – bay window (béi uíndou)
zócalo / rodapiés – baseboard (béis bord)

TÉRMINOS DE LAS PAREDES
Wall Terms

bloque de concreto – concrete block (cónkrit blok)
concreto vaciado – poured concrete (pórd cónkrit)
drywall – drywall (drái uól)
enmarcado – framed (fréimd)
empapelado para las casas – house wrap (jáus rap)
empanelado – paneling (pánelin)
estuco – stucco (stáco)
friso – wainscot (uéinscot)
paredes con bases – foundation walls (faundéishon uóls)
páneles de vidrio para paredes – glass wall panels (glas uól pánols)
papel para pared – wall paper (uól péiper)
tablero para paredes – bead board (bid bord)
yeso / plaster – plaster (plaster)

TIPOS DE MADERA
Wood Types

abedul – alder (ólder)
abedul – birch (berch)
álamo – poplar (póplar)
álamo – aspen (áspen)
arce – maple (méipol)
bambú – bamboo (bambú)

caoba – mahogany (majógani)
cereza – cherry (chérri)
cereza brasileña – Brazilian cherry (brazílian chérri)
ceniza – ash (ash)
haya – beech (bich)
nogal – hickory (jíkori)
pino – pine (páin)
presurizado – pressure treated (préshur tríted)
roble – oak (óuk)
teca – teak (tik)

HERRAMIENTAS DE CARPINTERÍA
Carpentry Tools

almádena – sledgehammer (slech-jámer)
arenador / lijador – sander (sánder)
cinsel – chisel (chísol)
cinta de medir – tape measure (téip méchur)
clavos – nails (néils)
compresor de aire – air compressor (éar comprésor)
cuadrado – square (Scuéar)
destornillador / desarmador – screwdriver (scru dráiver)
lima – file (fáil)
línea de tiza / gis – chalk line (chok láin)
manguera de aire – airhose (éar-jous)
martillo – hammer (jámer)
nivel – level (lévol)
palanca – pry bar (Prai bar)
pistola de clavos – nailgun (néil gan)
saca clavo – nail puller (néil púler)
sierra circular – circular saw (cir-quiu-lar so)
sierra de mesa – table saw (téibol so)
sierra rebanadora – chop saw (chop so)
taladro – drill (dril)

PROVISIONES DE CARPINTERÍA
Carpentry Supplies

andamiaje – scaffolding (scáfoldin)
burros / caballetes – horses (jórses)
cable de extensiòn – extension cord (Eks-tén-chon cord)
calentador – heater (Jíter)
cinturón herramientas – tool belt (Tul-belt)

clavos – nails (néils)
escalera – ladder (láder)
estribo para viguetas – joist hangers (llóist jánguers)
lija – sandpaper (sand péiper)
mascarilla para el polvo – dust mask (dast mask)
protectores de rodillas / rodilleras – knee pads (ni pads)
stud finder / busca montantes – stud finder (stad-fáinder)
tiza / gis – chalk (chok)
tornillos – screws (scrus)
ventilador – fan (fan)

FRASES DE PISOS – MADERA / BALDOSA / ALFOMBRA

FRASES DE ALFOMBRA
Carpet Phrases

Vea pagina 28 para preguntas, respuestas y afirmaciones básicas en el trabajo y Frases básicas en el lugar de trabajo

¿Cuánto hace que trabaja colocando alfombra?
How long have you been installing carpet?
(¿Jáu long jav iú bin instólin cárpet?)

Hace _____ años que trabajo colocando alfombra.
I have been installing carpet for _____ years.
(Ái jav bin instólin cárpet for _____ iérs)

Necesitamos tomar medidas para la alfombra.
We need to measure for carpet.
(Uí nid tu mésher for cárpet)

La alfombra ya está pedida.
The carpet is on order.
(De cárpet is on order)

Mañana entregarán la alfombra.
The carpet will be delivered tomorrow.
(De cárpet uíl bi dilíverd tumórrou)

Necesitamos ir a recoger la alfombra.
We need to go pick up the carpet.
(uí nid tu góu pik ap de cárpet)

Necesitamos descargar el camión.
We need to unload the truck.
(uí nid tu anlóud de trak)

Necesitamos traer la alfombra para acá.
We need to bring the carpet in here.
(uí nid tu bring de cárpet in jíar)

Necesitamos la plancha caliente y la cinta.
We need the hot-iron and tape.
(Uí nid de jot-áirn and téip)

Necesitamos el aplanador para alfombra.
We need the carpet stretcher.
(Uí nid de cárpet strécher)

Necesitamos cuchillas de navaja afiladas.
We need sharp utility blades.
(Uí nid sharp iutílity bléids)

Necesitamos colocar primero el bajoalfombra.
We need to install the pad first.
(Uí nid tu instól de pad ferst)

Necesitamos instalar una cartelera / tabla de tachuelas.
We need to install the tack boards.
(Uí nid tu instól de tac bords)

Necesitamos alfombrar la habitación / el closet.
We need to put the carpet in the bedroom / closet.
(Uí nid tu put de cárpet in de bed rum / clóset)

Necesitamos limpiar el área de trabajo a diario.
We need to clean up the job site daily.
(Uí nid tu clin ap de llob-sáit déili)

FRASES DE BALDOSA
Tile Phrases

¿Cuánto hace que trabaja colocando baldosas?
How long have you been installing tile?
(¿Jáu long jav iú bin dúin flors?)

Hace _____ años que trabajo colocando baldosas.
I have been installing tile for _____ years.
(Ái jav bin dúin flors for _____ iérs)

¿Adónde está la baldosa?
Where is the tile?
(¿Uéar is de táil?)

Necesitamos más baldosa.
We need more tile.
(Uí nid mor táil)

Necesitamos ir a recoger las baldosas.
We need to go pick-up the tile.
(uí nid tu góu pik ap de táil)

Necesitamos traer las baldosas para aquí.
We need to bring the tile in here.
(uí nid tu bring de táil in jíar)

Necesitamos descargar el camión
We need to unload the truck.
(uí nid tu anlóud de trak)

Necesitamos apilar las baldosas aquí.
We need to stack the tile here.
(uí nid tu stak de táil jíar)

¿Adónde está la lechada?
Where is the grout?
(¿Uéar is de gráut?)

Necesitamos más lechada.
We need more grout.
(Uí nid mor gráut)

Necesitamos limpiar la lechada.
We need to clean off the grout residue.
(Uí nid tu clin of de gráut résidu)

Necesitamos un balde de 5 galones.
We need a five-gallon bucket.
(Uí nid a fáiv gálon báket)

Necesitamos agua limpia.
We need clean water.
(Uí nid clin uóter)

Necesitamos una esponja limpia.
We need a clean sponge.
(Uí nid a clin sponch)

Necesitamos el serrucho para baldosa.
We need the tile saw.
(Uí nid de táil so)

Necesitamos el molinillo.
We need the grinder.
(Uí nid de gráinder)

¿Puede cortar baldosa?
Can you cut tile?
(¿Can iú cat táil?)

¿Adónde está el serrucho?
Where is the saw?
(¿Uéar is de so?)

Necesitamos instalar baldosa cerámica en el baño / la cocina.
We need to install ceramic tile in the bathroom / kitchen.
(Uí nid tu instól cerámic táil in de baz rum / kíchen)

Necesitamos limpiar el área de trabajo a diario.
We need to clean up the job site daily.
(Uí nid tu clin ap de llob-sáit déili)

FRASES PARA PISOS DE MADERA
Wood Floor Phrases

¿Cuánto hace que trabaja colocando pisos de madera?
How long have you been installing and refinishing wood floors?
(¿Jáu long jav iú bin instólin and rifínishin uud flors?)

Hace _____ años que trabajo colocando pisos de madera.
I have been installing and refinishing wood floors for _____ years.
(Ái jav bin instólin and rifínishin uud flors for _____ iérs)

Necesitamos ir a recoger los pisos de madera.
We need to go pick up the hardwood floors.
(uí nis tu góu pik ap de jard uud flors

Necesitamos descargar el camión.
We need to unload the truck.
(uí nid tu anlóud de trak)

Necesitamos traer la madera para pisos para acá.
We need to bring the hardwood in here.
(uí nid tu bring de jard uud in jíar)

Necesitamos apilar las baldosas aquí.
We need to stack the wood here.
(uí nid tu stak de uud jíar)

¿Adónde están los protectores de rodillas?
Where are the knee-pads?
(¿Uéar ar de ni-pads?)

¿Adónde están las máscaras protectoras?
Where are the safety masks?
(¿Uéar ar de séifti masks?)

¿Adónde está el aguarrás?
Where are the mineral spirits?
(¿Uéar ar de míneral spírits?)

Necesitamos colocar este piso.
We need to lay this floor.
(Uí nid tu léi dis flor)

Necesitamos realizar el acabado de los pisos de madera.
We need to refinish the hardwood floors.
(Uí nid tu rifínish de járd uúd flors)

Necesitamos arenar los pisos.
We need to sand the floors.
(Uí nid tu sand de flors)

Necesitamos más papel de lija.
We need more sandpaper.
(Uí nid mor sand péipar)

Necesitamos el bordeador.
We need the edger.
(Uí nid di écher)

Utilice el bordeador para ir alrededor del perímetro de la habitación.
Use the edger to go around the perimeter of the room.
(Iús de écher tu góu aráund de perímeter ov de rum)

Necesitamos trapos limpios.
We need clean rags.
(Uí nid clin rags)

Necesitamos limpiar el piso.
We need to wipe the floor down.
(Uí nid tu uáip de flor dáun)

Necesitamos tres capas de poliuretano en los pisos.
We need three coats of poly on the floors.
(Uí nid zri cóuts ov poli on de flors)

Necesitamos los pisos con una terminación satinada.
We need a satin finish on the floors.
(Uí uánt a sátin fínish on de flors)

Necesitamos los pisos con una terminación brillosa.
We need a high-gloss finish on the floors.
(Uí uánt a jái glos on de flors)

Necesitamos los pisos con una terminación clara.
We need a clear-coat finish on the floors.
(Uí uánt a clíar cóut on de flors)

Necesitamos los pisos con una terminación suave.
We need a light-coat finish on the floors.
(Uí uánt a láit cóut on de flors)

Necesitamos los pisos con una terminación oscura.
We need a dark-coat finish on the floors.
(Uí uánt a dark cóut on de flors)

Una vez que el piso se seque, necesitamos colocar papel para protegerlo.
We need to put paper down after the floor dries to protect it.
(Uí nid tu put péipar dáun áfter de flor dráis tu protéct it)

Mañana podremos caminar sobre los pisos.
We can walk on the floors tomorrow.
(Uí can uók on de flors tumórrou)

Necesitamos limpiar el área de trabajo a diario.
We need to clean up the job site daily.
(Ui níd tu clin ap de llob-sáit déili)

FRASES DE ENMARCAR
Framing Phrases

¿Cuánto hace que trabaja en enmarcar?
How long have you been framing?
(¿Jáu long jav iú bin fréimin?)

Hace _____ años que trabajo en enmarcar.
I have been framing for _____ years.
(Ái jav bin fréimin for _____ iérs)

Mañana entregarán los materiales.
The supplies will be delivered tomorrow.
(De sapláis uíl bi dilíverd tumórrou)

¿Adónde está el martillo?
Where is the hammer?
(¿Uéar is de jámer?)

¿Adónde están los clavos?
Where are the nails?
(¿Uéar ar de néils?)

Necesitamos más clavos.
We need more nails.
(Uí nid mor néils)

¿Adónde está la cinta de medir?
Where is the tape measure?
(¿Uéar is de mésherin téip?)

¿Adónde está el nivel?
Where is the level?
(¿Uéar is de lével?)

¿Adónde está el nivel láser?
Where is the laser level?
(¿Uéar is de léiser lével?)

Mire en la caja de herramientas
Look in the toolbox.
(Luk in de túl-boks)

¿Adónde están las tejas de madera?
Where are the shake shingles?
(¿Uéar ar de shéik shíngols?)

Necesitamos instalar tejas de madera.
We need to install shake shingles.
(Uí nid tu instól shéik shíngols)

Necesitamos más madera.
We need more wood.
(Uí nid mor uúd)

Necesitamos más de 2x4 / 2x6 / 2x8 / 2x10.
We need more 2x4 / 2x6 / 2x8 / 2x10.
(Uí nid mor tu bái for /tu bái six / tu bái éit / tu bái ten)

Necesitamos apilar la madera allí.
We need to stack the lumber there.
(Uí nid tu stak de lámber déar)

Necesitamos más andamiaje.
We need more scaffolding.
(Uí nid mor scáfoldin)

Necesitamos tablas para caminar.
We need walk boards.
(Uí nid uók bords)

Necesitamos la clavadora automática.
We need the framing nail gun.
(Uí nid de fréimin néil gan)

Necesitamos la pistola para clavos enrollados en tiras / pistola de clavos con tambor.
We need the coil nailer.
(Uí nid de cóil néiler)

Necesitamos construir un armazón / una estructura conforme los planos del arquitecto.
We need to frame this floor according to the blueprints.
(Uí nid tu fréim dis flor acórdin tu di blu-prins)

¿Puede realizar cortes?
Can you cut?
(¿Can iú cat?)

Necesitamos arreglar los sofitos.
We need to fix the soffits.
(Uí nid tu fix de sófits)

Necesitamos construir una cubierta / un balcón.
We need to build a deck.
(Uí nid tu bíld a dek)

Necesitamos revestir con tablas con traslapo / solapo la parte trasera del edificio.
We need to lap side the rear of the building.
(Uí nid tu lap sáid de ríar ov de bíldin)

Necesitamos darle las terminaciones a la casa una vez finalizado el drywall.
We need to trim-out the house after the drywall is done.
(Uí nid tu trim-áut de jáus áfter de drái uól is dan)

Necesitamos construir un armazón / una estructura para un techo a cuatro aguas.
We need to frame for a hip roof.
(Uí nid tu fréim for a jíp ruf)

Necesitamos construir un armazón / una estructura para las canaletas.
We need to frame for the gutters.
(Uí nid tu fréim for de gáters)

Necesitamos construir un bastidor / marco para una ventana aquí.
We need to frame for a window here.
(Uí nid tu fréim for a uíndou jíar)

Necesitamos construir un armazón / una estructura para una ventana vertical de buhardilla / un aposento salidizo.

We need to frame for a dormer.

(Uí nid tu fréim for a dórmer)

Necesitamos un hastial / gable.

We need a gable.

(Uí nid a guéibol)

Necesitamos colocar las escaleras.

We need to get the stairs in.

(Uí nid tu guet de sters in)

Las escaleras van aquí.

The stairs go here.

(De stéars go jíer)

¿Cuál es la inclinación del techo?

What is the pitch of the roof?

(¿Uát is de pich ov de ruf?)

Necesitamos secar esto mientras llegua el techista.

We need to dry this in until the roofer gets here.

(Uí nid tu drái dis in antíl de rúfer guets jíar)

Necesitamos instalar las puertas / ventanas.

We need to install doors / windows.

(Uí nid tu instól dors / uíndous)

Hay que enrasar esa pared.

That wall needs to be furred out.

(Dat uól nids tu bi ferd áut)

Necesitamos colocarle plomería a esto.

We need to plumb this.

(Uí nid tu plamb dis)

Necesitamos más apoyo aquí.

We need more support here.

(Uí nid mor sapórt jíar)

Necesitamos una viga especial aquí.
We need a special beam here.
(Uí nid a spéshal bim jíar)

Necesitamos obtener una inspección.
We need to get an inspection.
(Uí nid tu guet an inspékshon)

Necesitamos limpiar el área de trabajo a diario.
We need to clean up the job site daily.
(Uí nid tu clin ap de llob-sáit déili)

Concreto

TÉRMINOS DE CONCRETO
Concrete Terms

agregado al descubierto – exposed aggregate (ekspóust ágregat)
aguafuerte – etched (eched)
acabado grueso / acabado con escoba – broom finish (brum fínish)
acabado liso – smooth finish (smuz fínish)
curado – curing (kiúrin)
cemento portland – portland cement (pórtland síment)
acabado / capa – screeding (scrídin)
mesones de concreto – concrete countertops (cónkrit cáuntertops)
piso de concreto – concrete floors (cónkrit flors)
teñido – stained (stéin)

HERRAMIENTAS DE CONCRETO
Concrete Tools

alisador mecánico – power trowel (páuer tráuel)
camión de concreto – concrete truck (cónkrit trak)
carretilla – wheelbarrow (uíl bárrou)
compactadora mecánica – power tamper (póuer támper)
flotador – float (flóut)
instalador de alfombras / rodillera – kicker (kíker)
lavadora de presión – pressure washer (préshur uásher)
llana flotante / aplanador – bull float (bul flóut)
mazo / mandarria – sledgehammer (slech jámer)
nivel – level (lévol)
nivel láser – lazer level (léiser lévol)
orillador – edger (éller)
pala – shovel (shável)
paleta / cuchara de albañil – trowel (tráuel)

PROVISIONES DE CONCRETO
Concrete Supplies

ácido muriático – muriatic acid (miuriátic ásid)
ataduras / amarres de alambre – wire ties (uáier táis)
barra de refuerzo – re-bar (ri bar)
botas de goma / botas de caucho – rubber boots (ráber buts)
clavos en dúplex – duplex nails (dúplex néils)
dos por cuatros – 2x4's (tu bái fors)

escoba – broom (brum)
estacas – stakes (stéiks)
lona impermeabilizada – tarp (tarp)
mancha de ácido – acid stain (ásid stéin)
manguera – hose (jóus)
mortero – mortar (mórtar)
pernos de anclaje – anchor bolts (éinkor bolts)
pliego plástico / hoja plástica – plastic sheet (plástic shit)
plywood / madera terciada – plywood (plái uud)
rejilla metálica – wire mesh (uáier mesh)
retardador – retardant (rítárdant)

FRASES DE CONCRETO
Concrete Phrases

Vea pagina 28 para preguntas, respuestas y afirmaciones básicas en el trabajo y Frases básicas en el lugar de trabajo

¿Cuánto hace que trabaja con concreto?
How long have you been working with concrete?
(¿Jáu long jav iú bín uérking uíz cónkrit?)

Hace _____ años que trabajo con concreto.
I have been working with concrete for _____ years.
(Ái jav bín uérking uíz cónkrit for _____ iérs)

¿Adónde está la tela metálica?
Where is the metal mesh?
(¿Uéar is de métal mesh?)

Necesitamos más barras de refuerzo.
We need more rebar.
(Uí nid mor ríbar)

¿Adónde está la barra de refuerzo?
Where is the rebar?
(¿Uéar is de ríbar?)

Necesitamos más barras de refuerzo y más alambre de anclaje.
We need more rebar saddles and anchoring wire.
(Uí nid mor ríbar sádels and ánkorin uáier)

¿Adónde está el rastrillo?
Where is the rake?
(¿Uéar is de réik?)

¿Adónde está la pala?
Where is the shovel?
(¿Uéar is de shávol?)

¿Adónde está el llana flotante / aplanador?
Where is the bull float?
(¿Uéar is de bul flóut?)

¿Adónde está la cinta de precaución?
Where is the caution tape?
(¿Uéar is de cóshon téip?)

¿Adónde está la cota / el punto de referencia?
Where is the bench mark?
(¿Uéar is de bench mark?)

¿Cuántas yardas de concreto se van a necesitar?
How many yards of concrete will be needed?
(¿Jáu méni iárds ov cónkrit uíl bi nídid?)

Necesitamos más bolsas de concreto.
We need more bags of concrete.
(Uí nid mor bags ov cónkrit)

El concreto debe ser de 3.000 libras por pulgada cuadrada / 5.000 libras por pulgada cuadrada.
The concrete needs to be 3,000 psi / 5,000 psi.
(De cónkrit nids tu bi zri záusand pi es ái / fáiv záusand pi es ái)

Necesitamos el concreto que está reforzado con fibra de vidrio.
We need the fiberglass reinforced concrete.
(Uí nid de fáiber glas rienfórst cónkrit)

El camión entregará _____ yardas de concreto mañana.
The truck will deliver _____ yards of concrete tomorrow.
(De trák uíl dilíver _____ iárds ov cónkrit tumórrou)

Necesitamos un nivel.
We need a level.
(Uí nid a lével)

Necesitamos más estacas.
We need more stakes.
(Uí nid mor stéiks)

Necesitamos más madera.

We need more lumber.

(Uí nid mor lámber)

Necesitamos más plywood / madera terciada.

We need more plywood.

(Uí nid mor plái uúd)

Necesitamos un borde recto.

We need a straight edge.

(Uí nid a stréit ech)

Necesitamos nivelar con el nivel láser.

We need to laser level.

(Uí nid tu léiser lével)

Necesitamos más tela metálica.

We need more wire mesh.

(Uí nid mor uáier mesh)

Necesitamos inspeccionar el cimiento antes de volcar el concreto.

We need to get the footings inspected before we pour the concrete.

(Uí nid tu guet de fútins inspékted bifór uí por de cónkrit)

Necesitamos construir encofrados aquí.

We need to build forms here.

(Uí nid tu bild forms jíer)

Vaciaremos el concreto mañana.

We will pour the concrete tomorrow.

(Uí uíl por de cónkrit tumórrou)

Necesitamos alisar ese punto en el concreto.

We need to smooth-out that spot in the concrete.

(Uí nid tu smuz-áut dat spot in de cónkrit)

Necesitamos darle a esto una terminación lisa.

We need to make this a smooth finish.

(Uí nid tu méik dis a smuz fínish)

Necesitamos apisonar este área.

We need to tamp this area down.

(Uí nid tu tamp dis éria dáun)

Necesitamos lavar el concreto a presión.
We need to power wash the concrete.
(Uí nid tu páuer uásh de cónkrit)

Necesitamos dejar esto fraguar.
We need to let this set.
(uí nid tu let dis set)

Necesitamos cubrir el concreto con plástico.
We need to cover the concrete with plastic.
(Uí nid tu cáver de cónkrit uíz plástic)

Necesitamos agregarle tinte / tintura a esto.
We need to add stain to this.
(uí nid tu ad stéin tu dis)

Vamos a usar ladrillos para el borde.
We will use bricks for the border.
(uí uíl iús bricks for de bórder)

Construiremos un patio aquí.
We will make a patio area here.
(uí uíl méik a pátio jíar)

Usaremos esto para los mesones.
These will be used for the countertops.
(dis uíl bi iúst for de cáunter tops)

Estas serán paredes vaciadas con concreto.
These will be poured concrete walls.
(dis uíl bi pord cónkrit uóls)

¿Lloverá?
Is it going to rain?
(¿Is it góin tu réin?)

Necesitamos limpiar el área de trabajo a diario.
We need to clean up the job site daily.
(Uí nid tu clin ap de llob-sáit déili)

TAMBÍEN VEA LA SECCIÓN DE MAMPOSTERÍA
ALSO SEE MASONRY SECTION

Demolicíon

HERRAMIENTAS DE DEMOLICIÓN
Demolition Tools

barra demoledora – wrecking bar (rékin bar)
barredor magnético – magnetic sweeper (magnétic suíper)
bola de demolición – wrecking ball (rékin bol)
camión para botar basura – dump truck (damp trak)
cinsel – chisel (chísol)
depósito de basura – dumpster (dámpster)
martillo – hammer (jámer)
mazo / mandarria – sledgehammer (slech jámer)
pala – shovel (shável)
pata de cabra / palanca – crow bar (cróu bar)
rastrillo – rake (réik)
saca clavos – nail puller (néil púler)

PROVISIONES DE DEMOLICIÓN
Demolition Supplies

carretilla – wheelbarrow (uíl bárrou)
casco de seguridad – hard hat (jard jat)
careta de polvo – dust mask (dast mask)
cinta de precaución – caution tape (cóshon téip)
escoba – broom (brum)
guantes – gloves (glovs)
lentes de seguridad – safety glasses (séifti gláses)
lona impermeabilizada – tarp (tarp)
pintura en atomizador / pintura sprey – spray paint (spréi péint)
tiza / gis – chalk (chok)

FRASES DE DEMOLICIÓN & LIMPIEZA DE OBRA
Demolition & Clean-up Phrases

¿Ha hecho antes trabajos de remoción / demolición?
Have you ever done tear-out / demolition work before?
(¿Jav iú éver dan téar-áut / demolíshon uérk bifór?)

Hace _____ años que hago trabajos de remoción / demolición.
I have been doing tear-out / demolition work for _____ years.
(Ái jav bín dúin téar-áut / demolíshon uérk for _____ iérs)

¿Adónde está el martillo?
Where is the hammer?
(¿Uéar is de jámer?)

Vea pagina 28 para preguntas, respuestas y afirmaciones básicas en el trabajo y Frases básicas en el lugar de trabajo

¿Adónde está la escoba?
Where is the broom?
(¿Uéar is de brum?)

¿Adónde está la pala?
Where is the shovel?
(¿Uéar is de shável?)

¿Adónde está el marro / mazo?
Where is the sledgehammer?
(¿Uéar is de slech jámer?)

¿Adónde está la pata de cabra / palanca?
Where is the crow-bar?
(¿Uéar is de cróu-bar?)

¿Adónde está la carretilla?
Where is the wheelbarrow?
(¿Uéar is de uíl bárrou?)

Necesitamos más guantes.
We need more gloves.
(Uí nid mor glavs)

¿Adónde están los guantes?
Where are the gloves?
(¿Uéar ar de glavs?)

¿Adónde están los lentes de seguridad?
Where are the safety glasses?
(¿Uéar ar de séifti gógols?)

Necesitamos usar nuestros lentes de seguridad.
We need to wear our safety glasses
(Uí nid tu uéar séifti glases)

Necesitamos usar nuestros cascos de seguridad.
We need to wear our hard hats.
(Uí nid tu uéar auer jard jats)

Necesitamos demoler todas las paredes y cielorrasos marcados con pintura anaranjada.

We need to tear-out all the walls and ceilings marked with orange paint.

(Uí nid tu téar-áut ol de uóls and sílins markt uíz órench péint)

Necesitamos quitar los ladrillos viejos.

We need to remove the old bricks.

(Uí nid tu rimúv de óuld briks)

Necesitamos apilar los ladrillos luego de retirarles el cemento viejo.

We need to stack the bricks up after we get the old cement off of them.

(Uí nid tu stak de briks ap áfter uí guet de óuld simént of ov dem)

Necesitamos apilar todas las rocas.

We need to put all the rocks in one pile.

(Uí nid tu put ol de roks in uán páil)

Necesitamos apilar todos los escombros en forma ordenada en el basurero.

We need to stack all the debris in the dumpster neatly.

(Uí nid tu stak ol de dibrí in de dámpster nítli)

¿Ya está lleno el basurero?

Is the dumpster full yet?

(¿Ís de dámpster ful iét?)

Avíseme cuando el basurero esté casi lleno.

Let me know when the dumpster is almost full.

(Let mi nóu uén de dámpster is ólmoust ful)

Necesitamos otro basurero.

We need another dumpster.

(Uí nid anóder dámpster)

Necesitamos limpiar el jardín.

We need to clean up the yard.

(Uí nid tu clin ap de iárd)

Necesitamos rastrillar el jardín.

We need to rake the yard.

(Uí nid tu réik de iárd)

Necesitamos barrer esto.
We need to sweep this up.
(Uí nid tu suíp dis ap)

Necesitamos barrer los pisos.
We need to sweep the floors.
(Uí nid tu suíp de flors)

Necesitamos taladrar este concreto.
We need to jackhammer this concrete out.
(Uí nid tu jak-jámer dis cónkrit áut)

Necesitamos utilizar la retroexcavadora.
We need to use the backhoe.
(Uí nid tu iús de bak jóu)

Necesitamos cubrir esto con una lona impermeabilizada.
We need to cover this with a tarp.
(uí nid tu cóver dis uíz a tarp)

Necesitamos demoler esto.
We need to tear this out.
(Uí nid tu téar dis áut)

Necesitamos quitar esto.
We need to remove this.
(Uí nid tu rimúv dis)

Necesitamos quitar el revestimiento viejo.
We need to remove the old siding.
(Uí nid tu rimúv di óuld sáidin)

Necesitamos quitar esta madera.
We need to remove this wood.
(Uí nid tu rimúv dis uúd)

Necesitamos salvar el marco de la ventana vieja.
We need to save the old window sashes.
(Uí nid tu séif de old uíndou sáches)

Necesitamos salvar eso.
We need to salvage that.
(Uí nid tu sálvech dat)

Necesitamos dejar esto.
We need to leave this.
(Uí nid tu liv dis)

Necesitamos limpiar el área de trabajo a diario.
We need to clean up the job site daily.
(Uí nid tu clín ap de llob-sáit déili)

Drywall

TÉRMINOS DE DRYWALL
Drywall Terms

acabado liso – smooth finish (smuz fínish)
textura – texture (téxcher)
techo de las palomitas – popcorn ceiling (popcorn síling)
spackled – spackled (spakold)

HERRAMIENTAS DE DRYWALL
Drywall Tools

andamio – scaffold (scáfold)
cuchillo – knife (náif)
clavadora para drywall – drywall nailer (drái uól néiler)
escuadra para drywall – drywall square (drái uól skúear)
línea de tiza / gis – chalk line (chok láin)
martillo – hammer (jámer)
paleta / cuchara de albañil – trowel (tráuel)
pistola para atornillar – screw gun (scru gan)
tablero para caminar – walk board (uók bord)
taladro – drill (dril)
zancos – stilts (stilts)

PROVISIONES DE DRYWALL
Drywall Supplies

balde de cinco galones – five-gallon bucket (fáiv gálon báket)
bandeja / platón para el barro – mud pan (mad pan)
sheetrock / cartón piedra – sheetrock (shit rok)
cinta – tape (téip)
cinta plana – flat tape (flat téip)
clavo – nail (néil)
clavos de extracción – pull nails (pul néils)
drywall impermeable – green board (grin bord)
esquinero – corner bead (córner bid)
lápiz – pencil (pénsil)
lodo / barro – mud (mad)
tornillos – screws (scrus)
yeso – gypsum (llípsom)
yeso / emplaste – plaster (pláster)

FRASES DE DRYWALL
Drywall Phrases

Vea pagina 28 para preguntas, respuestas y afirmaciones básicas en el trabajo y Frases básicas en el lugar de trabajo

¿Cuánto hace que trabaja colocando drywall?
How long have you been hanging drywall?
(¿Jáu long jav iú bin jánguin drái uól?)

¿Cuánto hace que trabaja en la terminación de drywall?
How long have you been finishing drywall?
(¿Jáu long jav iú bin fínishin drái uól?)

Hace _____ años que trabajo con drywall.
I have been working with drywall for _____ years.
(Ái jav bin uérkin uíz drái uól for _____ iérs)

¿Cuándo entregarán las tablas?
When will the boards be delivered?
(¿Uén uíl de bords bi dilíverd?)

Necesitamos más tablas.
We need more boards.
(Uí nid mor bords)

¿Cuántas tablas va a necesitar?
How many boards will you need?
(¿Jáu méni bords uíl iú nid?)

Necesitamos apilar las tablas allí.
We need to stack the boards there.
(Uí nid tu stak de bords déar)

¿Adónde están las herramientas de terminación?
Where are the finishing tools?
(¿Uéar ar de fínishin tuls?)

Necesitamos más andamiaje.
We need more scaffolding.
(Uí nid mor scáfoldin)

Necesitamos utilizar tornillos de 2 pulgadas / de 1 pulgada.
We need to use 2" screws / 1" screws.
(Uí nid tu iús tu inch scrus / uán inch scrus)

Necesitamos utilizar drywall de 1/2 pulgada / de 5/8 pulgada.
We need to use 1/2" / 5/8" drywall.
(Uí nid tu iús jaf inch / fáiv éits inch drái uól)

¿Adónde está el barro?
Where is the mud?
(¿Uéar is de mad?)

Necesitamos más barro.
We need more mud.
(Uí nid mor mad)

Necesitamos utilizar el barro de 20 minutos / 45 minutos.
We need to use the 20 minute / 45 minute mud.
(Uí nid tu iús de tuénti mínit / fórti fáiv mínit mad)

Necesitamos más cinta.
We need more tape.
(Uí nid mor téip)

¿Adónde está la cinta?
Where is the tape?
(¿Uéar is de téip?)

Necesitamos utilizar cinta de tela aquí.
We need to use mesh tape here.
(Uí nid tu iús mesh téip jíar)

Necesitamos cubrir esta área con cinta.
We need to flat tape this area.
(Uí nid tu flat téip dis éria)

Necesitamos colocar cinta esquinera aquí.
We need to use corner tape here.
(Uí nid tu iús córner téip jíar)

Necesitamos utilizar cinta de tela para arreglar las rajas / grietas.
We need to use mesh tape for fixing cracks.
Uí nid tu iús mesh téip for fíxin cráks.

¿Cuántos esquineros se necesitarán?
How many corner beads will be needed?
(¿Jáu méni córner bids uíl bi nídid?)

Necesitamos más esquineros.
We need more corner bead.
(Uí nid mor córner bid)

Necesitamos reparar este yeso.
We need to repair this plaster.
Uí nid tu ripéar dis pláster.

Necesitamos arreglar las rajas / grietas en la pared.
We need to fix the cracks in the wall.
Uí nid tu ripéar de craks in de uól.

Necesitamos darle a esto una terminación lisa.
We need to finish this to a smooth finish.
(Uí nid tu fínish dis tu a smuz fínish)

Necesitamos arenar más éste área.
We need to sand this area more.
(Uí nid tu sand dis éria mor)

Necesitamos razar esta área una vez más.
We need to skim this area one more time.
(Uí nid tu skim dis éria uán mor táim)

Necesitamos colgar primero los cielorrasos.
We need to hang the ceilings first.
(Uí nid tu jan de sílins ferst)

Necesitamos colocar el ventilador aquí.
We need to put the fan in here.
(Uí nid tu put de fan in jíar)

Necesitamos colocar el drywall de desecho en el basurero.
We need to put scrap drywall in the dumpster.
(Uí nid tu put scrap drái uól in de dámpster)

Necesitamos limpiar el área de trabajo a diario.
We need to clean up the job site daily.
(Uí nid tu clin ap de llob-sáit déili)

ELECTRICO

TÉRMINOS DE ELECTRICIDAD
Electrical Terms

alambres tw / alambres tipo taiwan – TW wires (ti dábol iú uáiers)
aislamiento plástico – plastic insulation (plástic insuléishon)
apagador del voltaje bajo – low voltage switch (lóu vóltach suích)
amperio – ampere (ámper)
apagador / interruptor – circuit breaker (sérkit bréiker)
apagador fotoelécrico – electric-eye switch (eléctric ái súich)
apagadores / interruptores – switches (suíches)
balasto – ballast (bálast)
balasto de arranque rápido – rapid start ballast (rápid start bálast)
cable – cable (kéibol)
cable con cobertura plástica – plastic-sheathed cable (plástic shizd kéibol)
cable de calefacción – heating cable (jítin kéibol)
cable UF / cable de ultra frecuencia – UF cable (iú ef kéibol)
caja enterrada / caja incrustada – buried box (bérid box)
caja GFI / caja del Interruptor de falla a tierra – GFI box (gi ef ái box)
calentador de agua de gas – water heater [gas] (gas uóter jíter)
calentador de agua eléctrico – water heater [electric] (eléktrik uóter jíter)
circuito – circuit (sérkit)
conector – connector (conéctor)
cable de doce / cable de catorce – 12/14 wire (tuélv/fortín uáier)
cable pre-embobinado – pre-wired cable (pri-uáierd kéibol)
cables del enchufe – plug wiring (plag uáirin)
cables del interruptor / apagador – switch wiring (suích uáirin)
cables en paralelo – parallel wiring (páralel uáirin)
cables en serie – series wiring (síris uáirin)
combinación de calefacción y aire acondicionado – dual heating and cooling (dúal jítin and cúlin)
conductores – conductors (condáctors)
controles automáticos para abrir las puertas del garaje – automatic garage door openers (otomátic garách dor ópeners)
corriente alterna – alternating current (ólterneitin cárrent)
corriente directa – direct current (diréct cárrent)
conexión a tierra – grounding (gráundin)
diodo – diode (dáiod)
descarga de alta intensidad – HID [high intensity discharge] (éich ái di [jái inténsiti díscharch])

difusor – diffuser (difiúser)
dispositivos resistentes al clima – weatherproof fixtures
(uéder pruf fíxchers)
elevador / ascensor – elevator (éleveitor)
enchufes – plugs (plags)
enchufe – socket (sáket)
energía – power (póuer)
generador – generator (llénereitor)
GFI – GFI (lli - ef - ái)
iluminar – illuminate (ilúmineit)
interruptor de falla de tierra – ground fault interrupter
(gráund folt interráptor)
interruptores / apagadores – breakers (bréikers)
kilovatio – kilowatt (kilo uát)
lazada – loop (lup)
LED – LED (el i di)
línea de voltaje – line voltage (láin vóltach)
motor eléctrico para la lámpara araña / candelabro – electric motor
for chandelier (eléctric mótor for shándelier)
oscurecedores / regulador de voltage – dimmers (dímers)
pánel principal de electricidad – main electric panel
(méin eléctric pánel)
piso con calefacción – heated floor (jíted flor)
pinzas / grapas – clips (clips)
plantilla / patrón – template (témplet)
receptáculo – receptacle (recéptacol)
receptáculo montado en la pared – wall mounted receptacle
(uól máunted recéptacol)
reflector – reflector (rifléctor)
relevo – relay (rílei)
resistencia – resistance (resístans)
resistente a la corrosión – corrosion proof (corróshon pruf)
resistente a la humedad – moisture-resistant (móischer resístant)
resplandor / destello – glare (gléar)
sistema de aspiración / vacío – vacuum system (vákium sístem)
sistema de intercomunicadores – intercom system (íntercom sístem)
sistema de seguridad – security system (sekiúriti sístem)
sistema de riego – sprinkler system (sprínkler sístem)
solar – solar (sólar)
tablero / pánel de servicio – service panel (sérvis pánel)
tamaño del alambre / cable – wire size (uáier sáis)
transportadores de cargas – dumb waiters (dom uéiters)
tubo – conduit (cánduet)

tubo de metal de pared fina – thin-wall metal conduit (zin uól métal cánduet)
ultra violeta – ultraviolet (última váiolet)
vatio(s) – watt[s] (uát[s])
voltaje – voltage (vóltach)
ventiladores de techo controlados termostáticamente
  – thermostatically controlled roof ventilators (zermostáticali contróld ruf véntileitors)
voltaje alto – high voltage (jái vóltach)
voltaje bajo – low voltage (lóu voltách)
voltios – volts (volts)

HERRAMIENTAS DE ELECTRICIDAD
Electrical Tools

cortadores de cable / alambre – wire cutters (uáier cáters)
cortadores para laterales – side cutters (sáid cáters)
destornillador / desarmador – screwdriver (scru dráiver)
martillo – hammer (jámer)
medidor de ohmnios – OHM meter (om míter)
pinzas pelacables – strippers (stríprs)
protectores para pisar sobre los cables – wire strippers (uáier stépers)
taladro – drill (dril)

PROVISIONES DE ELECTRICIDAD
Electrical Supplies

bombilla / foco – lightbulb (láit bolb)
cable de extensión – extension cord (esténchon cord)
casquillos para empalmes de cables – wire nuts (uáier nats)
casquillos para empalmes de cables a tierra – ground wire nuts (gráund uáier nats0
cinta para bedir – tape measure (téip mésher)
clavos – nails (néils)
cubiertas – covers (cóvers)
guantes – gloves (glovs)
grapa de metal – wire staples (uáier steipels)
tapas de los enchufes – faceplates (féis-pleits)
tira de la energía – power strip (páuer strip)
tómá de corriente – outlet boxes (aut-let bókses)
tornillos – screws (scrus)
placa interruptora – switchplates (suích-pleits)

ESTILOS DE LUCES Y ACCESORIOS
Lighting Styles & Fixtures

accesorios de cobre – copper fixture (cóper fixcher)
antorchas – torches (tórches)
bombilla – bullet light (búlet láit)
estaca – stake (stéik)
farol – post lantern (póust lántern)
faroles / linternas – lanterns (lánterns)
fluorescente – fluorescent (florésent)
halógeno – halogen (jálollen)
iluminación de ambientación – accent lighting (áksent láitin)
iluminación arquitectónico – architectural lighting (arkitékchural láitin)
iluminación del balcón – deck light (dek láit)
iluminación de paisaje – landscape lighting (land skéip láitin)
iluminación para el jardín – garden lighting (gárden láitin)
iluminación para el sitio de trabajo – task lighting (task láitin)
iluminación para la pared – wall washing (uól uáshin)
incrustado – recessed (rísest)
lámpara – lamp (lamp)
lámpara araña / candelabro – chandelier (shándelíer)
lámparas / candelabros de muro – sconces (scónces)
luces del entrecortinado – valance light (válans láit)
luces de trabajo – task lights (task láits)
luces que alumbran debajo del mezón – under counter lights (ánder cáunter láits)
luz direccional – spotlights (spat láits)
luz industrial / reflector – floodlight (flad láit)
luz de paso – step light (step láit)
luz de sendero / de pasillo – pathway light (paz uéi láit)
luz del pozo – well light (uél láit)
luz que alumbra hacia abajo – downlight (dáun láit)
luz que alumbra hacia arriba – uplight (ap láit)
plafón – can light (can láit)
poste de luz – lamp post (lamp póust)
trayecto / riel – track (trak)
ventilador de techo con luz incorporada – ceiling fan with light kit (cílin fan uíz láit kit)

FRASES DE ELECTRICIDAD
Electrical Phrases

Vea pagina 28 para preguntas, respuestas y afirmaciones básicas en el trabajo y Frases básicas en el lugar de trabajo

¿Cuánto hace que es electricista?
How long have you been an electrician?
(¿Jáu long jav iú bin an electríshan?)

Hace _____ años que soy electricista.
I have been an electrician for _____ years.
(Ái jav bín an electríshan for _____ iérs)

Necesitamos conectar la electricidad.
We need to get the electricity turned on.
(Uí nid tu guet di electrísiti ternd on)

Necesitamos desconectar la electricidad.
We need to get the electricity turned off.
(Uí nid tu guet di electrísiti ternd of)

Is it on or off?
¿Está prendido o apagado?
(iz it an or auf)

Necesitamos instalar el poste temporario.
We need to get the temporary pole installed.
(Uí nid tu guet de témporari póul instóld)

¿Adónde está el cortacables?
Where are the wire cutters?
(¿Uéar ar de uáier cáters?)

¿Adónde está el destornillador / desarmador?
Where is the screwdriver?
(¿Uéar is de scru dráiver?)

¿Adónde está el martillo?
Where is the hammer?
(¿Uéar is de jámer?)

¿Adónde está la caja de fusibles?
Where is the fuse box?
(¿Uéar is de fiús box?)

¿Adónde está el dobla conducto/tubo?
Where is the conduit bender?
(¿Uéar is de kónduit bénder?

Necesitamos el dobla conducto / tubo.
We need the conduit bender.
(Uí nid de kónduit bénder.

Necesitamos más conductos / tubos.
We need more conduit.
(Uí nid mor kónduit.

Necesitamos más cable Romax.
We need more Romax.
(Uí nid mor róumax.

Necesitamos cables para parlantes en la casa.
We need speaker wires in the house.
(Uí nid spíker uáiers in de jáus.

En esta casa estamos usando fibra óptica
We are using fiber-optic cable in this house?
(¿Uí ar iúsin fáiber-óptic kéibol in dís jáus?

¿Cuántos enchufes / interruptores hay en esa habitación?
How many plugs / switches are in that room?
(¿Jáu méni plags/suíches ar in dat rum?

Necesitamos colocarle las tapas a los enchufes y a los interruptores.
We need to put the faceplates on the plugs and switches.
(Uí nid tu put de féis-pléits on de plags and suíches.

Necesitamos hacer las conexiones de tubería y de electricidad a la casa.
We need to rough-in the house.
(Uí nid tu ráf in de jáus.

Necesitamos una caja metálica para dos enchufes / interruptores aquí.
We need a two gang box here.
(Uí nid a tu gang box jíar.

Necesitamos una caja metálica para tres enchufes / interruptores aquí.
We need a three gang box here.
(Uí nid a zri gang box jíar.

Necesitamos un tres vías desde aquí hasta allá.
We need a three-way from here to here.
(Uí nid a zri-uéi from jíer tu jíar.

Necesitamos 110 voltios aquí.
We need 110 volts here.
(Uí nid uán jándred ten volts jíar.

Necesitamos 220 voltios aquí.
We need 220 volts here.
(Uí nid tu jándred tuénti volts jíar.

Necesitamos cablear el lavadero con electricidad de 220 voltios.
We need to wire the laundry room for 220 volts.
(Uí nid tu uáier de lóndri rum for tu jándred tuénti volts.

Necesitamos cablear para luces debajo de la alacena en la cocina.
We need to wire for under-cabinet lights in the kitchen.
(Uí nid tu uáier for ánder-kábinet láits in de kíchen.

¿Llegaron ya los accesorios?
Are the fixtures in yet?
(¿Ar de fíxchers in iét?

Necesitamos instalar los accesorios de iluminación.
We need to install the light fixtures.
(Uí nid tu instól de láit fíxchers.

Necesitamos instalar plafones en esta habitación.
We need to install can lights in this room.
(Uí nid tu instól can láits in dís rum.

Necesitamos colocar los plafones aquí, los del centro primero.
We need to put can lights here, center first.
(Uí nid tu put can láits jíer, sénter férst.

Necesitamos colocar esta luz en el dormitorio / baño / la cocina.
We need to put this light in the bedroom / bathroom / kitchen.
(Uí nid tu put dís láit in de bed rum / baz rum / kíchen.

Necesitamos colocar esta lámpara araña / candelabro en el comedor / vestíbulo.
We need to put this chandelier in the dining room / foyer.
(Uí nid tu put dís shandelíer in de dáinin rum / fóier)

Necesitamos colocar el ventilador de techo en esta habitación.
We need to put the ceiling fan in this room.
(Uí nid tu put de sílin fan in dis rum)

Jale el cable a través de la pared.
Pull the wire thru the wall.
(Pul de uáier zru de uól)

No toque el botón rojo brillante .
Don't touch the shiny red button.
(Dont tách de sháini red báton)

Necesitamos poner cable.
We need to run cable.
(Uí nid tu ran kéibol)

Necesitamos obtener una inspección.
We need to get an inspection.
(Uí nid tu guet an inspékshon)

Necesitamos hacer un chequeo final.
We need to do a final check.
(Uí nid tu du a faínal chek)

Necesitamos colocar los escombros en el basurero.
We need to put the debris in the dumpster.
(Uí nid tu put de dibrí in de dámpster)

Necesitamos limpiar el área de trabajo a diario.
We need to clean up the job site daily.
(Uí nid tu clin ap de llob-sáit déili)

HVAC

TÉRMINOS DE HVAC
HVAC Terms

aceite / petróleo – oil (óil)
aire forzado – forced air (forst éar)
barómetro – barometer (barómeter)
bomba de calefacción – heat pump (jit pamp)
BTU – BTU (bi ti iú)
calentador de agua elèctrico – water heater [electric]
(uóter jíter [eléktrik])
calentador de agua de gas – water heater [gas]
(uóter jíter [gas])
calor por radiación através del piso – radiant floor heat (réidient flor jit)
eléctrico(a) – electric (eléctric)
factor R – R-factor (ar fáctor)
flujo hacia abajo – down flow (dáun flóu)
gas natural – natural gas (náchural gas)
horno – furnace (férnes)
kelvin – kelvin (kélvin)
propano – propane (própein)
radiación – radiation (radiéishon)
radón – radon (Réidon)
rankin – rankin (ránkin)
retorno – return (ritérn)
sistema de gas compacto de calefacción y aire acondicionado / gas pack – gas pack (gas pak)
termostato – thermostat (zérmostat)
válvula reguladora de aire – damper (dámper)

HERRAMIENTAS DE HVAC
HVAC Tools

alicates – pliers (pláiers)
destornilladores / desarmadores – screwdrivers (scru dráivers)
detector de monóxido de carbono – carbon monoxide detector
(carbon monóksaid ditéctor)
manómetro de presión – pressure gauge (préshur guéich)
pistola para engrapar – staple gun (stéipol gan)
taladro – drill (dril)
indicador láser de temperatura – laser temperature gauge (láser témperacher guedz)
tijeras para metal – snips (snips)

PROVISIONES DE HVAC
HVAC Supplies

aislamiento – insulation (insuléishon)
clavos – nails (néils)
colgadores de metal – metal hangers (métal jánguers)
conductos de metal – metal ducting (métal dáctin)
conductos flexibles – flexible ducting (fléksibol dáctin)
filtro de aire – air filter (éar fílter)
rejillas cobertoras – register covers (réllister cóvers)
tornillos – screws (scrus)

FRASES DE HVAC
HVAC Phrases

Vea pagina 28 para preguntas, respuestas y afirmaciones básicas en el trabajo y Frases básicas en el lugar de trabajo

¿Cuánto hace que trabaja con calefacción y aire acondicionado?
How long have you been working with heating and air?
(¿Jáu lon jav iú bin uérkin uíz jítin and éar?)

Hace _____ años que trabajo con calefacción y aire acondicionado.
I have been working with heating and air for _____ years.
(Ái jav bin uérking uíz jítin and éar for _____ iérs)

¿Adónde está el termómetro?
Where is the thermometer?
(¿Uéar is de zermómeter?)

Necesitamos más planchas de metal.
We need more sheet metal.
(Uí nid mor shit métal)

¿Adónde está el conducto flexible?
Where is the flex duct?
(¿Uéar is de flex dact?)

Necesitamos un conducto flexible en el ático / sótano.
We need to use flex duct in the attic / basement.
(Uí nid tu iús flex dact in di átic/béisment.

Necesitamos rejillas para el piso.
We need floor grills.
(Uí nid flor grils)

Necesitamos quitar la unidad / el equipo viejo de la casa.
We need to remove the old unit from the house.
(Uí nid tu rimúv di óuld iúnit from de jáus)

¿Qué tamaño de unidad / equipo de calefacción y aire acondicionado se necesita para esta casa?
How big of an HVAC unit is needed for this house?
(¿Jáu big ov an éich-vee-éi-si iúnit is nídid for dis jáus?)

Necesitamos una unidad que tenga el sistema combinado de calefacción y aire acondicionado
We need a split heating and cooling system.
(Uí nid ei split jitin and culin system)

Necesitamos saber cuántas unidades se van a usar.
We need the number of units to be used.
(Uí nid de namber of yúnits tu bi yust)

Necesitamos saber el tamaño de la unidad.
We need the size of the unit.
(Uí nid de sáis of de yúnit)

Necesitamos instalar una bomba de calefacción.
We need to put in a heat pump.
(Uí nid tu put in a jit pamp)

Necesitamos instalar una unidad / un equipo de gas.
We need to put in a gas unit.
(Uí nid tu put in a gas iúnit)

La unidad / el equipo estará lista / o mañana para conexión.
The unit will be ready to hook up tomorrow.
(De únit uíl bi rédi tu juk ap tumórrou)

Necesitamos instalar la unidad aquí.
We need to set the unit here.
(Uí nid tu set de yúnit jíer)

Necesitamos instalarle el protector contra la lluvia a la unidad / el equipo.
We need to install the rain guard on the unit.
(Uí nid tu instól de réin gard on de únit)

¿Cuántas porciones salen de cada unidad / equipo?
How many feeds come off the unit?
(¿Jáu méni fids cam of de iúnit?)

Necesitamos una bandeja recolectora debajo de la unidad / el equipo.
We need an overflow pan under the unit.
(Uí nid an óuver flow pan ánder de iúnit)

¿Cuál es el período de garantía de la unidad / el equipo?
What is the warranty of the unit?
(¿Uát is de uárranti ov de iúnit?)

Necesitamos una tableta de concreto asi de grande
We need a concrete pad this big.
(Uí nid ei cónkrit pad dis big)

Necesitamos instalar un tubo de ventilación a través de allí.
We need to install a vent pipe thru there.
(Uí nid tu instól a vent páip zru déar)

Necesitamos instalar los conductos de aire en la casa.
We need to run the duct work thru the house.
(Uí nid tu ran de dact uérk zru de jáus)

Necesitamos aislar y engrapar todos los ductos duros.
We need to insulate and staple all hard ducting.
(Uí nid tu ínsuleit and stéipol ol jard dáctin)

Necesitamos conectar el gas a la cocina / estufa.
We need to hook up the stove for gas.
(Uí nid tu juk ap de stóuv for gas)

Necesitamos instalar desviadores aquí.
We need to install diverters here.
(Uí nid tu instól daivérters jíer)

Necesitamos ventiladores en todos los baños.
We need vent fans in all bathrooms.
(Uí nid vent fans in all baz rums)

Chequee el interruptor de circuito.
Check the circuit breaker.
(Chek de sérkit bréiker)

Necesitamos colocar el interruptor de circuito en encendido / apagado.
We need to turn the circuit breaker on / off.
(Uí nid tu tern de sérkit bréiker on / of)

Necesitamos colocar el termostato aquí.
We need to put the thermostat here.
(Uí nid tu put de zérmostat jíar)

Necesitamos obtener una inspección.
We need to get an inspection.
(Uí nid tu guet an inspékshon)

Necesitamos limpiar el área de trabajo a diario.
We need to clean up the job site daily.
(Uí nid tu clin ap de llob-sáit déili)

TAMBIÉN VEA LA SECCIÓN DE ELÉCTRICO
ALSO SEE ELECTRICAL SECTION

MAMPOSTERÍA

TÉRMINOS DE MAMPOSTERÍA Y PIEDRAS
Masonry & Stone Terms

agregado / en bruto – aggregate (ágregat)
apilado en seco – dry stack (drái stak)
asfalto – asphalt (ásfalt)
entrada – driveway (dráiv uéi)
concreto – concrete (cónkrit)
equipo delgado – thin set (zin set)
grava / granzón – gravel (grávol
fogón / fosa de fuego – fire pit (fáier pit)
ladrillo – brick (brik)
ladrillos para pavimentar – paver bricks (péiver briks)
patio – patio (pátio)
patio de ladrillo – brick patio (brik pátio)
pared de ladrillo – brick wall (brik uól)
pared de piedra – stone wall (stóun uól)
pasillo / sendero – walkway (uók uéi)
piedra – stone (stóun)
piedra y mortero – stone and mortar (stóun and mórtar)

HERRAMIENTAS DE MAMPOSTERÍA
Masonry Tools

canalizador – groover (grúver)
cinsel – chisel (chísol)
compactadora – tamper (támper)
cubeta para mezclar – mixing tub (míxin tab)
cuchara / paleta de concreto – concrete trowel (kónkrit tráuel)
cuchara puntuda – pointing trowel (póintin tráuel)
dinteles – lintels (lintels)
ensamblador – jointer (llóinter)
flotador – float (flóut)
instrumento para la orilla interna – inside corner tool (in sáid kórner tul)
instrumento para la orilla externa – outside corner tool (áut sáid kórner tul)
instrumento para la orilla interna –
línea del albañil – mason line (méison láin)
martillo – hammer (jámer)
martillo para masonería – mason hammer (méison jámer)
mezcladora – mixer (míksor)

nivel – level (lévol)
nivel láser – laser level (léiser lévol)
orillador – edger (éller)
pala – shovel (shávol)
paleta / cuchara de albañil – trowel (tráuel)
regla doblable para el albañil – mason's folding rule (méisons fóldin rul)
sierra para concreto – concrete saw (kónkrit so)
vibrador – vibrator (vaibréitor)

PROVISIONES DE MAMPOSTERÍA
Masonry Supplies

acelerador – accelerator (aksélercitor)
agua – water (uóter)
arena – sand (sand)
baldes – buckets (bákets)
bloque – block (blok)
botas de goma / caucho – rubber boots (ráber buts)
carretilla – wheelbarrow (uíl bárrou)
concreto – concrete (kónkrit)
dos por cuatro – 2x4 (tu bái for)
encofrados – forms (forms)
escoba – broom (brum)
estacas – stakes (stéiks)
dinteles – lintels (líntols)
grava / granzón – gravel (grávol)
impermeabilización – waterproofing (uóter prúfin)
ladrillo – brick (brik)
madera tratada – treated lumber (tríted lámber)
malla / red – mesh (mesh)
mezcladora de cemento – cement mixer (simént míxer)
mortero / argamasa – mortar (mórtar)
pernos de anclaje – anchor bolts (ánkor bolts)
plástico – plastic (plástic)
plástico de soporte – sill plastic (sil plástic)
refuerzos para praredes – wall ties (uól táis)
resguardo – flashing (flásin)
retardador – retardant (ritárdant)

NOMBRES DE PIEDRAS
Stone Names

arenisca – sandstone (sand stóun)
cuarzita – quartzite (cuártsait)
esteatita / talco natural – soapstone (sóup stóun)
piedrita / guijarro – pebbles (pébols)
granito – granite (gránit)
grava / granzón – gravel (grávol)
adoquíne / guijarro – cobbles (cóbols)
ladrillo – brick (brik)
ladrillo rescatado / recuperado – salvaged brick (sálvacht brik)
ladrillo viejo – old brick (óuld brik)
laja – flagstone (flag stóun)
mármol – marble (márbol)
mármol travertino – travertine (trávertin)
piedra artificial – manmade stone (man méid stóun)
piedra azul – bluestone (blu stóun)
piedra caliza – limestone (láim stóun)
piedra caliza de corte arquitectónico – architectural cut limestone
  (arkitékchural cat láim stóun)
piedra de campo – fieldstone (fild stóun)
piedra de lava – lava rock (láva rok)
piedra natural – natural stone (náchural stóun)
piedra para pavimentar – pavers (péivers)
roca – rock (rok)
pizarra – slate (sléit)
piedra – stone (stóun)

FRASES DE MAMPOSTERÍA – LADRILLO Y PIEDRA
Masonry – Brick
& Stone Phrases

*Vea pagina 28 para preguntas, respuestas y afirmaciones
básicas en el trabajo y Frases básicas en el lugar de trabajo*

¿Cuánto hace que trabaja con ladrillo / piedra?
  How long have you been working with brick / stone?
  (¿Jáu lon jav iú bin uérkin uíz brik / stóun?)

Hace _____ años que trabajo con ladrillo / piedra.
  I have been working with brick / stone for _____ years.
  (Ái jav bin uérking uíz brik / stóun for _____ iérs)

¿Adónde está el nivel?
  Where is the level?
  (¿Uéar is de lével?)

¿Adónde está el nivel láser?
Where is the laser level?
(¿Uéar is de léiser lével?)

¿Adónde está el mortero / argamasa?
Where is the mortar?
(¿Uéar is de mórtar?)

¿Cuántas bolsas más de mortero / argamasa se necesitarán?
How many more bags of mortar will be needed?
(¿Jáu méni mor bags ov mórtar uíl bi nídid?)

Necesitamos mezclar más mortero / argamasa.
We need to mix more mortar.
(Uí nid tu mix mor mórtar)

Necesitamos que el acabado de el mortero / la argamasa sea áspero.
We need the mortar to be a rough finish.
(uí nid de mortar tu bi ei raff fínich)

Necesitamos quitarle el mortero / la argamasa al ladrillo.
We need to clean the mortar off the brick.
(Uí nid tu clín de mórtar of de brik)

¿Adónde está la paleta?
Where is the trowel?
(¿Uéar is de tráuel?)

¿Adónde está la carretilla?
Where is the wheelbarrow?
(¿Uéar is de uíl bárrou?)

Necesitamos más andamiaje.
We need more scaffolding.
(Uí nid mor scáfoldin)

Por favor, tráigame más ladrillos / piedras.
Please bring me more brick / stone.
(Plis brin mi mor brik / stóun)

¿Cuántos ladrillos más se necesitan?
How many more bricks are needed?
(¿Jáu méni mor briks ar nídid?)

Mañana entregarán los ladrillos.
The bricks will be delivered tomorrow.
(De briks uíl bi dilíverd tumórrou)

Necesitamos apilar los ladrillos aquí.
We need to stack the bricks here.
(Uí nid tu stak de briks jíar)

Necesitamos colocar ladrillo en este lado de la casa.
We need to brick this side of the house.
Uí nid tu brik dis sáid ov de jáus)

Necesitamos limpiar las juntas de lechada.
We need to clean the grout joints.
(Uí nid tu clin de gráut llóints)

¿Cuántas piedras más se necesitan?
How many more stones are needed?
(¿Jáu méni mor stóuns ar nídid?)

Necesitamos apilar las piedras aquí.
We need to stack the stones here.
(Uí nid tu stak de stóuns jíar)

Necesitamos construir una pared de piedra.
We need to build a stone wall.
(Uí nid tu bild a stóun uól)

Necesitamos emparejar los bordes de las piedras.
We need to chip the sides off the stone.
(uí nid tu chip de sáids of de stóun)

Necesitamos nivelar esta pared.
We need to level this wall.
(Uí nid tu lével dis uó)

Necesitamos un balde de 5 galones.
We need a 5-gallon bucket.
(Uí nid a fáiv gálon báket)

Necesitamos agua limpia.
We need clean water.
(Uí nid clin uóter)

Tense el hilo por encima para formar una línea recta.
Pull the string across the top for a straight line.
(Púl de strin acrós de top for a stréit láin)

Necesitamos instalar / levantar una pared aquí.
We need to dry stack a wall here.
(Uí nid tu drái stak a uól jíar)

Necesitamos obtener una inspección.
We need to get an inspection.
(Uí nid tu guet an inspékshon)

Usaremos ladrillos para esta parte de la entrada.
We will use bricks for this part of the driveway.
(uí uíl yús briks for dis part of de dráiv-uei

Necesitamos usar estos ladrillos para la chimenea.
We need to use these bricks for the chimney.
(uí nid tu yús diis briks for de chímni)

Necesitamos poner el / la _____ por encima de la ventana.
We need to put the _____ above the window.
(uí nid tu put de _____ abóv de uíndou)

Necesitamos tres hileras de bloques para la fundación / la base.
We need three rows of block for the foundation.
(uí nid sri róus of blok for de faun-déichon)

Necesitamos sellar la fundación / la base.
We need to seal the foundation.
(uí nid tu siil de faun-déichon)

Necesitamos poner estuco en esa área.
We need to stucco that area.
(uí nid tu stuco dat érea)

Necesitamos construir una pared de contención.
We need to build a retaining wall.
(uí nid tu bild ei ritéinin uól

Necesitamos construir un buzón de piedra.
We need to build a stone mailbox.
(uí nid tu bild ei stóun méilboks)

Necesitamos construir una entrada de piedra.
We need to build a stone entrance.
(uí nid tu bild ei stóun éntrans)

Necesitamos limpiar el área de trabajo a diario.
We need to clean up the job site daily.
(Uí nid tu clín ap de llob-sáit déili)

TAMBIÉN VEA LA SECCIÓN DE CONCRETO
ALSO SEE CONCRETE SECTION

PINTURA

TÉRMINOS DE PINTURA
Painting Terms

aceite – oil (óil)
colores primarios – primary colors (práimeri cólors)
 [see basic's section]
colores secundarios – secondary colors (sécondari cólors)
exterior – exterior (extérior)
imprimador / pintura base – primer (práimer)
látex – latex (léitex)
mancha / broncear – stain (stéin)
masilla – spackling (spáklin)
mural – mural (miúrol)
oscuro – dark (dark)
pastel – pastel (pástel)
pintura con textura – texture paint (téxcher péint)
pintura en atomizador / pintura sprey – spray paint (spréi péint)
recortar / cortar – cut-in (cat in)
resistente al moho – mildew resistant (míldu resístant)
retocar – touch-up (tach ap0
suave / liviano / claro – light (láit)

HERRAMIENTAS DE PINTURA
Painting Tools

abre latas – can opener (can ópener)
boquilla – nozzle (nósol)
cerda china – china bristle (cháina brísol)
cinsel – chisel (chísol)
hojilla / navaja – razor blade (réisor bléid)
pincel / brocha / cepillo – brush (brash)
pincel / brocha de látex – latex brush (léitex brash)
poste de extensión – extension pole (exténshon póul)
rociador / atomizador – sprayer (spréier)
rodillo – roller (róler)
orillador – edger (éller)

PROVISIONES DE PINTURA
Painting Supplies

aceite de linaza – linseed oil (ínsid óil)
agua ras – mineral spirits (míneral spírits)

balde / cubo / **cubeta** – bucket (báket)
bandeja / **platón de pintura** – paint tray (péint tréi)
carta de pinturas – paint chart (péint chart
cepillo de alambre – wire brush (uáier brash)
cinta – tape (téip)
esponja – sponge (sponch)
goma / pegamento / **cola** – glue (glu)
lija – sandpaper (sand péiper)
masilla – caulk (cok)
masilla de pintor – painter's putty (péinters páti)
palo / **barilla para revolver** – stir stick (ster stik)
relleno para madera – wood filler (uud fíler)
removedor de pintura – paint remover (péint rimúver)
trapos de limpieza – drop cloths (drop clozs)

ACABADOS DE PINTURA
Painting Finishes

acabado con rodillo forrado con trapo – rag rolling (rag rólin)
antiguo – antiqued (ántikt)
cepillado – brushed (brasht)
embadurnado en aceite / embarrado de aceite – oil rubbed (óil rabd)
envejecido / maltratado – distressed (distrést)
esponjado – sponging (spónllin)
esténsil – stenciling (sténcilin)
estallido – crackling (cráklin)
glaseado – glaze (gléis)
mancha – stain (stéin)
pintura – paint (péint)
pulido – polished (pólisht)
simulacro / **falso** – faux (fóu)
texturizado – texturing (téxchurin)

FRASES DE PINTURA
Painting Phrases

Vea pagina 28 para preguntas, respuestas y afirmaciones básicas en el trabajo y Frases básicas en el lugar de trabajo

¿Cuánto hace que pinta?
How long have you been painting?
(¿Jáu long jav iú bin péintin?)

Hace _____ años que pinto.
I have been painting for _____ years.
(Ái jav bin péintin for _____ iérs)

La pintura y las provisiones serán enviadas mañana
The paint and supplies will be delivered tomorrow.
(De péint and sapláis uil bi dilíverd tumórrou)

¿Adónde está el aguarrás?
Where are the mineral spirits?
(¿Uéar ar de spírits?)

Necesitamos más trapos.
We need more rags.
(Uí nid mor rags)

¿Adónde están los rodillos?
Where are the rollers?
(¿Uéar ar de róulers?)

Necesitamos más rodillos.
We need more rollers.
(Uí nid mor róulers)

¿Adónde están los pinceles / las brochas?
Where are the brushes?
(¿Uéar ar de bráshes?)

Necesitamos más pinceles / las brochas.
We need more brushes.
(Uí nid mor bráshes)

Necesitamos limpiar los pinceles / las brochas aquí.
We need to clean brushes over here.
(Uí nid tu clín bráshes óuver jíar)

Necesitamos guardar los pinceles / las brochas aquí.
We need to store the brushes here.
(Uí nid tu stor de broches jíer)

Necesitamos más cinta.
We need more tape.
(Uí nid mor téip)

Necesitamos más trapos para limpiar.
We need more drop cloths.
(Uí nid mor drop clozs)

Necesitamos el poste de extensión.
We need the extension pole.
(Uí nid di exténshon póul)

¿Adónde está el poste de extensión.
Where is the extension pole?
(¿Uéar is di exténshon póul?)

Necesitamos la escalera.
We need the ladder.
(Uí nid de láder)

Necesitamos un balde de agua.
We need a bucket of water.
(Uí nid a báket ov uóter)

Necesitamos guardar los baldes de pintura aquí.
We need to store the paint buckets here.
(Uí nid tu stor de péint bóquets jíer)

Necesitamos más pintura.
We need more paint.
(Uí nid mor péint)

Necesitamos pintura para el interior/ exterior.
We need interior / exterior paint.
(Uí nid intírior / ekstírior péint)

Necesitamos pintura con base de aceite para las molduras.
We need oil base paint for the trim.
(Uí nid óil béis péint for de trim)

Necesitamos pintura de látex.
We need latex paint.
(Uí nid léiteks péint)

Necesitamos raspar / rasquetear y realizar el trabajo preparativo.
We need to scrape and do the prep work.
(Uí nid tu scréip and du de prep uérk)

Necesitamos raspar la pintura vieja.
We need to strip the old paint off.
(Uí nid tu strip di óuld péint of)

Necesitamos raspar / rasquetear las ventanas.
We need to scrape the windows.
(Uí nid tu scréip de uíndous)

Necesitamos arenar / lijar.
We need to sand.
(Uí nid tu sand)

Necesitamos enmasillar.
We need to caulk.
(Uí nid tu cok)

Necesitamos colocarle una capa de protector a esto antes de instalarlo.
We need to prime this before installing.
(Uí nid tu práim dis bifór instólin)

Necesitamos arenar esto antes de colocar la capa final de pintura.
We need to sand this before the final coat of paint.
(Uí nid tu sand dis bifór de fáinal cóut ov péint)

Necesitamos enmasillar aquí.
We need to caulk here.
(Uí nid tu cók jíar)

Necesitamos retocar aquí.
We need to touch-up here.
(Uí nid tu tach-ap jíar)

Necesitamos una capa de protector y dos capas de base.
We need one coat of primer and two coats of base.
(Uí nid uán cóut of práimer and tu cóuts ov béis)

¿Adónde está la pintura para esta habitación?
Where is the paint for this room?
(¿Uéar is de péint for dis rum?)

Necesitamos colocar la primera capa de pintura en las paredes y en los cielorrasos.
We need to get the first coat of paint on the walls and ceilings.
(Uí nid tu guet de ferst cóut ov péint on de uóls and sílins)

Necesitamos colocar el color principal aquí.
We need to put the body color here.
(Uí nid tu put de bódi cólor jíar)

Necesitamos colocar el color para la madera moldeada aquí.
We need to put the trim color here.
(Uí nid tu put de trim cólor jíar)

Necesitamos colocar el tercer color aquí.
We need to put the 3rd color here.
(Uí nid tu put de zerd cólor j`íar)

Necesitamos broncear / pintar los zócalos .
We need to stain / paint the kick plates.
(Uí nid tu stein / péint de kik pléits)

Necesitamos broncear / pintar los peldaños de las escaleras.
We need to stain / paint the stair treads.
(Uí nid tu stein / péint de stéar treds

Necesitamos broncear / pintar la puerta principal.
We need to stain / paint the front door.
(Uí nid tu stéin / péint de frant dor)

Necesitamos broncear / pintar la repisa de la chimenea.
We need to stain / paint the mantel.
(Uí nid tu stéin / péint de mantel)

Necesitamos pintar la habitación / la cocina / el baño.
We need to paint the bedroom / kitchen / bathroom.
(Uí nid tu péint de bed rum/kíchen/baz rum)

Necesitamos pintar las contraventanas
We need to paint the shutters.
(Uí nid tu péint de chóters)

Necesitamos limpiar el área de trabajo a diario.
We need to clean up the job site daily.
(Uí nid tu clin ap de llob-sáit déili)

PLOMERÍA

TÉRMINOS DE PLOMERÍA
Plumbing Terms

abrazadera metálica – mission coupling (míshon cáplin)
accesorio / artículo – fixture (fíkscher)
acoplar – coupling (cáplin)
adaptador – adaptor (adáptor)
aireador – aerator (eiréitor)
agua negra – black water (blak uóter)
base – base (béis)
boca de acceso / tapa de alcantarilla – manhole (man jóul)
boca de la tubería – stem (stem)
caja / estuche / recinto – casing (kéisin)
caño / llave de agua – water tap (uóter tap)
circuito de ventilación – circuit vent (sérkit vent)
cloaca / alcantarilla – sewer (súer)
codo – elbow (élbou)
colector de rebalse – sump (samp)
colgador – flapper (fláper)
cámara de aire – air chamber (éar chéimber)
condensación – condensation (condenséishon)
deflector – baffle (báfol)
delantal – apron (éipron)
desaguadero / escurridero – drain (dréin)
desaguadero final – end drain (end dréin)
desagüe para las tormentas – storm drain (storm dréin)
desviador – diverter (divérter)
empacado – packing (pákin)
empacadura – gasket (gásket)
empacadura de anillo / O-ring – O ring (óu ring)
entrada / aporte – input (in put)
entrada para los servicios – service entrance (sérvis éntrans)
esponja de aislamiento – foam insulation (fóum insuléishon)
flexionar – flex (flex)
flujo en reverso – backwash (bak uásh)
fragmento de tubería – stub-out (stab áut)
hierro colado / fundido – cast iron (cast áirn)
líneas de percolación – leach lines (lich láins)
llave / grifo / canilla – spigot (spígot)
manga – sleeve (sliv)
manijas – handles (jándols)

medidor de agua – water meter (uóter míter)
mesa de agua subterránea – water table (uóter téibol)
pánel / tablero de acceso – access panel (ákces pánol)
pata de cuervo / cabra – crow's foot (cróus fut)
pozo séptico – septic (séptic)
preventor de reflujo – backflow preventor (bak flóu privéntor)
principal / madre – main (méin)
punto de chequeo de aire – air check (éar chek)
recolector de rebalse – overflow hood (óuver flóu jud)
reflujo – backflow (bak flóu)
rosca hembra – female threads (fímeil zreds)
salida / descarga – outlet / discharge (áut let / díscharch)
sellador – sill caulk (sil cok)
soldadura – solder (sáder)
soldar – weld (uéld)
solvente para soldar – solvent weld (sólvent úeld)
tapón – plug (plag)
tapón de vaciado total – knockout plug (nok áut plag)
tetilla – nipple (nípol)
terreno percolado – leach field (lich fild)
trampa – trap (trap)
tubería de agua – water service pipe (uóter sérvis páip)
tubería de cobre – copper pipe (cóper páip)
tubería de PEX – PEX pipe (PEX páip)
tubería de PVC / tubería plástica – PVC pipe (pi vi ci páip)
tubería L – L tubing (el túbin)
tubería M – M tubing (em túbin)
tubería para el rebalse – overflow tube (óuver flóu tiúb)
tubería subterránea de agua – culvert (cálvert)
tubo de escape – flue (flu)
tubo vertical – riser (ráiser)
tuerca de traba – lock nut (lok nat)
uniflex – uniflex (iúniflex)
unión – union (iúnion)
unidad de accesorio – fixture unit (fíkscher iúnit)
unión / empalme / junta – joint (llóint)
unión / empalme / junta de presión – slip joint (slip llóint)
válvula de cierre automático – ball cock (bol cok)
ventilación común – common vent (cómon vent)
válvula de seguridad de cierre – safety shut off valve
(séifti shat of valv)
válvula – valve (valv)
ventilación – vent (vent)

HERRAMIENTAS DE PLOMERÍA
Plumbing Tools

agujereador – hole-saw bit (jóul so bit)
alicates de presión – channel pliers (chánol pláiers)
alicate puntudo – needle-nose pliers (nídol nóus pláiers)
antorcha – torch (torch)
cinta para medir – tape measure (téip mésher)
cortador de tubos – pipe cutter (páip cáter)
cortapluma – utility knife (iutíliti náif)
culebra destapa cañerías – plumber's snake (plámers snéik)
escuadra – square (skúear)
llave – wrench (rench)
llave alen – allen wrench (álen rench)
llave de tubo – pipe wrench (páip rench)
llave de tubo ajustable – adjustable wrench (adllástabol rench)
nivel – level (lévol)
serrucho para drywall – keyhole saw (ki jóul so)
sierra circular – circular saw (sérkiular so)
soplete – blowtorch (blóu torch)
stud finder / busca montantes – stud finder (stad fáinder)
taladro – drill (dril)

PROVISIONES DE PLOMERÍA
Plumbing Supplies

acoplados – couplings (cáplins)
arandelas – washers (uáshers)
cinta de plomería – plumber tape (plámer téip)
cinta de teflón / teflón – teflon tape (téflon téip)
codos – elbows (élbous)
conexiones hembras – female fittings (fímeil fítins)
conexiones machos – male fittings (méil fítins)
llaves / grifos – faucets (fósets)
manijas – handles (jándols)
masilla de plomero – plumber putty (plámer páti)
masilla de silicón – silicone caulk (silikóun)
sopapo / destapa cañerías – plunger (plánller)
tapas – caps (caps)
tes – tees (tis)
tubería de PVC / tubería plástica – PVC pipe (plástic pi vi si páip)
tubería de cobre – copper pipe (kóper páip)
tubería de gas – gas pipe (gas páip)

válvula de regadera – shower valve (sháuer valv)
válvula montada en la pared – wall-mount valve (uól máunt valv)

ACCESORIOS DE PLOMERÍA
Plumbing Fixtures

aerosol para el cuerpo – body spray (bódi spréi)
bañera – bathtub (baz tab)
bañera con patas – claw foot tub (clo fut tab)
bañera de hidromasajes – whirlpool bath (uérpul baz)
bañera incrustada – recessed tub (rícest tab)
batea – vegetable sink (vélletabol sink)
bidet – bidet (bidét)
calentador de agua [electrico] – electric water heater (uóter jíter)
calentador de agua [gas] – gas water heater (uóter jíter)
calentador de agua sin tanque – tankless water heater
(tank les uóter jíter)
jacuzzi – jacuzzi® (llakúzi)
lavamanos de pie – undermount sink (ánder máunt sink)
lavamanos – sink (sink)
lavamanos de acero inoxidable – stainless steel sink
(stéinles stil sink)
lavamanos con pedestal – pedestal sink (pédestal sink)
lavamanos de cerámica – ceramic sink (cerámic sink)
lavamanos de cobre – copper sink (cóper sink)
lavamanos con gabinete – utility sink (iutíliti sink)
lavamanos de granja – farmhouse sink (farm jáus sink)
lavamanos de la lavandería – laundry sink (lóndri sink)
llave de agua del baño principal – master bath faucet
(máster baz fócet)
llave de agua de la cocina – kitchen faucet (kíchen fócet)
llave de agua automática – touchless faucet (tach les fócet)
poceta – commode (comóud)
poceta / excusado / retrete – toilet (tóilet)
poceta de consumo bajo – low-consumption toilet
(lóu consámshon tóilet)
poceta sin cloaca o pozo séptico – composting toilet
(compóustin tóilet)
regadera con vapor – steam shower (stim sháuer)
regadera / ducha – shower (sháuer)
regadera fuera de la casa – outdoor shower (aút dor sháuer)
seauna – sauna (sóna)
urinal / urinario – urinal (iúrinal)

FRASES DE PLOMERÍA
Plumbing Phrases

¿Cuánto hace que es plomero?
How long have you been a plumber?
(¿Jáu lon jav iú bin a plámer?)

Hace _____ años que soy plomero.
I have been a plumber for _____ years.
(Ái jav bin a plámer for _____ iérs)

Necesitamos conectar el agua.
We need to get the water turned on.
(Uí nid tu guet de uóter ternd on)

Necesitamos desconectar el agua.
We need to get the water turned off.
(Uí nid tu guet de uóter ternd of)

Necesitamos hacer las conexiones de tubería y de plomería a la casa.
We need to rough in the house.
(Uí nid tu raf in de jáus)

Necesitamos destapar la obstrucción.
We need to fix the clog.
(Uí nid tu fix de clog)

¿Cuántos grifos habrá en la casa?
How many faucets will there be in the house?
(¿Jáu méni fósets uíl der bi in de jáus?)

¿Llegaron ya los accesorios?
Are the fixtures in yet?
(¿Ar de fíkschers in iét?)

Necesitamos más cañería de cobre.
We need more copper pipe.
(Uí nid mor cóper páip)

Necesitamos más PVC.
We need more PVC pipe.
(Uí nid mor pee-vee-si páip)

Necesitamos más PEX.
We need more PEX pipe.
(Uí nid mor PEX páip)

Necesitamos colocar este grifo en la cocina / el baño / la lavandería.
We need to put this faucet in the kitchen / bathroom / laundry room.
(Uí nid tu put dis fóset in de kíchen / baz rum / lóndri rum)

Necesitamos excavar una nueva línea de agua en el jardín del frente.
We need to dig a new water line in the front yard.
(Uí nid tu dig a niú uóter láin in de front iárd)

Necesitamos soldar ese caño.
We need to solder that pipe.
(Uí nid tu sólder dat páip)

¿Ha encontrado el escape?
Have you found the leak?
(¿Jav iú fáund de lík?)

¿Adonde esta la llave de tubo?
Where is the pipe-wrench?
(¿Uéar is de páip-rench?)

¿Adónde está la pala?
Where is the shovel?
(¿Uéar is de shávol?)

¿Adónde está el martillo?
Where is the hammer?
(¿Uéar is de jámer?)

¿Adónde está el antorcha de propano?
Where is the propane torch?
(¿Uéar is de propéin torch?)

¿Adónde está el pegamento / la goma / la cola?
Where is the glue?
(¿Uéar is de glu?)

¿Adónde está el pozo séptico?
Where is the septic system?
(¿Uéar is de séptic sístem?)

¿Adónde está la bomba?
Where is the pump?
(¿Uéar is de pamp?)

Necesitamos desconectar el agua de la calle.
We need to turn the water off at the street.
(Uí nid tu tern de uóter of at de strit)

Necesitmos sacarle los detalles a la casa.
We need to trim out the house.
(Uí nid tu trim uót de jáus)

Necesitamos colocar una bandeja de desagüe / drenaje aquí.
We need to put a drain pan here.
(Uí nid tu put a dréin pan jíar)

Necesitamos quitar esta cañería.
We need to pull this piping out.
(Uí nid tu pul dis páiping áut)

Necesitamos obtener una inspección.
We need to get an inspection.
(Uí nid tu guet an inspékshon)

Necesitamos conectar con la tubería de la calle.
We need to tap into the street line.
(uí nid to tap ínto de strit láin)

Necesitamos chequear la presión del agua.
We need to check the water pressure
(uí nid tu chek de uóter présher)

Necesitamos instalar el sistema de riego.
We need to install the sprinkler system.
(uí nid tu instól de sprínkler sístem)

Necesitamos instalar una bomba extractora.
We need to install a sump pump.
(uí nid ti instól a samp pamp)

Necesitamos instalar el pozo séptico.
We need to install the septic system.
(uí nid tu instól de séptic sístem)

Necesitamos hacer un examen de tierra.
We need to get the soil tested.
(uí nid tu guet de sóil tésted)

Necesitamos demarcar el terreno percolado.
We need to mark off the leach field.
(uí nid to mark of de lich fild)

Necesitamos instalar los accesorios.
We need to install the fixtures.
(uí nid tu instól de fíkschers)

Necesitamos limpiar el área de trabajo a diario.
We need to clean up the job site daily.
(Uí nid tu clin ap de llob-sáit déili)

TECHADO

TÉRMINOS DE TECHADO
Roofing Terms

alero – eave (iv)
alquitrán – pitch (pich)
asfalto – asphalt (ásfalt)
balcón – deck (dek)
caballete / cumbrera – ridge (rich)
caballete / vértice – hip (jip)
canalete – drip edge (drip ech)
cobertizo – shed (shed)
curso – course (cors)
declive / nivelar – grade (gréid)
hastial / gable – gable (guéibol)
inclinación – slope (slóup)
plano – flat (flat)
resguardo – flashing (fláshin)
revestimiento con tablas al final – end lap (end lap)
revestimiento con tablas en los lados – side lap (sáid lap)
techo con hastiales / gambrel – gambrel (gámbrol)
techo de caucho – rubber roof (ráber ruf)
techo levantado – built-up roof (bilt ap ruf)
tragaluz – skylight (scái láit)
tubo vertical – rise (ráis)
ventanilla sobresaliente / dórmer – dormer (dórmer)
ventilaciones del techo – roof vents (ruf vents)

HERRAMIENTAS DE TECHADO
Roofing Tools

cinta para medir – tape measure (téip mésher)
cuchillo – knife (náif)
escalera de extensión – extension ladder (eksténshon láder)
extractor de clavos – nail pullers (néil púlers)
hacha – hatchet (jáchet)
horquilla – fork (fork)
levantador de escalera – ladder lift (láder lift)
martillo – hammer (jámer)
pala – shovel (shávol)
palanca de fuerza – pry bar (prái bar)
palanca / pata de cabra / cuervo – crowbar (cróu bar)

rastrillo – rake (réik)
tijeras para cortar metal – shears (shíars)
tijeras – snips (snips)

PROVISIONES DE TECHADO
Roofing Supplies

abrazaderas – cleats (klits)
barredor magnético – magnetic sweeper (magnétic suíper)
barretilla – wheelbarrow (uíl bárrou)
bolsa de clavos – nail bag (néil bag)
brea – tar (tar)
caballete de ventilación – ridge vent (rich vent)
cemento plástico – plastic cement (plástic címent)
clavos – nails (néils)
extractor a motor – power vent (páuer vent)
fieltro – felt (felt)
línea de tiza / gis – chalk line (chok láin)
lona impermeabilizada – tarp (tarp)
pintura sprei / en atomizador – spray paint (spréi péint)
plywood / madera terciada – plywood (plái uud)
protectores de rodillas / rodilleras – knee pads (ni pads)
resguardo – flashing (fláshing)
soportes – brackets (brákets)

FRASES DE TECHADO
Roofing Phrases

Vea pagina 28 para preguntas, respuestas y afirmaciones básicas en el trabajo y Frases básicas en el lugar de trabajo

¿Cuánto hace que es techista?
How long have you been roofing?
(¿Jáu long jav iú bin rúfin?)

Hace _____ años que soy techista.
I have been roofing for _____ years.
(Ái jav bin rúfin for _____ iérs)

¿Sabe trabajar con techos de metal?
Can you do metal roofs?
(¿Can iú du métal rufs?)

¿Sabe cómo trabajar con techos de cobre?
Can you do copper roofs?
(¿Can iú du cóper rufs?)

Necesitamos arrancar y desechar el techo viejo.
We need to tear off and dispose of the old roof.
(Uí nid tu téar-of and dispóus ov di óuld ruf)

Necesitamos primero arrancar las tejas.
We need to tear off shingles first.
(Uí nid tu téar-of shíngols ferst)

Necesitamos utilizar una lona para atajar las tejas.
We need to use a tarp to catch shingles.
(Uí nid tu iús a tarp tu cach shíngols)

Necesitamos colocar las tejas y los escombros en el basurero.
We need to put shingles and debris in the dumpster.
(Uí nid tu put shíngols and dibrí in de dámpster)

Necesitamos un basurero.
We need a dumpster.
(Uí nid a dámpster)

¿Adónde están las tejas?
Where are the shingles?
(¿Uéar ar de shíngols?)

Necesitamos más tejas.
We need more shingles.
(Uí nid mor shíngols)

Mañana entregarán las tejas.
The shingles will be delivered tomorrow.
(De shíngols uíl bi dilíverd tumórrou)

¿Adónde está el fieltro?
Where is the felt?
(¿Uéar is de felt?)

Necesitamos más fieltro.
We need more felt.
(Uí nid mor felt)

¿Adónde están los clavos?
Where are the nails?
(¿Uéar ar de néils?)

Necesitamos más clavos.
We need more nails.
(Uí nid mor néils)

Necesitamos más andamiaje.
We need more scaffolding.
(Uí nid scáfoldin)

¿Adónde está el martillo?
Where is the hammer?
(¿Uéar is de jámer?)

¿Adónde está el serrucho?
Where is the saw?
(¿Uéar is de so?)

¿Adónde están las tenazas para techar?
Where is the roofing fork?
(¿Uéar is de rúfin fork?)

¿Adónde está la pistola para clavos enrollados en tiras / pistola de clavos con tambor?
Where is the coil nailer?
(¿Uéar is de cóil néiler?)

Necesitamos colocarle cubrejuntas a esto.
We need to flash this.
(Uí nid tu flash dis)

Necesitamos colocar cubrejuntas alrededor de la chimenea.
We need to flash around the chimney.
(Uí nid tu flash aráund de chímni)

Necesitamos colocarle cubrejuntas de cobre a la chimenea.
We need to flash the chimney in copper.
(Uí nid tu flash de chímni in cóper)

Necesitamos colocar cubrejuntas alrededor de los tragaluces / las claraboyas.
We need to flash around the skylights.
(Uí nid tu flash aráund de skái láits)

www.ingramcontent.com/pod-product-compliance
Lightning Source LLC
LaVergne TN
LVHW051503080426
835509LV00017B/1899